FORGOTTEN CONSCRIPTS

PRELUDE TO PALESTINE'S STRUGGLE FOR SURVIVAL

ERIC LOWE

Trafford.
PUBLISHING

Order this book online at www.trafford.com/06-2523
or email orders@trafford.com

Most Trafford titles are also available at major online book retailers.

Note for Librarians: A cataloguing record for this book is available from Library
and Archives Canada at www.collectionscanada.ca/amicus/index-e.html

ISBN: 978-1-4251-0765-9

Second Edition 2007

*We at Trafford believe that it is the responsibility of us all, as both individuals
and corporations, to make choices that are environmentally and socially sound.
You, in turn, are supporting this responsible conduct each time you purchase a
Trafford book, or make use of our publishing services. To find out how you are
helping, please visit www.trafford.com/responsiblepublishing.html*

*Our mission is to efficiently provide the world's finest, most comprehensive
book publishing service, enabling every author to experience success.
To find out how to publish your book, your way, and have it available
worldwide, visit us online at www.trafford.com/10510*

 www.trafford.com

North America & international
toll-free: 1 888 232 4444 (USA & Canada)
phone: 250 383 6864 ♦ fax: 250 383 6804 ♦ email: info@trafford.com

The United Kingdom & Europe
phone: +44 (0)1865 722 113 ♦ local rate: 0845 230 9601
facsimile: +44 (0)1865 722 868 ♦ email: info.uk@trafford.com

10 9 8 7 6 5

DEDICATIONS

To the memory of the 784 members of the British
Armed Forces who lost their lives in Palestine
during the final years of Britain's Mandate.

1945 – 1948

To my wife, Dorothy Joyce, who patiently tolerated the
inconvenience that the preparation of this book created.

Palestine Veterans validate

Forgotten Conscripts – Prelude to Palestine's Struggle for Survival

A special print run of *Forgotten Conscripts – Prelude to Palestine's Struggle for Survival* was sold to five hundred men and women who served in Palestine between 1936 and 1948. It was a test run for viability and validation prior to the book's general release. Without any solicitation the content was approved by numerous letters and telephone calls. The consensus was that it was accurate in its content and reflected the veterans views.

Here are a few of the comments extracted from letters:

…thanks for Forgotten Conscripts, which I found to be enjoyable, interesting and informative. I am more enlightened.

–Trevor Hall, (Royal Artillery) and author of 'Enduring the Hour'

It is an enjoyable and informative read which I am surely going to refer to many times.

–Dr. H. de la Haye Davies M.A. (Oxon) B.M, B.Ch, D.M.J (Royal Artillery)

Once started I couldn't put it down, and must congratulate you on the information you have put together in such an interesting and absorbing way.

–John Tarran (RAOC)

I heartily congratulate you on a very impressive account which must have entailed an enormous amount of research.

–Peter H. Steele (REME)

…an accurate account of the frustrations, hazards and loss of life that was experienced by the men and women who were conscripted into what transpired to be an unsustainable campaign…

– W Allen-Muncey (RAOC)

Please accept my congratulations on the way all your work has turned out. The book was an eye-opener for me.

– Harry Piper, (Argyll & Sutherland Highlanders)

Many, many thanks for your excellent book 'Forgotten Conscripts'… you excelled in your account of the history of the Holy Land from time long past to the present day.

– Howard Allen (RAOC)

……a good read that captures the difficult circumstances we were all in at the time. Your book also helps to highlight the political situation which was there but which we were quite ignorant of at the time.

– Peter Marsh (4th – 7th Royal Dragoon Guards)

You've done a fine job.

– Alan Rose (Royal Signals)

Acknowledgements

Palestine veterans are scattered throughout Great Britain and communication with them has been largely by telephone and letter. In eight years over 200 Palestine veterans wrote over 2500 letters. Their diaries, memoirs and experiences form a personal insight into the life of an army made up mainly of conscripts and serving in the first post war terrorist conflict. I am indebted to them all. They provided articles and photographs for fifteen issues of *Palestine Scrapbook,* and a bank of material some of which I have used in the text. The names and addresses of former comrades collected by former Staff Sergeant Alex Monaghan, Corporal Brian Cross and Sergeant John Tarran formed the nucleus of the subscription/contributor list. My son Andrew then made the idea of a magazine a reality. I also have to thank him for editing the photographs used in the book.

Unpublished memoirs from Sergeant Ken Brown, Sergeant Charlie Eyles, Corporal 'Gus' O'Brien, Private Ken Parker, prewar material from Major Bill Howard and the seditious libel case, researched by Leslie Morgan were of substantial value to the manuscript.

I thank them all, including those whose material I haven't been able to use.

A special thanks goes to Mrs. Irene Collins for the photograph and the BBC report of her husband's kidnap.

To put our personal experiences into the context and sequence of the political situation at that time it was necessary to rely on the research of others, they are credited in the notes at the end of each chapter. However, Nicholas Bethell's *Palestine Triangle* was my main reference source. In his comprehensive book Lord Bethell covers the entire Mandate period without the odour of propaganda.

Indeed, A.J.P. Taylor said of *Palestine Triangle* 'A story that no Englishman can read without shame.'

No single book will cover every political statement, every document written or every bitter incident of the Palestine problem. Bethell used extensive hitherto unused research.

He in turn acknowledges, justifiably the years Olwen Gillespie spent in the Public Records Office researching government documents.

The one ingredient I was never short of during the eight years was the help and encouragement from many veterans, friends and experts. Not only the veterans whose names are to be found in the index, but also the many whose material is not yet published but still remaining in my archives.

The interest taken over a number of years by notable personalities including Robert Fisk, Middle East correspondent of *The Independent,* Brian Sewell, author and broadcaster and the late Dr. Mo Mowlam have served to boost my confidence.

Lady Michele Renouf whose interest from the book's inception led to filming my interview with journalist Philip Knightley to use on her lecture tours.

In January 1991 former Corporal Malcolm Astley typed the first four chapters of the manuscript and the prospect of getting a book into print took a big leap forward.

Malcolm born in the same year as myself, served in the same camp in Palestine and worked in the same depot but we never knowingly met. Good fortune brought us together in this publishing venture. Malcolm transcribed my scribbling onto a disc. But he was much more than a typist; he lifted my morale when the going was heavy. He took the alterations, corrections and even the rewriting all in his stride. Because we had shared a dramatic period in our lives we had a common aim, to get our story into print.

Cover photograph: 3rd Infantry Division Ordnance Field Park members.
Photograph supplied by John Darnell.

Contents

Introduction   v

1   Seeds of Discontent   1

A short resume of the events in Palestine from 1917 when Britain took it from the Turks. The British army's involvement from 1936.

2   War and Peace Palestine 1939 to 1945   13

The establishment of a large military ordnance to support the forces in the Western Desert Campaign and the landings in Italy.

3   Movement Orders   36

The logistics of getting men and materials to Palestine and the Middle East by land and sea. First hand accounts of the troops involved.

4   The First Post War Conflict   55

Some of the major incidents of modern terrorism for which Britain was not prepared.

5   Not So Soft Targets   74

The defensive measures that made the large valuable military installations out of reach of the terrorists.

6   Palestine Realised   92

The reactions of the troops arriving in the Middle East and Palestine for the first time. For new recruits it was their first time overseas.

7   A Way Of Life   119

Initial reactions over. How the conscripts managed to find pleasure living in siege conditions.

8   Time Out   138

> When normal duties and camp life paused for pleasure, pain and punishment. Experiences in leave centres, hospitals and detention barracks.

9   Clifty Wallahs   155

> Or in real Arabic 'Clefty Whallads,' thieves, who missed no opportunity to liberate anything that was unguarded. Soldier, Arab or Jew were at it from towels to Tommy guns.

10   The Gun Runners   161

> A scandal that rocked not only the RAOC but also the nation. How a war hero, a colonel, and a bullying major stole weapons and sold them to the Jewish terrorists.

11   An Atrocity Too Far   178

> A double murder that shocked the world, raised tempers in Parliament created race hatred in Britain and put an editor in High Court and the terrorists claimed they drove the British out of Palestine.

12   The End is in Sight   188

> The ending of the Mandate is announced but the violence increases and spreads to Arab civilians.

13   The Bitter End   203

> Mixed feelings about leaving a job unfinished. The problems of moving machinery, vehicles, weapons and ammunition in a hostile environment.

Epilogue   224

Index   230

Introduction

National service as it is recalled today is accepted as commencing in 1947 and ending in 1962. However conscription started in April 1939 as Britain prepared for the war in Europe. The last drafts of conscripts were called up in 1960.

World War 2 ended in 1945 but conscription was deemed to be necessary to deal with post-war unrest. Men called up for the armed services between the end of the war and the commencement of National Service were not given a firm commitment regarding their length of service. They were given an 'age and service' number, better known as a Demob Group number. After the hostilities in Europe ceased several nations within the British Empire resumed their quest for independence. The first of the post war trouble spots to erupt was Palestine. It was a dispute that had simmered throughout the war years and rapidly came to the boil again in 1945.

Following so quickly in the wake of the terrible war that had raged in Europe and Asia its significance was not fully realised. Certainly the politicians of the day had not realised the tragic consequences that would still be with us sixty years later.

'Forgotten Conscripts' is about those conscripts caught up in that conflict that had an unacceptable loss of life for what was after all, only a 'peacetime conflict.' It was not a fight on the scale of World War 2, there were no epic battles, there was no visible enemy, and it was war against terrorism. It didn't make the same major headlines that Britain's battles with Germany did; it shared the newspaper columns with the domestic post war problems.

Post war conscripts were children in 1939 when World War 2 broke out. They had lived through the depressions of the thirties, were accustomed to hardship and accepted the disciplines that service life demanded of them. Very few had ever been out of the country some had never even been to the coast and seen the sea and the prospect of an overseas posting was seen as an adventure.

The number killed in the Palestine conflict is not accurately known. What is known is that 784 members of the armed services who died between 1945 and 1948 are buried in Palestine. Of the post war conflicts only in the Korean War was the death toll higher.

When newspapers listed post war conflicts they didn't include Palestine. Even the B.B.C. omitted it from every Armistice Sunday broadcast. Many wars claim to be forgotten and many armies have made similar claims. However none deserved that distinction more than the post war Palestine Campaign. It is inexistent in public awareness. This book has been written to go perhaps some way to filling that void.

Many books have been written on the subject of Palestine, by a variety of people, some of who were there and most who were not.

Books have been written by politicians and government officials, books by Jewish terrorists and a few by army officers who had had a unique personal experience. Scholars and historians who weren't even born in 1945 have written many more books. Most of what has been written is biased and contaminated with lies, misconceptions and propaganda.

There has been little concern for the injustice meted out to the indigenous population of Palestine and no insight into the lives and feelings of the young conscripts who were thrust into that cauldron of hate. No book to my knowledge has been written by a private soldier, featuring the personal accounts of his comrades in Palestine who were not members of fighting units. They were conscripts trained mostly to be clerks, storemen, drivers and mechanics. They left the UK not knowing where they were going and when they got to their destination, not knowing why they were there.

On arrival they knew little of the Arab-Jewish conflict and only a little more when they left. The Jews made much of the Balfour Declaration but until the eighteen years olds reached Palestine, it is doubtful if they had even heard of the name Balfour.

By working alongside the Jewish and Arab employees we got to know them well. The Arab workers were gregarious and had a comradeship that the troops recognised. The affinity that I personally had, as did many others, with the Arabs was understandable, because we had lived through the distressing times of the thirties and the deprivations of the war and immediate post war years. This gave rise to the empathy we felt for the Arabs and their struggle to feed and clothe their families. The situation created by Jewish militants inevitably led to a mistrust of Jewish workers. It was after all, their terrorists that were killing and maiming Britons. Subsequent events justified our mistrust.

Israel's boastful Golden Jubilee in 1998 jolted us into action. Memories that had lain dormant for fifty years were stirred. Discontent rippled through our dispersed ranks, discontent that focussed on the manner in which the second and more vicious Palestine conflict within ten years had been sidelined. The outcome was a combined services Veterans Association, with an annual reunion at Eden Camp, North Yorkshire, every October.

No memorial existed for those who died between 1945 and 1948 until we paid for and erected our own memorial at the National Memorial Arboretum at Alrewas, Staffordshire.

My ambition was to write a book about Palestine from a conscripted private soldier's point of view. To obtain the experiences and memories of my comrades I published a journal entitled 'Palestine Scrapbook' for members of the Royal Army Ordnance Corps and the Royal Electrical and Mechanical Engineers to submit and record their recollections and experiences.

Over a thousand letters were received in response from 212 veterans of the two regiments.

'Forgotten Conscripts' is not intended to be, nor is it, a book detailing heroic deeds. We were not chasing terrorists or searching houses and settlements.

It is a simple story of the lives of young conscripts in a hostile land. It was our opportunity to observe first hand the Arabs and Jews who worked with us. We were there to witness the final stages of Britain's Palestine Mandate.

Upon arriving at Camp 153 near Haifa, when Jewish terrorism was at its height, my draft was told that the Jews claiming Palestine as their country was similar to the Romans returning to claim England. Even though that was an oversimplification it seemed plausible to eighteen year olds who had quickly become close to the Arabs. Until we reached there Palestine was regarded by many as the 'Land of the Jews'

During my research it became apparent that to fully understand the reasons for Britain's involvement one needed to put on hold our views based solely on what we had seen.

It was necessary to study the events before 1945 back to the time when, in 1917, Britain and her Allies took the Arabian peninsula from the Turks, although Zionism, a Jewish national movement had been conceived in the mid nineteenth century.

Britain's involvement in 1917 when Balfour produced his declaration and the Zionist dream came closer to a reality.

'Palestine Scrapbook' received letters describing the experiences of RAOC veterans as far back as 1936 (REME was formed in 1942 from part of the RAOC).

References to the years before 1936 come entirely from the historical works of other authors. It was not my intention to write a book that merely duplicated information that can be read elsewhere. It does cover some of the most shocking events, simply because those events were to shape the course of the ensuing conflict.

Palestine veterans ask why is it that this unhappy episode in Britain's' history has been overlooked by many historians, ignored by all newspapers and conveniently sidelined by successive governments.

I would hope that it is not for the fear of appearing anti-Semitic or politically incorrect.

Before May 1948 there was no Israel and the Palestinians were either Jews or Arabs and it was only when the Jews declared the state of Israel did they begin to be called Israelis.

PALESTINE

Miles

Kilometres

REFERENCE

- Standard gauge railways
- Narrow gauge railways
- 1st class roads
- 2nd class roads
- Principal tracks
- Airfields
- Landing grounds
- Seaplane moorings

Previous page: Official Communicatons Map c 1945, issued to all units.

Seeds of Discontent

Britain's long and troublesome burden of Palestine began when General Sir Edmund H.H. Allenby's forces captured Jerusalem after 400 years of Turkish rule on December 11 1917 when he walked through Jaffa Gate into the historical city. Although Allenby actually walked through the gate he rode up to it on a white horse to fulfill a local legend that Jerusalem would be liberated by a man on a white horse. As far as the population of Jerusalem was concerned the legend of Allenby was completed by the very sound of his name, Allenby sounded like Al Nebi 'The Prophet' in Arabic. In 1920 Britain was given the responsibility for Palestine by the League of Nations and it became a British Mandate. Arab leaders, from the tribes in the southern territories, tired of Turkish rule, had lent their support in the battle for the Arabian peninsular and in October 1915 in return were promised self-rule. The Anglo Arab alliance was impaired when former ally Russia, in 1918 a newly proclaimed communist state, exposed the secret Anglo-French agreement known as the Sykes-Picot Agreement. In 1916 Monsieur Georges-Picot on behalf of the French Government and Sir Mark Sykes for Britain agreed, unbeknown to the Arabs that Britain would retain Iraq, Jordan and Palestine and France would retain Lebanon and Syria. Disagreeable as it was it to the Arabs it was tolerated by them.

At that time, Palestine, a country roughly the size of Wales, had a population of approximately one million. There was one Jewish town, thirty four Jewish colonies, fourteen Arab towns, 612 Arab villages and five mixed population towns. Arabs formed 92 percent of the population.

After Turkey entered the First World War as an ally of Germany thousands of Jews left the country.

By the end of the war the Jewish population according to Israeli sources was about 65,000.

The desire to be rid of Turkish rule was more prevalent in the southern desert regions of the Arabian peninsular than in the north. The countries that Britain and France were interested in was the more settled region known as the Fertile Crescent. As Muslims, the Turks revered its holy places and historical significance and they admired the occupants for their gentle stewardship. In the 19th century Palestine was a popular tourist attraction for British and European Christians. In addition to the excellent accommodation to be found in the hotels Christian visitors would stay in the various monasteries. It was even possible to get from London to Jerusalem in eight days.

In 1908 the Anglo-Persian Oil Co. discovered oil in neighbouring Persia where the terrain was similar to that in Iraq. A large oil field was found in 1927 at Kirkuk in northern Iraq and a 600-mile pipeline was laid to the Mediterranean ports of Haifa and French controlled Tripoli in the Lebanon.

This accounted for Britain's desire to control Iraq and Palestine.

Those of us who served in Palestine between 1945 and 1948 assumed the contentious situation we found ourselves in was due to a series of ill conceived decisions over the preceding thirty years. However Pierre Van Passen cautiously advanced the theory in 1943 that it was a deliberate plot by the British government to retain Palestine permanently. Passen was Dutch by birth, Canadian by adoption and worked as a Journalist in America. His theory was that it was a divisive plot by Britain to keep the Jews and Arabs in contention and Britain permanently in control of the situation. *[1]

In 1917 the British Prime Minister David Lloyd George plainly favoured the burgeoning wave of Zionism, probably because it afforded some relief from the waves of Russian and Eastern European Jews that were migrating westward. The Americans may have had similar motives but neither the British or the Americans could have foreseen the eventual outcome. A homeland was promised for the Jews within Palestine in a controversial document which became known as the Balfour Declaration. It was a secret letter from Arthur James Balfour, the Foreign Secretary and a former Prime Minister to Lionel Walter, 2nd Baron Rothschild, Chairman of the British Zionist Federation, the leading Zionist in Britain. The Rothschilds were a powerful family of moneylenders established in 1747 and were able to influence governments. In 1875 Benjamin Disraeli was able to buy Britain's share in the Suez Canal with a £4 million loan from Rothschild. The wording of the document was suitably vague and disappointing for those Zionists who were looking for statehood. It clearly said nothing would be done which may prejudice the civil and religious rights of existing non-Jewish communities.

Foreign Office

November 2nd, 1917

Dear Lord Rothschild:

I have much pleasure in conveying to you, on behalf of His Majesty's Government, the following declaration of sympathy with Jewish Zionist aspirations which has been submitted to, and approved by the Cabinet. "His Majesty's Government view with favour the establishment in Palestine of a national home for the Jewish people, and will use their best endeavours to facilitate the achievement of this object, it being clearly understood that nothing shall be done which may prejudice the civil and religious rights of existing non-Jewish communities in Palestine, or the rights and political status enjoyed by Jews in any other country."

I should be grateful if you would bring this declaration to the knowledge of the Zionist Federation.

Yours sincerely,

Arthur James Balfour

This lone document, more than anything else, sowed the seeds of discontent, which was to cost the British taxpayer a lot of money and the lives of many young men in bitter conflict.

Balfour and the then British Prime Minister, Lloyd George were the first politicians to give substance to the aspiration of a Jewish homeland in Palestine before the First World War. Several approaches were made by Zionists to persuade the Turkish Government had failed.

Quietly and stealthily the Jewish colonisation of Palestine started when Sir Moss Montefiore purchased an estate near Jaffa in 1855. In 1861 the London Hebrew Society was founded to further the colonization of the Holy Land. In the same year an agricultural school, Mikveh Israel, was established again near Jaffa with one of its main aims being to settle more Jews in Palestine.

The first Zionist Congress was held in Basle in August 1897. Its Director was Theodore Herzl an author and playwright who is credited with being the founder of the Jewish State. In his book 'The Jewish State' he outlined its conception. As a journalist and playwright he used a slogan, which the Zionists have unashamedly used despite its lack of substance. It was 'A Land without a people, Palestine, and a people without a land, the Jews.'

Over one hundred years later ardent Zionists still use and believe the slogan.

By 1899 nine Jewish settlements, covering two thirds of the Jewish owned land in Palestine, was owned by and entirely dependent on Rothschild.

Chaim Weizmann a Jew born in Russia and by 1917 a naturalized British subject was a key figure in the drawing up of the Balfour Declaration and in 1948 was Israel's first President.

When George Bush, the American President, visited Britain in 2003 he made several references to the 'Special Relationship' between Britain and America. He traced it back to 1917 and America's decision to participate in the First World War. A war which President Woodrow Wilson strove to keep America out of until German U-Boat activity affected America's trade. The Balfour Declaration was submitted for his approval before it was passed to the Zionists.

The American Ambassador to Britain, Walter H. Page, whilst well informed of the Government's Pro Zionist plan had no idea of the impact it was to have thirty years later. In a letter to his son on January 19, 1918, Page wrote, 'I have never been able to consider the Zionist movement seriously. It is mere religious sentiment, which will express itself in action by very few people. *[2] Such was the light-mindedness of the politicians of the warring nations in 1918.

How, all these years later we wonder, could the government of one of the world's leading democracies be so crass? The fact is, Britain still had an Empire and the right of conquest was accepted amongst the leading nations. Balfour had already earned himself the sobriquet of 'Bloody Balfour' for his drastic handling of the unrest in Ireland whilst Chief Secretary of State for Ireland.

The seeds of discontent planted by Balfour germinated when Lloyd George appointed Herbert Samuel, a practicing Jew to be the first High Commissioner to Palestine on June 30, 1920. No matter how impartial Samuel claimed his intentions were he was destined to be viewed with more than a little suspicion by the agitated indigenous Palestinian Arab population. Samuel was the first Jew to govern Palestine in 2000 years. He was considered a prince by the Jews in Eastern Europe and was equated with Cyrus the King of Persia who liberated the Jews from captivity in Babylon. *[3] In his first two years as High Commissioner there was an influx of 14663 Jewish immigrants. This was enough to incite the Arabs to outbursts of violence against the Jewish population.

Following riots between Jews and Arabs in August 1929 extra forces were needed to supplement the Palestine Police Force. The first party of infantry was flown in from Cairo. An infantry brigade, a squadron of armoured cars and supporting units followed by rail. A small ordnance dump was established at Lydda Railway Station. The small headquarters staff included SQMS (Staff Quarter Master Sergeant) Hewitt as BOWO (Base Ordnance Warrant Officer) and his office was a railway truck. The tension eased and the military force was reduced and by 1937 it was down to six battalions and supporting units. *[4] It was not to last, the troubles flared again early in 1938 and reinforcements were brought in again from Egypt and India. Despite the Arab reactions to the arrival of immigrants Jewish immigration continued and took on a new impetus when Hitler came to power in Germany. For example in 1932 there were 353 Jewish immigrants and in 1933 it rose to 5,392. Overall the annual influx rose rapidly to a peak of 61,844 in 1935. Some absentee Arab landowners sold land to Jews and the Arab tenant farmers were turned off the land. Jewish employers replaced Arab workers with Jewish labour, not always happily because the Eastern Europeans were union members and had to be paid more.

Allowing the Jewish National Fund to purchase land was causing concern among the small tenant Arab farmers who possessed and worked the land. Much of the land was owned by the Turkish Government or absent landowners and tenants paid for it by a tithe system. The Arab National Movement had voiced their objections to the Turkish Government before the outbreak of the First World War. Several Arab poets saw the dangers and wrote about selling the land. One leading poet, Ibrahim Tuqan targeted the sellers and brokers warning of the danger of selling land to the Jews. He showered them with bitter, critical words in several of his poems. Needless to say the selling of the land continued. The words may have been critical but they couldn't penetrate the deaf ears of the pro Zionist British Government. Tuqan, whose father was imprisoned by the British for being an activist in the Arab National Movement, was a member of an affluent Nablus Arab family.

Several of Tuqan's poems predicted disaster at the hands of 'two powerful enemies' of the Palestinian Arabs and that could mean none other than the British and the Zionists.

This is an extract from one of Ibrahim Tuqan's poems written about the time (1935) when he was a teacher in the American University in Jerusalem.

'We have two enemies; one is mighty and powerful, the other, a swindler and an opportunist.

From the friendship they have maintained with each other, we have reaped humiliation and evil.

Our eradication has been planned according to lucid methods and carried out sometimes by force, sometimes gently.' *[5]

By 1936 the Royal Army Ordnance Corps (RAOC) was more organized in Palestine, the 5th Division went to the northern part of the country with an HQ at Haifa and the 1st Division covered the southern part of the country with the Divisional and Corps HQ at

Jerusalem. A Forward Ordnance Depot and an Ordnance Mobile Workshop were opened at Sarafand. By August a depot and vehicle reception park were established at Haifa. *[6]

In September 1936 Major Bill Howard, then a Lance Corporal in the RAOC boarded a troop train in Aldershot Field Stores Military Sidings bound for Southampton. He was a clerk in the office of a Major Harry of the Indian Army Ordnance Corps. They boarded the SS Laurentic, destination Haifa. In 1936 the Laurentic was a civil ship built to carry a total of 1500 passengers of which 594 would travel in cabins and Bill was lucky enough to travel in a cabin. No doubt the urgency of the situation created this rare opportunity to travel in luxury, a privilege normally accorded only to senior officers. Later this coal-fired ship was converted to a trooper carrying more than double its original quota of passengers. The ship docked at Haifa which, in 1936, the British made into Palestine's main port.

'Most of the Ordnance contingent were destined for an Ordnance Depot at Haifa. My posting was to HQ Palestine and Transjordan in Jerusalem. On arrival by train in Jerusalem, we were accommodated in tents in an olive grove near the King David Hotel. Our offices were to be on the third floor of the hotel. All other ranks had to use the side entrance to the hotel and we had to change from our army boots into plimsoles so as not to damage the marble stairway.' wrote Bill.

Except for the third floor the King David Hotel flourished as a hotel it was a lively venue for a cosmopolitan social life. It had all the amenities of a first class European hotel. It had an Oriental ambience of opulence, a meeting place for all who could afford to frequent its glamorous bar and plenteous dining rooms. Well beyond a lance corporal's income. However Bill and all the other "other ranks" were quite happy with the facilities that the nearby YMCA offered.

'The YMCA had excellent facilities; shower baths, indoor swimming pool, squash court, football ground, a very good library, an excellent canteen with table tennis facilities. From time to time there were certain events such as trips to the Dead Sea and at Christmas time a visit to the Shepherd Fields at Bethlehem to experience a scene very similar to those at the time of Christ's birth.'

Sergeant Brian Clark was posted from 12 section RAOC to Sarafand in 1938.

'Our troubles in those days lay mainly with the Arabs who would take pot shots from ambushes and place mines where army vehicles were likely to pass. Whilst in Sarafand I was detailed along with Joe Hiscock another sergeant to take a convoy of 13 vehicles loaded with camp equipment to a map reference in the desert South of Gaza to set up an advanced camp for a Base Ordnance Depot.(BOD) When we got there we found an empty stretch of sand upon which the Royal Engineers had kindly installed a water tank-nothing else!

We pitched the first store tents and set up camp. This was Rafah and it was to become quite a large complex, but we were glad to hand it over to the advance party of the BOD when they arrived.'

1938 was probably the peak year of the Arab unrest and they paid the biggest price. The recorded deaths in fighting were 69 British, 292 Jews and at least 1600 Arabs, rebels and others. Mixed British and Jewish units know as 'Special Night Squads' led by pro Zionist Orde Wingate were feared by the rebels and the Arab population generally for their ruthlessness. Wingate very often worked outside the law, was capable of torture and he would imprison suspected rebels in cages in the hot sun for hours on end. One of Wingate's more bizarre habits was to scrub his naked body in public with a toothbrush. Despite his unorthodoxy and eccentricities he was a great tactician and proved to be a great asset in World War Two.

Community punishments were commonplace, if an incident was traced to a village one house, not necessarily a house harbouring a rebel, would be blown up. Collective fines were probably the most oppressive punishment; they made poor people poorer and punished the innocent as well as the guilty. Sydney Burr, a downhearted Palestine Policeman wrote home to his family of his job as a policeman in Haifa '...our only job out here seems to be clearing up the mess after the crime has been committed, we are on the defensive all the time.' The police relied on informers who were according to

Burr, now all dead. He went on to write 'what I dislike about this war is that more often than not it is the innocent that suffer. Our hospitals here are filled with women and children maimed and blinded for life... Life for the police is now all work and no play.' *[7]

The police station was the receiving centre for the goods and chattels of those who could not pay the collective fine, usually about 400 mils (40p in today's British currency). For a population who were generally destitute it was a difficult sum to raise.

The Haganah benefited from the Arab rebellion when at the insistence of the Jewish leaders the police force was expanded and 14,500 Jewish men were recruited all of whom were members of the Haganah. Moshe Dayan was one of those recruits and he accompanied Wingate on his illegal missions. Britain's treatment of Arab rebels was far more ruthless than that was to be meted out to Jewish terrorists between 1945 and 1948.

Throughout the Arab Rebellion Britain armed and employed Jews as a supernumery force. These supernumeries were the foundation of the illegal Haganah that was prepared to take arms against the British when Germany was defeated. With the ending of the Arab Rebellion and when Arabs were still being hanged for carrying arms, it was not a wise decision to supply Jews with weapons.

Alarmed by the ominous situation by the end of 1938 King Ibn Saud of Saudi Arabia was moved to write a lengthy letter to President Roosevelt.

He plainly believed, with some justification, that the citizens of America were not fully aware of the growing injustice that was being inflicted on the indigenous population of Palestine. The King's eloquent letter touched on every aspect of the situation and gently reminded the reader of the shameful behaviour of Britain and America. He started by answering the Zionist claim to Palestine with these words;

'The argument on which they depend in these claims regarding Palestine is that they (the Jews) settled there for a time in the olden days and they have wandered in various countries of the world, and that they wish to create a gathering place for themselves in Palestine where they may live freely. And for their action they rely upon a promise they received from the British Government, namely; the Balfour Declaration.

As for the historical claim of the Jews, there is nothing to justify it; because Palestine was and has not ceased to be occupied by the Arabs through all the periods of history, and it's sovereign was their sovereign. If we exclude the interval when the Jews were established there, and a second period when the Roman Empire ruled there, the ruler of the Arabs has been the ruler of Palestine from the oldest times to our own day.'

He then went on to say 'If this principle (the Jewish claim) be now held in esteem, then it is the right of every people to reclaim the country it formerly occupied by force for a certain time. This would bring about astonishing changes in the map of the world, and would be irreconcilable with right, with justice or with equity.'

With the events of 1936 to 1938 in mind the King wrote of the Balfour Declaration that it had surely 'brought the limit of oppression and iniquity to a peaceful and tranquil country. It was given by a government that at the time of the gift did not possess the right to impose it upon Palestine.'

The Times picked up the note to President Roosevelt in its columns on January 10 1939.

It quotes an important part of the letter:-

'It seems to us that the Palestine question has been viewed in the United States of America solely from the point of view of the Zionist Jews and that the freedom loving people of America have been so much misled on this question by extensive Zionist propaganda that they have come to look upon the Jewish attempt to crush the Arabs of Palestine as a humane act, when as a matter of fact it is nothing but a horrible crime on a peaceful people in their own homeland. A distinction must be made between political Zionism and the world problem of the persecuted Jews, to which Palestine cannot possibly be the solution, although she has already done more than any other country in the world by accommodating the greatest possible number of Jews for her size.' *[8]

According to their diaries the government officials and army officers enjoyed a lifestyle as close as they could arrange to the country set in Britain. At Ramleh they hunted, chasing jackals through the cactus. On Lake Huleh they took duck shooting trips by boat and at Ludd, point to point racing. However Major McNeill had to rough it a bit at times according to this extract from his diary on one shooting trip.

'Our quarters were in the house of a little Jew farmer and quite comfortable but the sanitary arrangements in most of these Jewish colonies are nil! Hearty meal, a couple of pipes and ditto a couple of "drams" and so the bed, and here endeth the year 1923. I wonder what 1924 will bring forth?' His diary was full of events of all descriptions, sporting and numerous celebrations of all kinds. *9

British politicians, after nineteen years of Mandate responsibility, were divided and their sense of purpose had dissolved. The behaviour of Government Officers left a lot to be desired and the world had changed since Lloyd George and Balfour made their promise to the Jews. Successive governments were beset with conflicting opinions from their appointed officials. There was no shortage of 'advice' from other countries, from both official sources and not least of all from journalists. Very few of these opionists had any sympathy or support for the indigenous Palestinian Arabs. Journalists held them in low esteem, as was the case of Van Passen who took every opportunity to denigrate the Palestinians in his pro Zionist book *The Forgotten Ally.'*

'Palestine was a wilderness before the war inhabited by a few hundred thousand poverty stricken fellahin, the most apathetic to the prospect of freedom in the whole Arabian Peninsular and culturally the most backward' was just one example of his derogatory comments. Despite the vicious racial conflicts, the numerous white papers, the endless commissions and the divided opinions about Britain's role in Palestine it was fortunate for Britain and her Allies, the Arabs and the Jews in particular, that Palestine was firmly in Britain's hands in 1939. For the next six years it was to be a strategic base for the Allies. Britain expanded its arsenal creating logistic support for the fighting units in the North African Desert, defeating Vichy France in Syria and the landings in Italy. In a war torn world, Palestine was a haven of rest and recuperation for battle weary servicemen and hospitals were built to accommodate the wounded. For European Jews it was seen as a safe haven and this little Arab country was expected to provide shelter and accommodations for displaced European Jews in such numbers that larger countries were refusing to accept them. Entry to Palestine was on a quota system but the quota was well exceeded as refugees were getting there illegally in barely seaworthy vessels, which became known as 'Little Death Ships.'

References

1. *Forgotten Ally.* Pierre Van Passen, Dial Press, New York 1943
2. *The Life and Letters of Walter H. Page,* Burton J. Hendric, William Heinemann
3. *Mandate Days,* A.J. Sharman, Thames A. Hudson, New York, 1997
4. *A History of the Royal Army Ordnance Corps.* RAOC Trustees
5. *Palestine and Modern Poetry,* Khalid A. Sulaiman, Zed Books Ltd. 1985
6. *A History of the Royal Army Ordnance Corps*
7. *Mandate Days*
8. *Arabia Unified,* Mohammed Almana, Hutchinson, 1980
29. *Mandate Days*

War and Peace

There had been wars and rumours of wars before the ultimate outbreak of World War 2. A series of crises was created by the aggressive actions of Germany and Italy, including the occupation of Czechoslovakia which brought the likelihood of war in Europe nearer. The occupation of Poland by Germany was the ultimate provocation and Britain and France declared war on Germany. The impending storm clouds of the recent crisis induced Britain to make some preparations. In Egypt there were already British troops and munitions to guard the Suez Canal and the tenuous roots of an ordnance structure were already in place but they needed strengthening. Territorial troops and conscripts were posted to Egypt to build up the ordnance depots and Lines of Communication. Troopships to Port Said, or Alexandria or Haifa via Gibraltar and the Mediterranean was the accepted route to the Middle East but many went overland by the Medloc (Mediterranean Line of Communication). One of the first conscripts to use the Medloc route was Howard Allen, who later was promoted to WO.II.

'After embarkation leave we returned to Victoria Barracks, Portsmouth where we had our T.A.B. jabs and were kitted out with thick underwear as well as topees. We wondered if we would be off to Finland then being invaded by Russian troops, or to the tropics.

On March 14, 1940, the draft marched smartly out of the barracks in full kit, with topees slung on the left shoulder, the Regimental Band playing the Corps March; we boarded a train and completed the journey at Reed Hall Barracks, Colchester.

The draft left Colchester on March 29, (after learning that our destination was the Middle East) by train to Southampton and the ferry Archangel to Le Havre. We were confined to the Le Havre railway station for the day. The posters on display told us to 'Keep your mouth shut and your bowels open.' After a lengthy train journey through another sleepless night we were in Marseilles and on to the troopship Devonshire. Hammocks were issued and with them came the necessary skill of getting into them for the night.

The ship anchored off Valetta Harbour, Malta and was soon surrounded by little boats with local vendors selling their wares. The morning of April 6 found us at Alexandria, our first sight of the Middle East. From the railway station the Palestine contingent was on its way to the Suez Canal.

After crossing the Suez Canal at Kantara by ferry we entrained on Palestine Railways for the long journey through the night. Sleep was almost impossible on the hard wooden slatted seats and we had our first glimpse of the Holy Land in the early morning as we travelled through orange groves. Before reaching Lydda Station an officer boarded the train to give us a lecture on the care of one's rifle and the penalty should it be stolen.

Our party was the first 'duration of the war' squaddies to reach the camp and our address became 'Details RAOC Sarafand.' As we debussed and formed up, a window of one of the adjacent huts opened and a regular called out 'What do you lot want?' Some greeting!'

Winston Churchill was made Prime Minister on May 10 and the Allies had to evacuate from Dunkirk. On June 14, 1940 Italy declared war on Britain and France capitulated in the same month and it was no longer safe to use the Mediterranean for the movement of troops. The war had taken a turn for the worse and henceforth troops bound for the Middle East would have to take a long, costly, time-consuming route around Africa and the Cape. German submarines, U-boats, in the Atlantic were prolific and playing havoc with shipping and to avoid them convoys of troopships crossed the Atlantic until they were within a few hours sailing of the Canadian coastline before turning south. 'Britain expected to be invaded but stood resolute like a solitary figure against a horde of bullies.'

Churchill made stirring speeches, which brought out the best of British determination and made that small stride across the Channel seem like a mighty leap into the unknown for Hitler. Churchill's 'We will never surrender.' speech was highly motivational for the British population and very intimidating for our enemies. Many valiant airmen lost their lives in the Battle of Britain when 350 fighter planes were shot down but the Luftwaffe lost almost 2700 aircraft. Unable to beat Britain in the air the Luftwaffe turned to bombing British cities.

In September 1940, the Italians invaded Egypt but by January 1941 the Allies had pushed them back and captured Tobruk. However Rommel arrived on the scene and by April 13 had encircled Tobruk and the long siege had started.

The war in the Middle East once more appeared to be swinging in favour of the Nazis.

In April 1941 Germany invaded Greece and an ominous change of power in Iraq occurred and a coup by Rashid Ali a pro-German Iraqi caused Prince Abdul Illah, the Regent for his infant nephew King Feisal II to flee south beyond Basra.

Meanwhile the German army had swiftly moved eastwards into Russia as far as Bessarabia and was in a position to easily turn south to the Iraq border that spanned the area between the Black and Caspian seas. Were that to happen, the British controlled oilfield at Kirkuk would be in enemy hands and Britain would lose the major oil supply to Haifa. Britain had an RAF airfield at Habbiniya which needed defending and a fighting force called Habforce was formed. Men and supplies for the force went over the Syrian Desert from Palestine to form a spearhead. That was followed by a large Indian army, including the Indian Army Ordnance Corp, landing at the port of Umm Qasr bound for Basra and the Ordnance Depot at Shuaiba.With the initial task of securing Habbiniya airfield and the oil refinery at Kirkuk completed it was then necessary to secure the country from any possible invasion. Habforce was rechristened Paiforce (Persia and Iraq Force) to protect a vital supply route to Russia. Five million tons of supplies took that route to Russia before the war ended.

It is doubtful if we will ever know how many Paiforce lives were lost, Private John McDowall an RAOC driver mechanic went from Palestine to Iraq in 1941 and was reported missing presumed killed. Although he was never in the North Africa campaign he is listed on the war memorial at El Alamein.

In three years Shuaiba, from a collection of stacks and tents in a wilderness west of Basra it had grown into an organized cantonment. The Base Ordnance Depot was now a town with an eight-mile wire perimeter fence. In addition to the store sheds, workshops, vehicle parks and laundries there were neat encampments for the troops, an open-air cinema, a church and a swimming pool. There were also other military installations in the proximity of Basra and its ports.

The Royal Electrical and Mechanical Engineers (REME) had Base Workshops at Maquil, Zubair and Rafadiya. Vehicles that came into the ports were assembled and no less than 16,000 were collected by Russian drivers and driven back, all loaded, to help the Russian war effort. *[1]

The unchanging scene in a static location can be very monotonous but in the hot oppressive climate of Southern Iraq could threaten the health of the troops. Craftsman George Nicolas arrived at Shuaiba when the facilities were being completed. Apart from the recreation facilities of the base a leave camp was opened at Karina in the Persian hills for the Indian troops and in 1944 another was opened at Beirut for British troops. George Nicolas spent a pleasant leave at Beirut with the cooler climate and even managed to get a day at the races.

In 1941 a total fifteen British convoys went round the cape, each with up to twenty troopships packed with servicemen and women. Former RAOC private, Sydney Parker sailed in a convoy, which consisted of nineteen troopships probably capable of carrying about 3,000 troops on each.

They were: Phemius, Andes, Orcades (the Commodore's Ship), Strathallan, Reina Del Pacifico, Windsor Castle, Diomede, Volendam, Stirling Castle, Niger Stroom, Indian Prince, Idrapoera, Highland Monarch, Cameronia, Nea Hellas, Warwick Castle,

Manchester Port.

Because this was the start of the Western Desert Campaign, some may have been carrying stores. *Palestine Scrapbook* received two accounts of that particular convoy. One from Sydney and one from John Tarran. Although both men were stationed a 2 BOD (Base Ordnance Depot) they did not know each other until over 50 years later. Not only were both in the same convoy which sailed from Gourock on the Clyde in August 1941, they were also on the Nea Hellas.

Sydney writes:

'I sailed on the Nea Hellas which had shortages in her crew of engineer officers which were made up by using army driver mechanics. They were also short of a wireless operator, which was made up by using our Corporal Brown. (He supplied me with the details of the convoy.) Warwick Castle collided with Windsor Castle in fog and they were escorted to Nova Scotia by the cruiser HMS Aux. The convoy sailed to within four hours of steaming off Nova Scotia before turning and heading for Freetown where the vessels anchored for four days. As we entered Freetown we passed an anchored aircraft carrier with bands on deck playing as we passed.

It started to rain and continued to rain until four days later when we steamed passed the carrier on our way to Durban. The rain was very welcome as we took soap on deck and bathed in the fresh water.'

Seventeen troopships escorted by HMS Edinburgh continued the journey. Sergeant John Tarran, in 1941, then a 19-year-old private, gave graphic details of the actual conditions on board the Nea Hellas:

'Some 3000 troops were housed in the most cramped and foul conditions for the next two months. My worst recollections are of the heads constantly overflowing and the lower decks being under water. Even so this was where we were expected to eat, and sleep in our hammocks. Fortunately the weather was fine and warm for most of the voyage and this allowed us to sleep on deck. However in rough weather we were driven below deck in spite of the dreadful stench. The sea was 'choppy' immediately we left the Clyde, and by the time we reached the Bay of Biscay there were very few of us who had not been violently seasick.

Happily, from then on we all seemed to have gained our sea legs. Our first port of call was Freetown in West Africa where the convoy stayed for a few days to refuel. Young boys rowed out from land and dived into the clear sea to recover coins thrown over by the troops. The next three weeks were spent in idyllic weather and the nights were magic and the sea was alive with marine life. Our days were spent in rehearsing emergency drill, Bren gun training, cookhouse fatigues, sporting activities, impromptu concerts and the inevitable 'housey housey' and card schools. Rumours of submarine attacks were rife, but our Naval escorts were always in evidence and frequently discharged their depth-charges, which were always a cause for worry.

All went well until we reached the Cape on our approach to Durban. Here the cross currents played havoc with us and most of us were violently ill until we reached the calm of Durban harbour. Britain had been blacked out since September 1939 and food was rationed. Here was Durban brilliant with light at night and there was lots of food – especially fruit – and the climate, even in the South African winter, was delightful. We were given a week's leave so long as we returned to the Nea Hellas at night.

The hospitality of the South Africans was incredible. Three of us were literally 'picked up' by an African couple before we had walked 300 yards from the ship, and adopted for a whole week. They took us sightseeing and fed us and generally treated us a VIP's.

We left Durban with a great deal of sadness and sailed for another three weeks up the Indian Ocean to the Red Sea where we stopped to refuel at Aden for a few days. The heat was intolerable and we were not allowed ashore.'

Sydney also has some pleasant memories of that one-week that the convoy moored in Durban.

'On the quayside was a stack of 4,000 cases of oranges and we were allowed a case each. Things were a little different from home, beer ten pence a half pint, tobacco for as little as a penny-ha'penny an ounce in the local Woolworth's. Being a pipe smoker at the time

I bought two 1lb tins of good flake tobacco at 6 shillings each. The vessel Diomede was listing badly due to her cargo shifting in the heavy seas around the Cape and was left behind at Durban. So what was left set off for Aden where we anchored and set off one at a time every 24 hours for Suez. Ships offloaded quickly at Suez because the Germans had managed to sink a ship in the harbour and she lay there with just her funnels sticking out of the water.'

Whilst going round the Cape to reach the Middle East was safer than going through the Mediterranean it was not an absolute guarantee against shipping losses. Two troopships bound for the East were torpedoed by U-Boats.

John Clegg was a passenger on the Mooltan in 1941 when it was part of a convoy going around the Cape to Port Suez. John was a seasoned sea traveler. He escaped from France after the evacuation of Dunkirk on the ill-fated SS Lancastrian. More than 7000 died when it was bombed and it sank ten miles from St. Nazaire on June 10 1940. John was one of about 1200 survivors. The Mooltan had only been converted to carry troops in 1941. Uniquely it published a ship's daily newspaper *der Tagerblitz* bringing the troops news of war and items of interest about the journey. It was quite ambitious considering its four tiny pages and very brave considering the way the war was proceeding in 1941. The Mooltan crossed the Equator twice on the journey around Africa and in the tradition of pleasure cruising issued crossing the Line Certificates for both crossings.

Every ship bound for the Middle East via the Cape in 1942 didn't sail in convoy. One ship made the journey in record time and was carrying 15,000 troops! That ship was RMS Queen Elizabeth doing the work of a convoy of approximately five troopships.

Ken Ingle was a member of Draft RKGYX that left Hilsea Barracks, Portsmouth in May 1942.

They marched to Portsmouth station behind the RAOC Regimental Band and on to an overnight train to Gourock. They arrived late afternoon and next day were on the Queen Elizabeth. The vessel had a crew of 1200. Bunks were five tiers high in the ship's library and those in the top two bunks had safety belts. Like many troopers the RMS Queen Elizabeth ran a daily mileage sweep and the average distance was 1000 miles per day. As far as Simonstown Ken was berthed on the forward sports deck. For the rest of the journey he shared a first class cabin with two others. There was no smoking below decks at any time, and none above decks after dark for security reasons. As Ken put it – 'But behind the locked door of the en-suite bathroom we could have a crafty drag.'

Whilst Britain battled valiantly in a war that was growing in intensity Palestine was presenting problems that would prove troublesome in the future. Arabs annoyed by the constant flow of Jews into Palestine were placated when the British Government took the decision to restrict further immigration to Palestine in 1939. It was essential that peace should reign in Palestine. Palestinian Jews were well aware that it was in their interest that Britain should continue to resist the advance of Nazism. However immigrants still came in overcrowded, unsanitary, leaking rusty vessels christened 'Little Death Ships.' Apart from concern over Arab reaction there was the very real possibility of Nazi agents using the influx of refugees to enter the country under cover. To overcome the two problems it was decided that the refugees should be sent to Mauritius. Nazi agents may or may not have come in with those sanctuary-seeking refugees from occupied Europe who managed to avoid the blockade. It was later discovered that within their ranks were elements that were to prove more problematical in the long term than Nazi spies. Amongst them were disruptive East European Jews including future terrorist leaders, Menachem Begin, Nathan Yalin Mor (real name Freidmann-Yellin) Ishtak Shamir, (real name Yzertitsky). Yalin Mor who later became leader of the Lehi (the fighters for the Freedom of Israel) arrived in Israel from Lithuania in January 1941 and openly declared that he hated Britain more than he hated Nazi Germany. Their posters urged Jews to fight the arch-enemy, (Britain) and to refrain from taking part in the 'imperialist war.' All of this was at time when thousands of Jews were being persecuted in Germany and the occupied countries and 43,000 British civilians were killed in the 16 months ending December 1941 in the Blitz.

On November 24 1940 the 'Atlantic,' a paddle steamer, arrived at Haifa from Cyprus with 1800 Jewish refugees on board. They along with 1760 refugees from two previous arrivals, the 'Milos' and the 'Pacific' were interrogated as they boarded the SS Patria to be taken to Mauritius for the duration of emergencies. Two hundred of them never made it; they were killed during the transfer to the SS Patria when an explosion sank the vessel. All manner of groups were suspected, some said the refugees did it as act of despair. In the end the Haganah were found to be the culprits. Their intention was to cripple the ship so that it could not leave the port. On board was a Palestine Police interrogator, Bill Taylor who was thrown into the sea and survived to help trap Abraham Stern in 1942.

The Zvai Leumi (National Military Organisation) later abbreviated to IZL became active by attacking Arabs in 1937. Their first acts of terrorism against Britain began just weeks before outbreak of the Second World War when they killed two British inspectors of the Palestine Police. The concept of Haganah, Hebrew for defence, was formed at Petah Tikva (Door of Hope) the first Jewish settlement in Palestine in 1878. Irgun strategies and tactics were not aggressive enough for the young terrorist, Abraham Stern, who formed a group of forty young men of the same opinion called Lohamei Herut Israel (Lehi). This group became known as the Stern Gang. Short of money the Stern Gang resorted to robbing banks and their couriers. They even approached and obtained funds from the agents of the Italian Government. In February 1942 Stern was killed whilst resisting arrest for the murder of Soloman Schiff, a Deputy Superintendent of the Palestine Police. He became a martyr and his gang carried on with their activities and the membership of the gang rose to 200.

Nazi propaganda aimed at the Arab population of Palestine, Iraq and Syria was inciting them to rise up against the British, who were, they said, intent on giving Palestine to the Jews.

Winston Churchill was a leader; a lateral thinker capable of making unpalatable decisions whose mind was set on one objective, to win the war with Germany and her allies. He believed, quite rightly, that was what the Jews of Palestine wanted. The British Army in Palestine had the full support and co-operation of the majority of the Jewish population, and the Jewish Brigade was formed.

On Jan 5 of 1941 it became necessary for British forces to invade the French Mandate of Syria which was in Vichy French hands. The campaign took just six days and Syria was secured.

To appreciate the totality of war and in particular the totality of Winston Churchill's involvement one only has to read the records of his correspondence for the first six months of 1941.

He sent out a constant stream of questions and directives to every head of every department, military or civilian, connected with the war effort. His missives included one to Chaim Weizman saying he was not in a position to give a decision to allow more Jewish immigrants into Palestine. Another was directed to the Secretary of State for war and the Chief of the Imperial General Staff (CIGS) on January 12 1944 querying why were 8,500 officers and men of the Cavalry Division kept in Palestine for security purposes. He asked for a calculation of the cost involved in-

(a) Sending them to the Middle East
(b) Maintaining them with rations, pay and allowances from the beginning of the war to the beginning of March 1942
(c) Transporting them home again.

Apparently when the question of this Cavalry Division had previously arisen it had been suggested that they would have to go back to the UK for retraining. Churchill would not accept that. His suggestions in addition to retraining them in the Middle East included equipping them with Bren Guns and Bren gun carriers, of which, we had plenty, or utilizing captured Italian tanks. However there was one problem he frequently brought up and that was employing soldiers as clerks, storemen, mechanics, drivers etc. These were duties that could be left to civilians he claimed. Whilst Churchill's thoughts were noted the decision to use a mixture of civilians and troops was the final and probably the wisest decision. 'Rearward Services' *2 was the expression he used to separate the support services from the Frontline Services. He was keen to have the maximum number of men fighting on the front line.

Ordnance installations in Egypt and Palestine had to be developed. A depot was under construction at Rafah and Sarafand workshop facilities for the repair and equipping of light tanks and carriers needed expanding. Even so the Ordnance facilities were far from adequate and installations continued to open up and develop all over Palestine, an ammunition factory and munitions dump at Wadi Sarar, a Base Ordnance Depot and workshop near Haifa, sub depots and workshops at Sarafand, Jerusalem, Bat Galim, Tel Aviv and in 1942 Kryat Motzkin.

War raged throughout the Western Desert, sometimes advancing sometimes retreating with the taking and retaking of towns and settlements by both sides. General Montgomery took command in the field in July 1941 and the same month the enemy under General Rommel reached El Alamein in Egypt and was only 100 miles or so from Cairo and several RAOC depots with their valuable hoard of munitions. This advance of the German army proved the strategic value of the RAOC installations in Palestine.

Water from the well sunk at Rafah was pumped round the clock to camps in the area. Each storage tank allocated so many hours each every day.

Sergeant Sydney Perkins was RTO (Railway Traffic Officer). The marshalling yard at 2 BOD had a 2000-gallon tank for supplying water to locomotives. It was the only supply for locomotives between El Kantara and Haifa and if the water level in the tank was low he could telephone the pumping station and get it refilled immediately. There were times when the army at the Front needed water for the men and vehicles every bit as much as they needed weapons. A call came reporting that water was urgently needed in the Western Desert. Sydney explained how he organised his supply system.

'The standpipes for the locomotives had branch pipes fitted with up to ten taps on each pipe. Lorries arrived filled with 2-gallon cans and local manufacturers started sending more in by rail.

Prisoners of war came from the local camp and were split into gangs, one gang for offloading the cans, one for laying them out and removing the tops, another gang on the hosepipes for filling, and yet another gang for putting the tops on and loading the cans into railway trucks.

Hassan, the stationmaster would do anything if you told him it was good for King George so I managed to get him to stop every goods train passing through and hitch on to the train as many trucks as we had ready and loaded. Many months afterwards we heard that in spite of being the furthest place from where the water was required 2 BOD Rafah supplied the most water in the shortest time.'

Tobruk was taken from the Italians in January 1941 and 500 Advanced Ordnance Depot was established there. Trained RAOC personnel were moved from Rafah and Sarafand.

At the end of August 1941,when the tide of the war in the Western Desert was going against us it was quite obvious that if we were to win this highly mechanized war there was a need for more tracked armoured vehicles with the necessary servicing facilities.

To meet the existing demands of unpacking and making new vehicles battle worthy and maintaining those vehicles that had been on the battle front, the men in the RAOC Sarafand workshops worked long hours in shifts.

Ken Brown kept detailed accounts of those critical months of the Second World War.

Ken's account gives an insight into the value of those men who assembled the armoured vehicles and serviced them when in use. From his account we can appreciate the need for a rapid growth in workshop capacity. However, more importantly, we can read of the men and details that Ken recorded so well. He remembers the mixed races who formed the workshop company, men like Pte. Zgornicki, a Polish Jew and Ken's friend.

Pte. Hammerman, an Austrian Jew. In particular he remembers Staff Sergeant Harold Hewitt who left the UK for the Middle East on the Windsor Castle on January 4 1941 and after a period in what was then the main workshop at Sarafand, was posted to 2 BOD, Haifa with its new huge purpose built facilities complete with railway sidings off the main Cairo – Haifa line. Harold's job was to prepare the workshops for the forthcoming move.

Howard Allen had been in Palestine just two months when Italy came into the war and he was posted to Abbassia. In February 1941 he was posted to the 6th Infantry Division in the Western Desert. In June the Division went to Syria to quell the Vichy uprising. In October they were taken by sea into the siege of Tobruk. As the siege

lifted and the Allies advanced westward Howard was transferred to
Tobruk. He worked at a Forward Ordnance Supply depot at El Aden
and then at a Sub Depot at Derna Camp, just outside Tobruk. Later
as the German army was once more advancing east, the unit was
split into platoons to defend the Depot. Each morning between 6.45
and 7.45 a.m., before normal duties commenced in the depot they
had basic military training, which included marching at the double
wearing gas masks. Howard wrote;

'An amusing item sticks in my memory – a Staff Sergeant had his
platoon marching up and down, about turn, about turn, about turn.
He admitted he had forgotten the word 'HALT' – he could only
remember 'STOP' and 'Whoa'

A few days later the bugler sounded the general alarm to fall in
on the parade area when we were told that Jerry was up the road. As
it was the case of longest in I was fortunate to hear my name called
to get out. I eventually reached Alexandria.

From there I was posted to 2 BOD, Palestine where I was stationed until leaving for Blighty in December 1944.'

Frank Bell who was at 2 BOD at the time of the fall of Tobruk
fortunately missed being taken prisoner. He explains:

'At one stage I was in charge of the dispatch riders, acting and
unpaid of course. On an off duty day I took a trip into Haifa but
when I returned I was informed that the rest of the dispatch riders
had been posted to Tobruk. Quite why they were required there I
never knew because three days later Tobruk fell and they were all
taken prisoner. I was due to follow them when southbound transport could be found. My day out in Haifa meant spending four more
happy years in Palestine. I always was dead lucky!'

Not so lucky was Harold Hewitt with the fall of Tobruk on June
20th 1942, he and another RAOC private, a German Jew, was taken
prisoner. However they managed to acquire German army clothing
and boldly walked out of the POW camp dressed as German soldiers
and hitchhiked to North Africa.

Their disguise failed them when they walked into an Italian camp
and they were recaptured.

In September 1942 Harold was sent to a POW Camp in Bologna

to work on agricultural implements, only to find he was expected to work on tanks and guns. Because he refused to do so he was sentenced to thirty days solitary confinement. In February 1943 he was moved to a non-working camp in Northern Italy and he escaped again this time dressed as an Italian soldier. He was again recaptured as he made his way to Yugoslavia and when Italy capitulated in September he was in a prison cell in Bologna.

The Italians were no longer allies of Germany and that part of Italy was occupied by the Nazis and Harold was thinking he might be moved to Germany. So naturally he escaped again and was befriended by a family who had already been sheltering two South African soldiers for two and a half months.

Late in November the three of them came out of hiding and made a run for it – on bikes. They cycled down the leg of Italy to the River Sangro. Harold and one of his companions made it through to the Allied lines eighteen months later after their capture at Tobruk they were at last free.

Shortly after the El Alamein victory in October the revitalized 8th Army swept westward taking Tobruk on November 13. The Germans were fighting hard and counter attacking but on January 23 the 8th Army entered Tripoli. The German and Italian armies surrendered in Tunis on May 13. One million German troops were killed or taken prisoner in the entire Western Desert campaign. Amongst the first to return into Tobruk was the RAOC. The manufacture, storing, inspecting, supplying and maintaining of ammunition was also the role of the RAOC. They placed the mines to defend Tobruk and were there to pick them up again when British forces retook the city. It was whilst unloading the mines that had been collected that Private Sam Flanagan lost his arm in an explosion. Sam was a friend of Private Stan Heath at Wadi Sara and Stan went to see the severely injured Sam in hospital shortly after the accident. Stan was told by the doctor not to tell Sam that he had lost an arm.

At the northern end of Tel Aviv, near the River Yarkon was the site of a pre war Industries Fair called the Levant Fair and it was the site for another RAOC Workshop.

By October 1942 the War Office at last realised that it was a highly mechanised war and the Royal Electrical and Mechanical Engineers (REME) was formed. As well as trained mechanics from the RAOC and suitable individuals from the Royal Engineers and Royal Army Service Corp were transferred to the new regiment. The workshops were the responsibility of the REME.

Germany started the war in a superior position but when Churchill took over the Premiership things began to change.

Ken Ingle was at 3 Base Sub-Workshops, Tel Aviv, in October 1942 when it became a REME installation. For Ken it was the same job, the same pay and the same workshops until February 1943 when most of the unit moved off to join the 8th Army in Libya.

He was now part of HQ 3 Advanced Base Workshops. Large convoys of vehicles stopped at Rafah en route to North Africa to pick up stores and equipment and some extra personnel. The next stop was at Tel-el-Kebir where they collected additional workshop machinery, lathes, milling machines, forging hammers etc. and more personnel.

For the next two weeks Ken's convoy trundled 1500 miles across North Africa to Tripoli. There they set up shop in an Italian Army Barracks with very good workshop facilities.

Ken said he was not in danger in North Africa but was impressed with the guards at Rafah.

The only danger from a military source came from trigger-happy guards, said Ken. 'At the time of leaving Palestine to go and tag onto the Eighth Army we had occasion to spend about three days at Rafah picking up equipment and stores. On the first day after an evening in the sergeants' mess we were warned most seriously not to take a short cut across open ground but to keep to the roads to get to our sleeping quarters. The depot was guarded by detachments from the 4th Indian Division and they had an amazing enthusiasm for doing guard duties and shooting at moving things. I was told that in certain units one of the punishments for misdemeanors was to be taken off the guard roster for a week or two. This was regarded as a terrible disgrace.'

Eventually the Germans were chased out of the Middle East and at last Hitler's reach was proving too long for his grasp. From the

Middle East the war moved to Europe with the landings in Sicily.

Ken wrote 'Our activities in Tripoli were quite intensive and the output of vehicles was impressive and the same could be said for the output of the gunshops. After fourteen months the workshops followed the Eighth Army into Italy.'

2 BOD and the Port of Haifa played a key role in the supply of weapons and war materials.

The men at 2 BOD were first at the growing depot at Rafah and then moved to Haifa because there was more civilian labour available, it was also Palestine's only deep-water port.

It was a move appreciated by all. A better camp, better recreation facilities and a more favourable climate.

Brigadier Hitchcock, known to the men as 'Scratch' had been their C.O from the very start at Rafah, moved with them. At the Haifa depot he was able to live in a flat in the town. From the Brigadier down to other ranks the entire depot was happy to be away from Rafah. The Brigadier was concerned about this disparity and sometime later decided it would be fairer if he allowed some of the men at Rafah to swap places with the men at Haifa.

The reactions were surprising; the men from Rafah didn't relish the idea of being in a depot so close to the Brigadier and the H.Q. 'They saw a definite advantage in being some 300 miles away' said John Tarran who was exchanged. But John was pleasantly surprised; Rafah had improved since he was there in 1941.

'They had facilities not available at Camp 153, a swimming pool, tennis courts, billiard rooms and regular weekend trips to Tel Aviv and Jerusalem. The labour problem had largely been solved; hundreds of Italian prisoners were now working in the depot seemingly content to see the war out in comparative safety and comfort.'

The population of Palestine was enjoying a better war than the population of the UK. More food was available in their shops and souks and the armed forces were providing employment for the civilian population. Both the Jewish and the Arab communities were more prosperous that at any time during or before the period of the Mandate. Many were employed by the army. Off duty service people and those on leave were generating revenue for cafés, bars and hotels. All the rearward services stationed in Palestine had local purchasing teams ordering items that could be made or grown locally.

Early in 1942 the troops camped under canvas in the olive trees at Camp 153 whilst permanent accommodation was being built. Brick built toilets were first to be erected then these Arab bricklayers built the Regimental Office. Mount Carmel is in the background. *Photo: John Farrow*

The men who sailed out of Britain in 1941 and were in Palestine for four years had by most standards a 'comfortable' war. John Tarran summed it up: 'we in the BOD as clerks and storemen were doing civilian jobs, but in uniform and a long way from home and under army discipline. The Regimental side of the BOD was administered quite separately from the Depot. The Officer Commanding and his Adjutant and Orderly Room staff were responsible for feeding, housing and seeing to the welfare. We were also required to update our training from time to time and provide guards for the camp and the Depot. This was generally regarded as a bind but all in all it was nothing worse than a minor irritation. We had a number of Sergeant Majors some from Guards regiments, who must have despaired at trying to make soldiers of us. R.S.M. Bradley stood head and shoulders above them as far as I was concerned.'

Regimental Sergeant Majors were welcome members of a rearward service unit; conscripts and junior officers alike appreciated them. It was an appreciation few recruits would have thought likely upon their first encounter with the R.S.M. of the training depot.

R.S.M's and experienced N.C.O's brought orderliness to otherwise inexperienced soldiers. They stabilized hotheaded young subalterns, soberised drunken captains and energised flagging soldiers.

Tide of war was beginning to turn. German lines of communication in Russia were stretched beyond a manageable limit and the Russians were winning back some of their lost ground. America was at last in the war. Thousand bomber raids were blasting German cities giving the British civilian population the satisfaction of knowing that the Germans were getting the bitter taste of their own medicine. With Rommel defeated and North Africa in Allied hands the Allies could enter Europe from the Mediterranean. On July 9, 1943 the Allies invaded Sicily. The strategic value of Palestine was again proved. In the pre war period, Britain had made Haifa into the country's major port and perfect for loading men and materials onto Liberty ships to establish a beachhead supply base. Palestine was now like a giant arsenal largely safe from attack except for a few ineffective air raids from bases in Italy. The Middle East Ordnance Base continued to expand to sustain the campaign in Italy and ease the strain on bases in Britain. It was also a vital link in the chain of supply to South East Asia a theatre where Allied forces were under considerable pressure. This expansion required more personnel both military and civilian.

Very rarely did troops leaving Britain have any idea of their final destination. Those bound for the Middle East knew they weren't going to Iceland or Finland only when they were sailing down the West Coast of Africa. They also knew when they reached the Red Sea that their destination was Egypt. From Egypt they wouldn't know whether they were going west to North Africa or north to Palestine until they were on the train. It was a popular theory that if you were fair you would be posted to the cooler zone of Palestine. Whatever the destination it was going to be a long, hot, tiring journey. Ken Brown was fair and this is his diary entry of his journey to 3 Base Workshops at Sarafand from Tel el Kebir.

Thursday 27th May 1941

We were on and off parades all morning, but by 3:00 pm we were ready to move off – embarking on a train at the sidings. This line was the main line to the Western Desert. Thankfully we were going in the opposite direction. Our route took us back through Zagazig, heading for El Kantara on the Suez Canal. Here we crossed the canal by lighter, and after a good meal of sausage, mash and peas we had a rest until 3:00 am when we assembled with a full kit etc. to proceed to the loading sheds. Twenty men were allocated to each goods van, with a corporal in charge. The officers enjoyed a carriage at the front of the train. In charge of our van was Corporal Walker, quite a jovial character. We eventually moved off at a slow speed across the Sinai Desert. The single line track ran on through the desert, with an occasional loop line at various stages. We took turns for three of us to sit in the open van doorway, the rest either sleeping or playing cards.

About midday, Jim Wade, Walter Speck and myself were sitting in the open doorway. I was awake, the other two dozing when, drawn by the horizon, I fell from the train! It was lucky that I fell into soft sand. I looked back towards the track only to see the guard's van pass. With only K.D. shorts, no topee, no money and only my army knife and feeling very drowsy I set off to follow the train in the hope that my disappearance had been noticed. After walking a couple of miles I was suddenly surrounded by 5 or 6 Arabs who came along and caught hold of my arms. This, for a 20-year-old novice, alarmed me. However, later on I found that they were checking to see if I had broken any bones. It would seem that my absence from the van had been noticed and Corporal Walker had fired his rifle to alert the driver of the engine – to no avail. But the Arabs had seen this and picked up the spent cartridges, which they showed me. This working party then put me on a line trolley and proceeded up the line towards El Arish.

About an hour later we heard the whistle of an engine and pulled off the track. It was the engine from the train with three officers on board. The M.O., a major from the Australian Army, together with the adjutant Captain Whiting and another officer. The engine driver was most concerned – he would have to report this to his employers, the Palestine Railways, to account for lost time. I was assisted to the engine which returned to the train, held up on a loop line. The C.O. had cleared a long bench seat in the officer's carriage where I was put down. The M.O. proceeded to wash my face and gave my eyes a good examination. I was told to rest, with a dose of Sal Volatile. Further treatment came along with cups of tea and some sandwiches, by which time we had reached El Arish station. The train halted for some time to take on water and I again received treatment from the M.O., apparently to see if I was still suffering from shock.

After leaving El Arish the C.O. came to see if I had recovered. I assured him that I was feeling much better, so he provided some books for me to read. The first book I opened, Tolstoy's *War and Peace*, was not a very good subject at that time!

We eventually crossed the border from Egypt to Palestine and on to the peacetime garrison at Sarafand where we detrained. We moved to our billets, Salamanca Barracks, and deposited our gear into Hut No.5. The garrison M.O. gave further treatment and inspected my eyes, which were still smarting, after which I was told to report in three days time.' *[3]

Charlie Eyles was born in 1905 and served in the RAOC from 1923 to 1929 and in that period served in Egypt and China. As a reservist who had received a shilling a day for ten years he was recalled to the colours on Sept 1 1939 and before the month was out he was crossing the Channel for France with the No. 7 Advance Ammunition Company RAOC. Events were such that on June 17 1940 they had to abandon the camp and leave on the last lorry to get away. They left France from St Nazaire on the 18 June on H.M.S. Destroyer Vanoc from which they were transferred to a rusty old freighter. Tired and hungry after a long roundabout journey they docked at Southampton on June 22.

As more and more men were needed in the Middle East it was not long before Charlie was taking the trip around the Cape on the troopship Rhuahine. Charlie's company, the No.28 Advanced Ordnance Ammunition Coy were posted to Abu Sultan in Egypt. Twelve of the company, including Charlie were sent to Sidi Haneesh in the desert.

'After three weeks we returned to Abu Sultan via Alexandria.

Next day we left for Palestine via Kantara. The orange groves were a sight after the desert and the scent of blossoms in the evening is unforgettable. Our destination was a place called Wadi Sarar, which, according to Biblical legend, is where David slew Goliath. To us it was 3 AAD, MEF.

Our commanding officer was Maltese; he did his rounds on a beautiful white horse. I seemed to cross swords with him at our first meeting. He accused me of dereliction of duty and gave me a dressing down using a fair number of swear words.

As an ex regular soldier, I informed him that officers just don't do that sort of thing. In military circles if you are likely to be awkward you are either posted away – or promoted! He could do very little of either but there is one thing he did do. Apparently a trainload of explosives had been sent from the Canal Zone to us and, believe it or not, it got lost. He gave me a lorry and four men to go and find it. It seemed a cockeyed sort of mission to me but I was delighted. I had always been interested in Biblical regions so I thought he'd done me a good turn.

We headed south. We had no map but with the sun and a watch it is fairly easy to navigate by day. In the Middle East, sun and stars are available for such uses 75% of the year. The sun and stars are so much brighter. We visited Hebron and Gath and attached ourselves to an Australian unit for food and petrol. I asked them to send a signal, a sort of telegram, to all units concerned. Normally only a commissioned officer can do this, but Australian units have a totally different attitude. It was to my own CO and Depot and ammunition depots and Rail Transport Officers throughout the Middle East, stating that I was looking for the train and that I was with an Australian unit. After seeing several places of interest, I signalled 'no train in sight, instructions please.' The reply eventually came telling me to return to Wadi Sarar. A few days later the CO informed me he was sending me to a place called Jisr-el-Majami. "Take a civilian lorry driver and four men" he said. "I don't know exactly where it is, but I think it's by the lake." Whether he wanted me to just go and get lost I've no idea, but the desire to get going was paramount. I didn't even ask why I was going. The Jewish driver and his lorry came from the local Kibbutz but he didn't know where the place was either.

'Jerusalem was some miles to the East. My plan was get going and ask no questions and buy a map in Jerusalem. The trip to Jerusalem was one of the most hair-raising trips I've ever made. The descent into the valley, around the hairpin bends with nothing but an abyss on one side and a cliff on the other, and a lorry that had long since seen the best of its days, driven by a maniac. However, we arrived safely.

In order to visit Jerusalem's wonderful places of interest we arranged for our Jewish driver to stage a breakdown, so we had an excuse should the Military Police be suspicious.' *4.

Storage of ammunition east of the Suez Canal and in Palestine developed piecemeal. A depot was constructed at Wadi Sarar between Jerusalem and Sarafand in 1941 and was then known as 3 Advanced Ammunition Depot. (AAD) Further developments were influenced by the campaign in Syria, and the threat from the north which continued to be serious even after the occupation of Syria. From being an AAD it was redesignated No. 2 BAD (Base Ammunition Depot) with a sub depot at Acre. At the peak period in December 1942 Wadi Sara held 18,000 tons of ammunition and Acre, 13,000 tons. Lance Corporal Charlie Kidd arrived at Wadi Sara in 1942 he writes of the conditions there:

'When we arrived at Wadi Sarar in 1942 there was not much in the way of facilities. No paths in the camp and our first winter was spent with mud up to our knees. The toilets were just buckets thirty yards away across a sea of mud. The water supply was more out of action than in. Our unit was made up of new arrivals to the Middle East. I was a new arrival but quite a few had been up in the Desert before coming to Wadi.

In the second year things were more organized. We had breeze huts and connecting paths to all the facilities. In the summer we were infested with bugs which took refuge in the gelignite bower. Our beds had straw palliasses, which, despite hanging them out daily were infested with the bugs. As we tried to sleep they would come out for supper every night.

The Filling Factory and Base Ammunition Depot RAOC staff

was supplemented by a variety of civil and military staff from the Commonwealth. There was such a high turnover of personnel we had the Palestine Buffs, a Jewish unit, an East African unit, and Indian unit and an Arab company. About the middle of 1944 approximately 25 ex Tank Corps members who had been wounded and recovered were posted to Wadi. This doubled the British strength.

There was one upset, when the Arab Company tried to go to the cinema on the night it was allocated to the Jewish Palestine Buffs. Three of them were shot and the rest started to go back for their guns from their camp on the hill. However a British officer and four men took a 15 cwt. truck got there before them and set up a table and Bren gun to discourage them. More of us followed and the RAOC saved the day. A unit of Military Police was sent up from Sarafand and the Arab company was taken away in trucks. Soon after the camp had a dog unit to guard the ammunition sheds and a mounted unit to patrol the perimeter.'

References

1. *Paiforce*. HMSO 1940
2. *The Second World War, Vol II,* Winston Churchill, Cassels
3. The unpublished *Life in the Army*, Ken Brown
4. The unpublished memoirs of Sergeant Charlie Eyles.

3.

Movement Orders

Other than in wartime overseas travel was no more than a dream
for thousands of youngsters. Few had visited foreign countries and
had little hope of doing so in civilian life. Service life gave the opportunity to travel abroad even though it incurred a degree of danger. Our dreams were inspired by travelogues at the cinema and
the glossy pages of the National Geographical Magazine. What we
experienced did not fulfil the dream, not even by half. The harsh
logistics of travelling as a member of a large army on the move as ec-
onomically as possible was far removed from the seductive descriptions of the travel journalist. Even so it brought with it its own form
of excitement and surprises for a conscripted soldier. Transporting
troops was literally the mother of all package tours. It began in 1884
when Thomas Cook was given the job of moving General Gordon's
Expeditionary Force to the Sudan.

The moment World War II ended the demand for military transport increased dramatically. There were Allied forces wanting to
return to their homeland, there were hundreds of thousands of
prisoners of war to be repatriated and displaced persons were add-
ing to the problem. Servicemen and women who had been away for
up to six years needed to be replaced by post war conscripts. More
were making the homeward journey than the outward journey. It
was a situation that was to exist beyond the evacuation of Palestine.
Despite the enormous scale of the operation it did present the occasional difficulty.

Troops on the move were exposed to terrorist activity not only in

Palestine but also in Egypt, which was showing considerable unrest in the immediate post war years. Whether it was a complete unit or a group of individuals a considerable amount of documentation was deemed necessary. There were roll calls before departure, on arrival at all overnight stops en route. An alarm was raised if one should be missing. Troops in transit afforded the opportunity for an individual to abscond. It was not expected to happen on the homeward journey but it did when Leo Chambers left 614 AOD in Palestine. Harold Draper said he was missing from his group unnoticed for six days. It was believed that he took unofficial 'leave' in Fayid together with pals from the leave centre.

In 1864 the most direct and quickest way to get from London to Jerusalem was by rail, sea and stagecoach via France, Italy, the Adriatic and the Mediterranean.

The final stretch was by stagecoach from Jaffa to Jerusalem. The total journey took eight days.

The route became popular when the Suez Canal opened in 1864 and the ancient Italian seaport of Brindisi was modernised to take large passenger ships. The overland route via France was a well used by the British Army until France was taken by Germany and Italy entered the war.

After the war the overland routes through France and Italy were reopened. Sergeant Jack Hayman who served at 2 BOD between 1941 and 1945 was among the first to use the reopened Medloc route.

Jack was a confirmed diarist and his journey home was quite detailed not just with days and dates but also with departure times at each stage of the journey. More than eighty years after the opening of the route it took Jack and his comrades a total of 59 days from leaving Camp 153 to reaching home. The logistics of moving a Company of soldiers are much greater than the moving of small independent groups of travellers.

Jack's diary allows us to sense his frustration after so long abroad.

Left Camp 153 on Monday September 17 1945 and the day began at the normal time, with a visit to the Medic for an FFI (free from infection) examination at 0700hrs. At 1200 hrs the troops and their kit were trucked to Haifa Central station and they were pulling out on a southbound train at 1355hrs.

After a sixteen-hour journey they arrived at Tel-el-Kebir at 0600hrs on Tuesday September 18.

Jack described the journey as 'terrible'; they had to change coaches at midnight in the middle of the Sinai desert. Transport took them to 5 BOD in time to be on parade at 0930hrs. they were paraded again at 1400hrs and then dismissed for the day.

For five days they became more and more "browned off" waiting for 'the boat.' There were lots of rumours but no action. They did however manage a visit to Shafto's, a civilian cinema. On Thursday September 25 eight days after leaving Camp 153 there was the usual 0800 hrs parade, but at last this was a day for action.

At 2310 hrs they left 5 BOD's railway sidings on a train that arrived at Alexandria at 0600hrs next day. The morning was taken up embarking on the MV Batory and much to the delight and surprise of Jack and his mates they were allocated cabins. They sailed at 1540hrs and out of sight of Egypt at 1800hrs.

On September 27 the clocks were put back one hour. On the 28th in much rougher seas Italy was in sight through the Straits of Messina. The MV Batory passed the small Lipari Island with its towering active volcano, Stromboli.

The clocks went back by a further hour and they were now on UK Time and home seemed that much nearer. After passing through the Straits of Bonifacio between Corsica and Sardinia the Batory docked at Toulon at 0700hrs on September 30 and by 1030hrs they were in Transit Camp 312. The weather was cold and miserable but the village of La Sayne was worth a visit.

Next day more parades and at 2215hrs on October 1 they left on a German train.

After thirty-five and quarter hours travelling through France seated on wooden seats they reached Dieppe at 0930hrs on October 3. It was to be almost twenty-four more hours before the travel weary troops boarded a ferry, the "Isle of Thanet" and seven hours, ten minutes later they disembarked on English soil.

Tea and cakes were distributed at the harbour and they were

on the train to Donnington Depot, Shropshire but the journey was not without a hitch. Jack wrote 'There was a long wait at Clapham Junction and some of the London lads were feeling exasperated.' The train arrived at Donnington at 2215hrs.

On the morning of Friday October 5 there were more parades. 'Everyone was cheesed off with the delay' wrote Jack. Pay and rations were collected at 1200hrs and Jack would finally leave for home at 1355hrs and he arrived home at midnight.

From the day he left the UK to the day he arrived back Jack had been away 1,526 days, the last 59 of them occupying just the journey home.

Young recruits going abroad for the first time were not quite so intent on counting the hours they were more interested in the detail and the novel experience of a journey beyond their wildest imagination. Stan Hayward left Aldershot to travel the Medloc route in the opposite direction going southwards across France three or four months after Jack and his train journey took longer. His party from 20 Vehicle Recovery Depot, Aldershot arrived at Newhaven at 1600hrs. Around midnight they were given breakfast and left the harbour on the "Royal Daffodil" a valiant little vessel used in the evacuation of Dunkirk. It was a very cold night and the ferry was crowded. To keep warm Stan sat close to the funnel which was still perforated with the bullet holes from the evacuation five years earlier.

The "Royal Daffodil" docked at Dieppe at dawn and after they were given a second breakfast they boarded the train. Six men were allocated to each compartment. They were seated on slatted wooden seats and the journey took four days and the men stretched out as comfortably as they could with the two lightest and shortest sleeping on the luggage racks, one of them being Stan.

Bridges over ravines that were being repaired, reduced the speed of the train down to only 5 mph at times. At Toulon the SS "Ascania" was waiting for troops to board her. The 'tween decks were boarded over to increase the accommodation capacity. The ship stopped once at Malta to take on fresh water. It took four days on a calm sea to reach Alexandria. No overnight stops were necessary in either of the transit camps in France or Egypt. They boarded a troop train in Alexandria bound for Tel-el-Kebir.

Early in 1946 Brian Cross made the same journey and made some interesting observations.

'On arrival at Dieppe after a five hour cross channel journey we were confronted with the debris of war including .303 ammunition on the beaches. The uncleared debris of demolished pillboxes remained as evidence of the Canadian raid on Dieppe in August 1942. For five days we were besieged in a transit camp at Dieppe by the locals, mainly women, who were offering the earth for the Lux soap and cigarettes we had purchased from the NAAFI.

'For a pound note we were offered five times the official exchange rate-alas we didn't have too many of those!' Brian's train journey took three days compared with Stan's four. Everywhere there was the wreckage of war including the big railway guns that had been pushed off the rails.

Brian continues; 'At Toulon we were again in a transit camp for a week. One thing I remember when we were allowed into town was an old man sitting in silence, on a chair who jerked his thumb to a side street. No doubt he had been doing that since France capitulated to the Germans, because up that street was the local brothel.

There were few takers, after all we were only 18 and had no desire to go where the Germans had gone before. We embarked on the old Liberty ship "Empire Mace," a real hell ship. No wonder the American army wouldn't sail in Liberty ships even though they were built in America.

We weren't given bread, only hard biscuits. Most of the time that this 'bath tub' of a boat thrashed its way to Alexandria many were seasick.'

Walter Horrocks of 614 AOD tells a very similar story. He left England in November 1946. He says the transit camp outside Toulon was at Hyeres, and it was there that they were issued with khaki drill uniforms. He writes:

"We were able to visit Toulon, our first experience of the Mediterranean climate. Even in November it was great to be away from the dull dark days of post war UK, although we were reminded of war by the sight of the French Fleet that had been scuttled in Toulon Harbour.

A nice memory of mine was the pavement artists who were willing to sketch a portrait for a few francs, also the very welcoming Church of Scotland Club for a much-appreciated cup of tea. Sorry no alcohol, strictly temperance.'

Denis Burns of 52 Mobile Laundry and Bath Unit went out by the Dover-Calais route in autumn 1946. Calais was still in a mess from the invasion. Denis and his fellow comrades spent the night before embarkation on straw palliasses in the attics of Dover Castle. He writes:

'The troop train journey was about 900 miles or so via Dijon and Lyon. We had one official stop somewhere for a brush up and food. Some of the bridges we crossed looked as if great parts were missing and at times looked as if we were travelling over rails in mid-air. After two days in Hyreres transit camp we boarded a troopship at Toulon for a five day voyage to Port Said.'

Arthur Hammond's draft went by what was known as the Medloc 'C' route that was via Calais, Germany, Austria and Italy the route tourists travelled in 1864. From Italy the route took them through the Adriatic and Mediterranean to Port Said.

Arthur was deeply moved by his journey through Europe in those immediate post war years. He cannot remember most of the places he went through but his most abiding memory is 'the hundreds of thousands of displaced persons that lined the route. We stopped at Karlsruhe, Stuttgart and Munich for cooked meals. We were also given sandwiches to eat on the train but we threw those to the homeless at each stop.

At Karlsruhe the bomb damage was severe. The damaged buildings that were still standing were being pulled down and immediately rebuilt.'

Very few of these post war conscripts had ever been abroad before, some had never seen the sea until the army took them abroad.

The events of 1946 brought about a change in Britain's strategy in Palestine and a large draft was mustered for transit to Palestine in the first days of 1947. They were to go by sea and the ships they went on to Port Said were to be used to take ATS personnel and the army wives of regular officers back to the UK. In December 1946 I was one of many RAOC conscripts given a combined Christmas and embarkation leave that was unfortunately marred during my leave by having to visit the nearest barracks for another injection. We reported to Feltham RAOC Holding Depot for transit only to be told to take some more leave. This didn't personally overwhelm me because I was sure we were going to Germany, a country of friendly frauleins and Leica cameras at knock down prices. Then there was all the business of saying farewell to parents, grandparents and neighbours again. The six-year-old boy next door had cried when I left the first time. We reassembled once more at Feltham and were allocated bunk beds in a vast unheated store shed. It was terribly cold and we slept in battle dress.

To make the next night, Saturday, more bearable we took the tube to Piccadilly to see for the first time in our lives, the famous heart of London. Also, for the first time in my life, I made myself drunk after visiting many pubs. We again slept fully dressed including boots and greatcoat not knowing that this was how it was to be for many nights to come.

We had not been in our bunks long on Sunday night when in the very early hours of Monday morning we were given a 'wakey-wakey rise and shine' call. In the dark we lined up and an officer asked every fourth man to fall out.

It was a cold, cold journey in an unheated train. At that time of night our journey should not have taken long. The train stopped on one occasion and we thought we may have arrived, but wiping the frost from the window I could see a dimly lit sign that told us we were at Basingstoke, so then we knew our destination was to be Southampton.

At Southampton we lined up again on the quay beneath a large departure canopy and in front of the SS Mooltan. Dawn was breaking and it was snowing gently. Everyone was given a bun and our mugs were filled with tea, which cooled off before we could put mug to lip. After at least a two hours wait we were directed on board.

Ray Machin, George Billings and myself plus a couple of hundred or so others were guided to the lowest deck. We were given hammocks and shown where to sling them. It was soon apparent just how tightly packed we were going to be. It was necessary to roll up the hammocks every morning in order to eat our meals on the tables that were directly beneath us and we had a demonstration on how to do this.

The Mooltan was built and registered in Belfast in 1923 and operated as a luxury liner capable of carrying 656 passengers until 1938 when she was converted to carry chilled beef. In 1941 she was converted again, this time to a troopship to carry up to 3000 passengers. This overcrowded vessel was to be our home for the next ten days.

What had started as a rumble of discontent turned into anger as no one to complain to could be found on our deck. On the dockside a line of Red Caps (Military Police) were obviously amused at our anger. The gangplanks had been pulled up and the ship moved away from the quay, too far to get off but no so far that we could not scoop up the thick layer of snow off the decks and superstructure to make into snowballs to throw at the jeering Military Police.

Under an intense barrage of snowballs they moved several paces backwards.

Most of the men on board were born in 1928 and were demob group 76 and by their appearance they didn't look like infantrymen. In fact many of us were bound for just one destination, 614 Advanced Ordnance Depot although we didn't know that until we got there.

Also on board were men that I was destined to meet again 50 years later. They were Harold"Brummie" Draper, Alex Monaghan, Eric Long, John White and Jack Hibbs. Alex was a sergeant and a couple of years older, it was his job to see that the men took showers, an impossible job until we reached Gibraltar.

When darkness fell we moved into the Solent but the weather was so stormy we had to anchor for the night in the lee of the Isle of Wight. The next day we thrashed our way through the English Channel. Such was the poor visibility and the sea so rough that we had no idea where we were for several days. Although in it's day the "Mooltan" was the biggest P&O ship built at 20,847 gross registered tonnage, in these stormy seas it was tossed about as if it were an empty can. The propellers were frequently out of the water and as Eric Long put it, "It did everything but turn over."

Most of the men were seasick and not only from the motion of the sea, everything conspired to nauseate. There was no escape on the recreation deck. Smells came from the two funnels, one emitting carbon monoxide from the ceaselessly throbbing engines and the other the odours from the ventilating system.

The latrines, or heads to use seafarer's language, were in a disgusting state; the cubicles were without doors and the contents of the lavatory basins were thrown out when the port side of the ship was hit by a wave and the latrine deck was awash with a mixture of seawater, vomit, undigested oranges and excretion. The oranges should have been a treat after being without them for so many years.

The food on the ship was good if you could eat it, freshly baked French bread sticks, Egyptian new potatoes and tinned fruit and cream. Harold Draper who was a small wiry, nimble man enjoyed all his food and followed to the letter the advice given to him by a former sailor – "Eat all that is put before you, before and during the voyage."

He was one of the few who was not seasick. Eric Long also stayed free of seasickness by continually walking around the deck, but it was cold and the ship's rails were covered in ice.

Eric recalls the lifeboat drill at the end of the ship on one occasion when the sea was rough and the ship's propellers came out of the water, and all but a few were dashing to the rail to be sick. Eric's deck was immediately below the galley and two men were detailed from each mess table, on a rota basis, to fetch the food from the galley. He remembers one morning when the breakfast was kippers; 'One of the men carrying a large tray of hot, steaming kippers was overcome by the smell, which contributed to his acute seasickness with the result that he added something extra to the breakfast tray.'

Troops relaxing on the deck of the *SS Mooltan* in the calmer waters of the Mediterranean.

The ship was very cold and we continued to sleep in our uniforms. Getting into a hammock was like a Laurel and Hardy farce; one got in one side and fell out of the other. Some men fell out of their hammocks and knocked the man out of the next hammock also. Eventually we all got the hang of it.

Once past Cape Finisterre the storm abated somewhat but it was still very cold and rough. There was still thick ice on the ship's rails and superstructure. It was not until we entered the Straits of Gibraltar that the waters calmed and the ice melted. Early in the morning, a few days later, as we were approaching Port Said an aircraft carrier was easing its way out. A little further in we were slowly passing the homeward bound troop ship 'Empress of Scotland' from the Far East. Happy time expired men were laughing and light heartedly jeering 'Get your knees brown!' and 'You'll be sorree!'

Even before The Mooltan dropped anchor the bumboats were alongside and throwing up ropes to establish lines for trading. All manner of goods were on offer from daggers to handbags, and including a product I had never heard of before called Spanish Fly!

British currency was mostly what they wanted and there were several moneychangers operating from these small boats. Small boys also swam in the murky water asking us to throw in coins for them to dive for. The coins never reached the bottom because they were caught as they flip-flopped downwards, glinting in the muddy light.

Homeward bound *Empress of Scotland* carrying troops from the Far East leaving Port Said, from the deck of the *SS Mooltan*.

Less than a month after the Mooltan sailed, another draft was embarking at Tilbury Docks for service in Germany.

Malcolm Astley was part of that draft but he was one of four disappointed men pulled out just hours before the troopship sailed. Like many other eighteen year olds he had never been on holiday in Britain in his life let alone overseas.

Germany was the most hoped for overseas posting but within days, like boarding a mystery tour charabanc, he was on the next troopship sailing from Tilbury, but this time it was more adventurous and hazardous destination, Palestine via Port Said.

Not surprisingly his train journey on the Cairo to Haifa Express took three days. Once aboard the train you couldn't be sure when you would arrive at your destination. He was surprised at the number and variety of vendors at every stop. He commented 'They were skilled salesmen and even more skilled pickpockets and thieves, however looking back now one realises what a pathetic and miserable existence they endured.'

At times there seemed to be no logic in troop movements. Stan Heath was posted to the No.2 Ammunition Repair Depot and Filling Factory at Wadi Sarar from Famagusta, Cyprus. Although it was only 70 miles to Haifa they left Cyprus for Sicily and then back to Port Said and then the long train journey to Palestine.

Throughout 1946 Bill Muncey spent his time in Calcutta. In May 1947 Bill was under canvas at Deolali Transit Camp, India. After four weeks waiting he got a berth on the SS Chitnal on it's way from Singapore to the UK. It was not unknown to wait for two months for a ship, which gave rise to the expression 'gone dolali.' True to form, he was not told what was to be his final destination and being a regular soldier he didn't build up his hopes for a return to Britain.

Bill wrote... 'On arrival at Suez we were informed that as there was an epidemic of Yellow fever in the Canal Zone all personnel due to disembark were to be inoculated. There was then to be a seven-day inoculation period before being allowed to disembark. As the ship was at berth the 'air conditioning' was in operation only for short periods, making it impossible to sleep below deck. Everyone made for the open deck at night where some sleep was possible. I eventually arrived at Port Suez transit camp where a number of us were told that in all the confusion our kit bags had not been unloaded from the ship before she had sailed on. We were, therefore, to report to the QM Stores where missing items of kit would be reissued. A few days later we boarded a train for Palestine and the ammunition depot at Wadi Sarar.'

Bill's next posting was in March 1948 to 522 Ordnance Depot, Khartoum. The first leg of the journey was to Abu Sultan by road across the Sinai Desert. Due to one small error in the documents he found himself at 525 Ordnance Depot, Asmara in the mountains of Ethiopia. Two weeks later a troopship took him back to Port Sudan and a 450 miles train journey took him to Khartoum and his intended destination 522 AOD.

All troop movements required a considerable amount of documentation to cover every contingency and detail. It involved documents with a bewildering array of numbers.

Bill was on an individual posting but in the case of a group of troops the most senior officer or NCO is delegated to act as Draft Conducting Officer (DCO) and he takes charge of all the documentation and the responsibility of his travelling companions. Take the case of Sergeant John Hardwick, the DCO of a party of four, himself, Sergeant C.A.Foulkes, Sergeant R.H. Barrass and Pte. I.K. Harris, 378 all going home for demob.

Copies of the Movement Order were sent to the COO, GHQ, MELD, Orderly Sgt. Pay Office, Post Office, records, the MO, the Unit Education Officer, the Quartermaster (3 copies) of R333, R/4/2 (whatever they might be). Sergeant Hardwick had to take three copies to the O.C. 163 Transit Camp (Acre) along with a sealed envelope containing individual documents, AFB122, AFH1157, AFB250, and AFKB861.

Everything in the Army had a number and to most men the numbers were meaningless. One number that no soldier could forget was 252, the number given to a charge sheet, often given for some minor misdemeanour and this was better known to the troops as a "fizzer."

In addition the sealed envelope contained the nominal roll (in triplicate) and three copies of the Movement Order, in this instance, 358.

Finally John had to make sure that each man had in his possession his AF A3690 (service sea landing permit for the UK) and had been vaccinated against smallpox within the past two years, which of course would be recorded in his AB64 Part 1.

It came as no surprise that the order stated 'Arms and ammunition will be kept with the person at all times and on no account will be left unattended. Sergeant Hardwick will warn his party that it is forbidden to be in possession of enemy arms or equipment.' This was an attempt to stop the taking of captured weapons as souvenirs. Under the heading, 'Rations' which in this case simply meant the weekly free issue of cigarettes and matches up to March 25 and certificates for NAAFI purchases of cigarettes and soap (at a special low price) up to March 27.

The Movement Order issued by Major R.S.T. Newman command-ing Depot Co., 614 AOD, authorising John and his companions to proceed from 614 AOD to Acre transit camp (Haifa) for onwards routing to the UK for Class 'A' release in Age and Service Group 69, better known to all as 'demob group.'

They linked up with men from other units at the end of the lane from Camp 153 and they formed a convoy that took the high road over Mount Carmel to avoid the fierce fighting between Jews and Arabs in Haifa. They got through the Jewish area intact but when they entered the Arab area they were forced to stop by armed Arabs. A Warrant Officer from one of the other groups wanted to take the Arabs on but John and the men close to demob persuaded him to desist and a conflict was avoided.

Troop trains in the Middle East, like the troopships that took the armed forces there were always overcrowded. They inevitably trav-elled through the night with little opportunity for the passengers to sleep. Some managed to sleep sitting in their seats, not an easy achievement on the wooden slats. Others slept on kit bags on the floor, some even slept on the luggage racks. There was no glass in the windows and that was a blessing in the hot climate. However, for safety's sake, or in bad weather, there were shutters. They were shut tight at night because thieving by the natives was prevalent. Even in seemingly uninhabited desert areas thieves were likely to be operat-ing. They occasionally travelled on the roof leaning over to sneak a look inside waiting for an unguarded moment when they would, with remarkable ease and agility, swing into the carriage and take away any loose item that was handy.

Unless you were at the end of a carriage getting to the latrine was almost impossible. In the early years the carriage lights had been fitted with globes but these had long since been taken for use as urinals.

Hot weather and very little to drink lessened the need to pass water but those who felt the need often relieved themselves out of the windows. With due consideration to passengers in the follow-ing coaches, the 'window method' was only used when the train was stationary or the speed had slowed down to walking pace.

Those that made the journey to the latrine at the end of a coach found that it was nothing more than a hole in the floor with a pivoted flap. It was a sight sufficient to deter even the most urgent calls of nature.

Vendors of all descriptions and all ages besieged stationary trains in Egypt. They advertised their wares by their cries 'Eggsy bread,' 'Ice cold limonada,' 'Cokey Cola' and 'water le melon.' Those selling other items were not so open; they would sidle up and say in a confidential hushed voice 'Dirtee book Johnny' or 'Dirtee pictures.'

However among the colourful characters there were some adroit thieves. More than one man has had his spectacles snatched from his nose. Many an unsuspecting rookie who may have had his arm out of the window of a stationary train has lost his wristwatch.

The thief would jump up and hook his finger in the watch trap and hang from it. The strap would snap and the thief and the watch were lost in the crowd. It was done so deftly and at a speed that indicated there had been a lot of practice on a lot of victims.

There was a regular courier service between the Base Depot at Tel-el-Kebir, and the various RAOC installations in Palestine. The couriers, generally sergeants, travelled on civilian trains and were armed with a revolver carried in a holster on the hip. Arthur Phillips was not a regular courier but R.S.M.Whitnell of 614 AOD selected him for a very special mission for Colonel Gore. The Colonel personally briefed Arthur who was surprised to find what this special mission was. He was given a massive onion inside a haversack to take to a particular officer in Tel-el-Kebir to settle a bet. The Colonel had the onion sent over from England to settle a wager that it was bigger than any other that his pal in Egypt had ever seen. Arthur travelled on a train full of Arabs who looked upon him with suspicion for the whole of the journey. He reached his destination only to find that the officer he sought had returned to England. Wearily Arthur made the return journey back to Haifa still carrying the wretched onion. The whole extravagantly childish venture could only have been the creation of a senior officer with little regard for the risks taken every time troops made that hazardous journey.

Just to describe how hazardous the journey was, Andrew Howe sent in this story. He was an official courier who frequently made the same journey that Arthur had made. He remembers one occasion late in 1947, which, in his words, turned out to be 'a hell of a journey.' An hour or so out of Tel-el-Kebir on the train back to Haifa he was told that one of the guards had fallen asleep and dropped his rifle on the rail track. Andrew stopped the train and sent out a patrol and retrieved the rifle. As dawn broke Andrew was tired and decided to take a nap He says – "I took off my holster and used it as a pillow under the impression that no one would be able to remove the revolver without waking me up. My false sense of security arose from the fact that the only other passenger in the compartment was a staff sergeant from a military detention centre.

Imagine my consternation on awakening and discovering the revolver missing. The staff sergeant indicated that he knew nothing about it, I searched the train but only succeeded in drawing a blank. When I got back to my compartment the staff sergeant handed me my revolver and said "Let that be a lesson to you". I did not require a second telling.

As the train approached Lydda Airport there was an almighty explosion and the carriage derailed on to its side. Extracting myself I went forward to the engine that was also on it's side and looked into the driver's cab and found the driver. Seeing a sheet of metal that appeared to be resting on his leg I put my hand down only to discover that the metal went right through the leg. It was a complete amputation.'

A rare opportunity occurred for Andrew to meet his father towards the end of December 1947. By using his privileged courier experience and various connections he managed to get to Port Said a few days before Christmas. A cablegram arrived for him at 614 AOD informing him that his father was on the way home from India and would be stopping at Port Said.

It so happened that Major Davidson from Tel-el-Kebir was on a visit to 614. Andrew knew the major well enough to seek his co-operation to get the necessary movement order signed by him.

Between them they concocted the reason that Andrew was

needed in Port Said was to inspect military vehicles. They travelled together as far as Port Said. At Port Said Andrew had an old school chum, Corporal MacDonnell in the Royal Signals. who, using his knowledge of Port Said took Andrew to the P & O Steamship's Company Building. The ship was due next day at midnight, an hour after the troops' curfew hour. MacDonnell took Andrew to a friendly baker who allowed them to stay under cover until the troopship docked. A P & O official they had met the day before agreed to take them on board. A cholera epidemic had been raging in Egypt since September and it had claimed many thousands of lives and precautions were taken to keep ships docking in Egyptian ports free from the contagion. As well as proving their identity they were able to prove from their AB 64's that they had recently been inoculated against cholera.

That night was spent chatting to Andrew's father in his cabin.

The main railway line was not solely used for business, at August Bank Holiday 1947 it was used to take a party of sports enthusiasts from 614 AOD to Rafah for 615 AOD's Sports Day. John White was a participant in that event. His diary records the seven-hour journey on August 4 to get there. The sports events took place on the next day with 614 winning all the open events. To return to Haifa John and his companions were called at 0300hrs next day stopping for breakfast at Gaza. Even though it was a long day it was back to duties on the following day.

The main south to north railway line was standard gauge and in part the sleepers were laid on bare sand without ballast and trains were frequently derailed by small but effective tulip bombs.

There was a branch line from Lydda that snaked its way past Sarafand and through many twists and turns to Jerusalem.

From Haifa there was a narrow gauge railway that joined the Hejaz to Damascus line. This was line that T.E.Lawrence and the Arabs repeatedly attacked in the First World War.

It was to the junction at Haifa, were the standard gauge and the narrow gauge lines met, that Charlie Eyles and Ian Napier were posted in order to assist the RTO (Rail Transport Officer).

After the Vichy French in Syria had surrendered in 1941 the captured French ammunition was taken by rail from Damascus to the Canal Zone in Egypt.

Charlie and Ian were in charge of two gangs of labourers, one Jewish and the other Arab, whose job it was to transfer the bombs and shells from the narrow gauge wagons to the standard gauge wagons. When eventually all the ammunition had been taken from the last train and sent on its long journey to Egypt Charlie and Ian decided to take an unofficial trip to Damascus. From the open wagons in which they sat they enjoyed an uninterrupted view of the countryside across the Plain of Esdraelon and over the River Jordan at Jsr-el-Majami.

Charlie wrote 'we passed up over the mountains, sometimes we could almost have shaken hands with the driver as we rounded some of the bends.' In Damascus they stayed with a detachment of their pals of the 6th Advanced Ammunition Depot and then hitch-hiked back to Haifa. It was a stolen joy ride in the middle of the war and they weren't even missed.

If it came to a matter of life and death it was theoretically possible to get back to the UK much faster by flying. Obviously, the Whitehall top brass could get in and out of Palestine very quickly whenever they needed to. But what about other ranks? For Corporal Gus O'Brien it did happen.

His story begins well before reveille on November 2 1947 when the orderly sergeant and Captain Jenkins, the adjutant, awakened him with the news that his father was at death's door and he was to be flown home. He had to pack his kit bag, have a cholera injection and get a travel warrant to take him to Fayid, Egypt.

It was twelve long tedious days in Fayid until his posting came. His time was spent between his bed, the NAAFI and the cookhouse except when he was called upon to issue blankets to a detachment of Coldstream Guards. When the time came along Gus with others was taken to an airfield

Gus writes; 'our kitbags were taken from us and carefully thrown into the baggage compartment whilst we climbed aboard. The officers had been directed to the rear of the plane, and we, the other ranks were directed forward.

I pulled rank and got a window seat. An RAF officer came from behind a green curtain that separated us from the cockpit told us to fasten our seat belts. Suddenly the plane shuddered and a loud roar filled the cabin. For ten minutes the plane stood quivering uncontrollably. Then the noise of the engines increased, I was thrust back into my seat and the plane was on the move. I watched sand speed by faster and faster until it became a uniform light brown blur. We gained height and from my little window I had a clear and uninterrupted view of one engine and miles of sand. No people, no camels, no houses, no sky, just sand. Miles and miles of sand. When Malta was in sight we touched down after circling the island as we descended. At the terminal building we were allotted beds for the night and in the dining room a hot meal was waiting for us. To my surprise I found that all those from the plane were sitting together, officers, NCO's and privates. On our table a sergeant major dished out the meat, a captain served out the greens and a full colonel did the honours with the spuds. During the meal the colonel informed us that from take off to landing we had taken seven hours. As we were in transit we were told we might be moved at any time and were confined to camp.

After a communal breakfast the coach took us to the plane, 'Gus had the same window seat but fell asleep. Somewhere during the flight they must have passed over or near Sicily, Sardinia or Corsica. When Gus awoke they were crossing the southern coast of France. Whilst flying over France he was surprised to see miles of roads without a single vehicle on them. Across the channel, in England, they noticed an immediate difference, nowhere was there a road without vehicles. They landed at Lyneham after a flight lasting another seven hours.

Gus's homeward journey was marginally quicker than those who travelled by sea or those that took the Medloc route. It was just as well that father was not at death's door as first imagined; in fact he lived for several years afterwards.

4.

The First Post-War Conflict

When the news came through that Germany had surrendered on May 8 1945 conscripts who were in Palestine knew they were soon to be on the way home. Except for the long absence from home, the war for the men of the rearward services had been more than bearable.

They knew they had enjoyed a comfortable war and were blissfully unaware of the trouble that was about to erupt within months of their departure. Their immediate replacements were being moved from Europe to the Middle East. They had been recruited during the later years of the war and had a couple of years, or so, of war service.

Lieutenant Jack Harris was attached to 158 Infantry Brigade, in the stores section. He joined the army territorials in 1939 and was with the Infantry Brigade when they landed at Normandy in 1944 and until they reached Hamburg. However, following the collapse of Germany he was transferred to the 3rd Infantry Division that was posted to Palestine in September 1945. His division shared the responsibility of policing Palestine with the 6th Airborne Division. Jack wrote, 'the northern border was a hot spot and therefore heavily patrolled. So many Jews were illegally infiltrating after a terribly haphazardous journey from Europe and even as far away as Poland. Our troops could not be other than sympathetic towards them. We had seen Belsen in Germany before coming here. They looked so desperate to get into Palestine, so many a blind eye was shown and they crept through. In spite of this, when we were in the more central parts of Palestine we met so much hostility they seemed to hate us more than the Germans had done. It was such a relief to get an occasional break by the Bitter Lakes in Egypt, which were recognised as a leave centre. The nine months I spent in the Middle East proved to be the worst time of my service. It seems so unfair that we received no recognition for this campaign.'

As Jack and his unit was arriving RAOC and REME troops were going home in little groups of thirty or so at a time. Each wartime soldier was given a Python number when on overseas service. It was a code introduced to replace a fixed period when the demands of war precluded a firm contract. John Farrow and Frank Bell had been in Palestine with 2 BOD for four years and they were going home to Britain on Python 30. They were part of a contingent of thirty men. whose Age and Service Groups (Demob Group) were numbered between 25 and 38. They left Haifa by train for Transit Camp 156, Port Said on November 7 1945. Both were returning home with happy memories of Palestine. Frank specially so because of the favourable finger of fate that saved him from being captured at Tobruk. Frank had volunteered at the start of the war and his Demob Group was 26. His friend John Farrow was Group 37 but they were both Python 30. Howard Allen one of the first wartime conscripts in 1940 was one of the first to return to England. He left before the end of the war in Europe and actually embarked on the *Stirling Castle* at Port Said on Christmas Day 1944. It was sixty years ago and now only one or two things stand out in his memory. The first was that Christmas Day breakfast was kippers. On New Years Eve they passed Gibraltar and searchlights illuminated the Rock and ships' sirens were sounding to welcome in the New Year. A year that was almost certainly going to end in peace. As they sailed up the British coast the snow-capped hills of Wales was their first sight of Britain and the *Stirling Castle* docked at Liverpool to the sound of a military band.

When peace appeared very imminent the streets of Europe were crowded with displaced persons and safe havens were in danger of being overwhelmed with immigrants. High-level talks on the future of Palestine were well under way by 1945. Politicians of all nationalities were putting their views forward, none more so than British and

American. The vociferous Jewish Agency put forward their views vigorously with little regard for the circumstances that were prevailing in Palestine. Although the problem of Europe was not created by the Arabs supporters of Zionism in America and Britain were obsessed with the idea of settling them in Palestine.

Only the people who were about to lose their country had no high level politicians to put their case. By any standard the Palestine Arabs case was the strongest and their need to be heard was the greatest. King Ibn Saud of Saudi Arabia made his views known but little attention was paid to them. Saudi Arabia was not then the rich and powerful nation it is today. World consumption of oil was only a fraction of what it is today. In fact some Arabs left Saudi Arabia looking for work with the British Army in Palestine, some were employed at 614 AOD. Nasir, a Saudi Arab, worked in the cookhouse at Camp 153, and he was saving to get married when he returned to Saudi Arabia.

It was through no fault of the Palestinian Arabs that they had no official spokesman. Britain made no attempt to prepare the Palestinians for independence even though the Jews were openly developing a self-governing administration. Britain could have been helping the Palestinians towards self-government. The Palestinians' chosen leader, the Mufti, Haj Amin el Husseini was still in exile for his part in the Arab uprising. Herbert Samuel had appointed el-Husseini as Mufti of Jerusalem in 1921 but he became hostile to the British for allowing so many Jews into the country. However there was one Palestinian, Musa El-Alami, an intellectual who had studied law at Cambridge. He was related to the Mufti by marriage, his sister was the Mufti's wife. although he himself had steered clear of the politics of the situation during the Arab uprising,

King Ibn Saud had, quite naturally, an interest in a satisfactory outcome to the Palestine situation. He was in correspondence with President Roosevelt who he saw as the Arab's best hope for a suitable solution. Roosevelt, like his predecessor, Woodrow Wilson, favoured a substantial Jewish homeland. In 1945 Musa El-Alami conferred with King Ibn Saud and the solution they offered was to let the Jewish population stay at its 1945 level. A level, which, in the eyes of the Palestinians was far too high at 400,000. It, had risen from 55,000 since 1919. Although the Jews only owned five per cent of the land they had made remarkable progress in the development of the area in which they worked and lived. American Senator Claude Pepper made the observation to El-Alami that the Jews had brought great prosperity to Palestine. This was a view that the troops were too frequently to hear for the next three years and many times since. It was discussed and was a view some held until the subsequent events in Israel dissuaded them.

Musa's reply to the Senator with simple Arabic logic was 'While Senator Pepper, being a richer man than El-Alami he could undoubtedly embellish the house of El-Alami and clothe the El-Alami children in finer raiment, certainly the Senator would agree that this was no reason why El-Alami should be willing to relinquish his house and his children to the distinguished Senator.' *[1]

The terrorists were not entirely inactive during the war years. There were violent incidents, but there was one that was to lose the Zionists a keen and powerful supporter, namely Winston Churchill. On November 6 1944 Lord Walter Moyne, former Colonial Secretary was murdered in front of his Cairo home by two Lehi members, Eliahu Hakin and Eliahu Bet Tsouri. Lord Moyne, an advocate for partitioning Palestine, was a personal friend of Churchill.

In a statement to the House of Commons on 17 November 1944 Churchill said 'If any dreams for Zionism are to end in the smoke of assassin's pistols and our labours for its future are to produce a new set of gangsters worthy of Nazi Germany, many like myself will have to reconsider the position we have maintained so consistently and so long in the past. If there is to be any hope of a peaceful and successful future for Zionism, these wicked activities must cease and those responsible for them must be destroyed root and branch.'

But the 'wicked activities' did not cease. As the war in Europe was over the Zionists changed their anti-British leaflet campaign into one of violence. In May 1945 they blew up oil pipelines, police stations and telegraph poles. In July they blew up a bridge.

Lord Moyne, a partitionist, was replaced by Edward Grigg who along with Lord Gort, the High Commissioner decided that partition would not be feasible. Privately Grigg advised Anthony Eden that 'partition would very likely bring into existence a Jewish Nazi state of a bitterly dissatisfied and therefore aggressive character. *2

On June 14 1944 a report appeared in the *Palestine Post* of a Stern Gang member, David Meiri, alias Begin receiving a 12-year prison sentence for carrying arms. The sentence was passed by the Military Court in Jerusalem,Meiri read out a long political address that he had written whilst on remand.

It took most of the morning session and concluded by saying "We the Fighters for the Freedom of Israel, members of the Jewish underground movement, stand face to face against you as enemies. Let us be open enemies with the status of belligerents. We should not be considered as criminals, but as prisoners of war."

Major G.W.Anderson MC President of the Court accused Meiri of aping Nazi methods and went on to say 'Your ideas only open the way to your own destruction.' In his conclusion the President said 'You have shown yourself to be familiar with bombs and firearms. You could have used this knowledge with honour and good effect as do the true fighting sons of Israel who are with the Allies against the Nazis, and whom we are proud to call brothers-in-arms.' *3

There is no photograph of Meiri in the article but his political address had the hallmark of Menachem Begin and the photograph of Meiri on the police posters looked like him. But the incident was not in *'The Revolt.'*

In June 1945 Winston Churchill sent a letter in reply to a request from Chaim Weizman saying he was withdrawing his support as the result of the murder of his friend Lord Moyne.

In July a disillusioned Churchill queried in his final ministerial note to the Chiefs of Staff 'why should Britain be responsible for this very difficult situation while the United States sat back and criticized?'

The true measure of the remorse and concern that the Jewish leadership displayed in 1944 over the murder of Lord Moyne became apparent on 26 June 1975 when bodies of the two murderers, Eliahu Hakim and Eliahu Bet-Tsuri were removed from their Cairo graves and reburied with full military honours at Mount

Herzle, Jerusalem.

Lehi and the Irgun formed an alliance. On July 13 the Irgun ambushed a lorry carrying explosives, killing the Palestine policeman escort, and drove it away. On the 25th, the day Britain was at the polls, the Irgun blew up a bridge on the Haifa-Kantara railway. July was a month of change. Labour Government had replaced the wartime coalition and Clement Attlee was the new Prime Minister.

The Jewish Agency welcomed Labour Government in Great Britain; it was, after all, the Parliamentary Labour Party who on April 23 1944 had raised their expectations. The Jews in Palestine read in the *Palestine Post*, the Zionist newspaper that was also read by the troops, that the National Executive Committee of the British Labour Party was to submit a report to the annual Labour Party Conference. The report said '. there is an irresistible case now, after the unspeakable atrocities against the Jews in Europe for allowing the Jews into Palestine and allowing them to become a majority.' It then went on to mention the case for the transfer of the indigenous population. 'The Arabs have many wide territories of their own, they must not claim to exclude Jews from the small area of Palestine' *4

Ten days later they read in the *Palestine Post:* -

The leader of the Parliamentary Labour Party, Arthur Greenwood, addressing the May Day rally of the Poalei Zion in London said the heart of the British Labour movement went out to the suffering European Jews. He referred to the executive's statement, which mentioned to the transfer of Arabs from Palestine, and said there was no question of the forcible expulsion of Arabs. It was only a matter of free choice. He stressed the solutions were based on friendship not hatred. 'Our intention is to establish a Jewish national home and let the Jews go there until they become a majority. We are convinced that the first real remedy for the Jews is a Jewish national home in Palestine, where it must raise the Jewish flag in the ancient Jewish homeland. *5

It is doubtful if Arthur, a Jew, had ever been to Palestine and met with the Christian and Muslim indigenous populations in their towns, villages and homes. If he had maybe, like we conscripts, he could put himself in their place.

Within six weeks of winning the election the solution that had seemed so simple around the Labour Party Conference table was so different when faced with the reality of the situation and the responsibility for dealing with it. The troops that were to follow in 'peacetime' Palestine quickly realised that to the Palestinian Arab his country was as sacred to him as Britain's was to them. It was not difficult for soldiers to understand why the Palestinians didn't want to be driven out of their land and homes. Hadn't the British just fought a savage war to keep their own country!?

In 1945 the world and Britain were appalled at the use of terrorism to achieve a political goal. Since the May 1944 Labour Party Conference, when the idea of transferring the non-Jewish population out of Palestine was of little consequence, the situation had changed.

Harry S. Truman, who became President of the United States upon Roosevelt's death in April advocated free Jewish immigration and in July was advising Attlee to allow 100,000 Jews into Palestine. This was too much for the Government and they proposed to restrict the influx to 1500 per month. Britain had annoyed the Arabs in trying to placate America and the Jewish lobby. The Jews wanted more and were demonstrating in Tel-Aviv. Taking advantage of the demonstrations a criminal element entered the situation. On September 22 Irgun extortionists demanded £300 from a Jewish café owner for employing Arabs. When he refused a mob burst into his café that evening and wrecked it. Six days later another group robbed a postmaster carrying £4760 on his way to the post office from Barclay's Bank in Tel-Aviv. The police constable escort was killed. By October the request from Truman to Attlee to allow 100,000 immigrants into Palestine was rejected. Truman promised Attlee not to divulge the request with its subsequent refusal but it never the less came into the public domain.

After being in his office as Foreign Secretary for three months and for much of that time studying the Palestine situation, Ernest Bevin was convinced that Zionism was unjust and unnecessary. From a soldier's point of view Palestine would not be the egalitarian society of the type that Labour had won the election for in Britain. It would not be a question of cultivating the desert; it was more likely to be the acquisition of more Arab land. Bevin was Foreign Secretary twenty-five years too late.

With the obvious intention of intimidating the Government a fully co-ordinated action by the Haganah, the Irgun and the Lehi occurred on the night of October 31. In a show of strength hundreds of explosive devices were used on soft targets, an intimidatory tactic that the Nazis had used on Cristal Nacht in their rise to power.

Two police launches were sunk in Haifa harbour by the use of limpet mines, explosives caused 242 breaks in the railway network. In Lydda goods yards a train and three locomotives were destroyed and three Arab civilians killed in an unsuccessful attempt to blow up the oil terminal at Haifa.

The situation was changing the nature of the British Army's role in Palestine.

They were engaged in more policing duties, more infantry and airborne troops were called in. Terrorist incidents increased and counter terrorist measures got tougher.

Ivan Lloyd Phillips, District Commissioner, Gaza and Beersheba summed up the situation on December 9 1945 in a letter to his father, – "Palestine would be almost ideal if it were only the Arabs and ourselves here." *6

In 1946 Britain granted independence to TransJordan and the Zionists claimed this was a breach of the Balfour Declaration. This indicated the gulf that existed in the interpretation of the Balfour Declaration. There was no doubt in British minds that Palestine and TransJordan were two countries separated by a border of which, the River Jordan and the Dead Sea formed part. Militarily they were administered jointly from the Allenby Barracks HQ in Jerusalem.

The Balfour Declaration did not promise the Jews a state, but a homeland in Palestine.

It was a period of intense meetings and talks with the plight of European Jews, rather than the future of non Jewish Palestinians, dominating the discussions.

With the end of World War II there were changes in the structure of the Army, less frontline troops were needed. On the other hand, the rearward services had been officered by older soldiers, many who, having served time in the First World War, were retiring. This resulted in wartime infantry officers being transferred to the rearward services. Some retained their infantry insignia and others, with appropriate training were transferred to the RAOC, REME, RASC and other support services.

Terrorist attacks were becoming more frequent and police stations were at that time soft targets although in February 1946 the terrorists attacked a bank and the radar stations on Mount Carmel. There was also no shortage of soft targets and almost every British establishment was vulnerable. This kind of reaction from a people that Britain had sought to free from the world's most evil regime seemed totally unwarranted. On the night of February 21 the terrorists attacked three police stations.

However, one attack failed, and four Haganah Palmach commandos were killed. The depth of support from the Jewish population for terrorist action came to light three days later when almost 50,000 lined the dead terrorists' funeral route. The date was chosen to coincide with Chaim Weizman's return to Jerusalem.

The following day RAF airfields at Qastina, Petah Tiqva and Lydda were attacked by the Irgun destroying or damaging twenty-two aircraft. The ever-increasing frequency and ferocity of the attacks continued but two incidents in April 1946 were to have consequences reaching far into the future. On April 23 1946 a raid on Ramat Gan police station by the Irgun resulted in one Arab policeman and one attacker being killed. Another Irgun terrorist, Dov Gruner was captured, seriously wounded and was hospitalised under guard.

Just two days later the most callous operation of all occurred, an event that was to bring the troops to the point of mutiny. There was an army car park on the Herbert Samuel Esplanade on Tel Aviv's sea front. It was guarded by fifteen 6th Airborne paratroopers. A gang of thirty or so terrorists commandeered a house overlooking the car park and the Airborne guards encampment. Some of the terrorists covered the car park from the house and the rest armed with Thomson sub machine guns (Tommy Guns) swept into the camp and murdered seven soldiers including the only man who was armed, the sentry. They went away as quickly as they had come taking with them twelve rifles.

Troops throughout Palestine were very unhappy with the lack of an effective counter-terrorist policy. Many of the troops arrived in Palestine having served in the liberation of Europe and had suffered great losses.

Major-General James Cassels was the GOC of the 6th Airborne Division and he was both angry and amazed at what his troops were encountering, he said – 'I don't think they (the Jews) realised that many of my men parachuted into Normandy in June 1944. Large numbers of them were killed and wounded, fighting to remove Hitler from the face of the earth.'

Terrorism could only have been countered by using the most brutal methods of repression on the entire Jewish population. Methods of the type they didn't hesitate to use against the Arabs in their rebellion eight years earlier. The 5th Parachute Battalion came close to going on a rampage, but while they held a secret meeting, officers, sensing trouble locked up all the firearms. The troops wanted revenge but the closest they could get to it was to break windows in Nathanya and Beer Tavya.

Major-General Cassels wanted a £1m fine on Tel Aviv's population but Lieutenant General Sir Alan Cunningham, the High Commissioner refused to sanction it.

He agreed to close all restaurants and places of interest at 8.0 pm.

The incident made Bevin even more reluctant to accede to Truman's request to let in 100,000 immigrants. Many of the arriving immigrants were not genuine refugees but fit young men carefully selected by the Jewish Agency to fight. Two ships, the *Fede* and the *Fenice* had recently brought in 1014 fit men between the ages of fifteen and thirty-five, they were obviously recruits to swell the ever growing secret army.

Day by day British tolerance was wearing thin; the army was trying to enforce the law impartially between the Jews and Arabs. Inevitably their attitude towards the Jews was more aggressive than it was towards the Arabs because it was the Jews that were doing the bombing and killing. The Arabs on the other hand were not only co-operative; they were trustingly loyal to the army. American Jewry and newspapers aimed a barrage of Zionist sponsored propaganda against Britain.

It served to spur further terrorist activity. Major Dare Wilson summed up the attitude of the British soldier who was intensely mystified on his arrival in Palestine – 'soon he was asking himself what had he been fighting for during the past five years?' *7

In June there were more attacks on bridges and railways all seen as soft targets but on June 17 a raid on the Kishon railway workshop went drastically wrong for thirty-five Lehi terrorists. They got into the workshop compound and set off numerous explosions destroy-ing a locomotive and a fire engine but in the process killed two of their own men. As the Lehi were making their escape their truck ran into an army roadblock and troops lining the ditch opened fire, killing seven and wounding eleven more. Twenty-six terrorists were captured complete with their Sten and Tommy guns.

It was only one year since the war in Europe had ended and not even a year since Japan was defeated. This added to the consterna-tion felt by the British over the reaction of the Jews in Palestine. In the war years Palestine was a place of rest and recuperation for Britain's' armed forces serving in the Mediterranean area. Jerusalem and Tel Aviv were popular leave centres. Jerusalem was ideal for those who wished to visit places of Biblical interest. Tel Aviv was for those who wanted a seaside holiday; it was like Bournemouth but with more sunshine. It had nightlife and sandy beaches and in wartime was far more congenial. In Britain many beaches were fenced with barbed wire and heavily guarded, food was rationed and the blackout curtailed the nightlife that was expected of popular holiday resorts. Knowledge of Palestine's gentle ambience and its hospitality spread to servicemen in Europe who judged it to be a 'cushy posting.'

Those taking leave in Tel Aviv reported to the Army Provost Marshall's Office (APMO) at 123 Hayarkon Street to have their leave passes stamped and to deposit their weapons until they were ready to return to duty. There was accommodation available at the Toc H,

War Comforts Hotel, St Andrew's House and Hibbert House.

In addition, for those who preferred a private hotel, there were sixty-six to choose from. John Clegg and three comrades chose the Hotel Yarkon a popular choice. The literature from the APMO also made the point that the civilians were hospitable also.

Hotel Yarkon had lost none of its popularity in 1946 until on June 18 a party of officers were gathering in the dining room for lunch when twelve Irgun men drove up to the door of the hotel. They were looking for hostages. Two of their gang had been caught in a raid on Sarafand Garrison in March and were sentenced to death on June 13 by a court martial. Seven of the terrorists stood guard outside the hotel and the other five went in armed with Tommy guns. They took two hostages with the intention of killing them if the two terrorists were executed. Both men were officers, Captain D T Rae and Flight Lieutenant Thomas Russell. They were spirited away in a specially fitted truck with long boxes built in under the floorboards. When the prisoner's death sentences were commuted the captives were released.

Throughout July the British Government was in high-level talks with America, without a loan Britain would be bankrupt. It wasn't a happy situation that we as a nation who had thrown our 'all' into a war to free Europe of Nazism should now be supplicants. That was the view of the vast majority of the British population. The Americans agreed the loan on July 13 despite the anti-British agitation over the Palestine issue.

The Jerusalem that Stan Hayward saw in July 1946 was a far different place from that which Bill Howard knew ten years earlier. Stan was there within days of the King David Hotel bombing-it was nothing like the hotel through which Bill Howard couldn't walk with his boots on. It was a scene of sheer devastation, an atrocity organised by the Irgun that killed more civilians than British servicemen. A total of ninety-one people were killed – forty-one Arabs, twenty-eight British, seventeen Jews and five others. Menachem Begin, no doubt was looking for a noble victory, if any act of terrorism or murder can ever be described as noble. In his book "*The Revolt*" he portrays the King David Hotel as a heavily armed British fortress. But, as in Bill's day, it still functioned as an hotel and restaurant and the main entrance was unguarded. It was Jerusalem's leading social centre. Part of the building was used as an office to which the public could go on matters of general administration. The terrorist gang, disguised as Arabs, entered through an unguarded service entrance and placed the kitchen staff under guard whilst others unloaded milk churns packed with explosives and placed them into position. In his book Begin claims there was a pitched battle to penetrate the cellar. In truth there was one British officer who was shot dead when he challenged the gang. One of the reasons why so many Arabs died was because a small extra bomb outside the hotel had been detonated to disperse people in the area. Unfortunately a No: 4 bus was passing and was caught by the blast. Some of the Arab passengers were injured and taken into the hotel for first aid. Hotel workers ran to the windows and balconies to see what was happening and they were directly over the exploding churns. There was a lot of controversy about whether a satisfactory warning was given or not. Begin says it was but was ignored by Secretariat Chief John Shaw. Shaw and all British witnesses deny this. The Irgun also claims to have warned the nearby buildings of the *Palestine Post* and the French Consulate, which was true, but in both cases it was after the explosion. The question about whether or not a warning was given cannot shift the blame from the thugs who perpetrated this odious crime aimed at the British army – they planted the bomb and lit the fuse, no one else.

Whilst it caused a slight blip in Begin's image with the Zionists it was insufficient to disrupt the prevailing anti-British attitude.

Irene Lewis was an ATS soldier inside the hotel on that fateful day. Irene was conscripted into the ATS at the RAOC Depot, Old Dalby, Leicester in 1944 and volunteered for overseas service in 1945. She was posted to H.Q. Palestine in the King David Hotel and went to work each day in a three-tonner truck from her quarters in Allenby Barracks. She gave this graphic account of the event.

'Jerusalem is such a beautiful city, who could imagine the evil already brewing in the minds of both men and women culminating in the appalling events of Monday 22 July 1946.

It was a normal working day, another gloriously sunny day, with, for me the added pleasure of anticipation as the next day would be my 23rd birthday. However at 12.20 pm we heard the sound of a large explosion followed by gunshots, but it was outside, after the initial shock we carried on working as it was close to lunchtime.

One of my ATS colleagues came in to ask if I would go with her to the roof to find out what was happening. Believing that discretion is always the better part of valour I declined the invitation. At 12.40 pm there was the most earth-shattering explosion, this time within the hotel. The whole building and equipment shook. We heard an avalanche of stonework and debris crashing into the street and saw an immense pall of smoke and dust drifting past the window. I turned to the next office where my friends worked and found them very shocked, looking down through a hole in the floor. A little later came the order to evacuate the building from the opposite end of the hotel. Standing in the street we could see the devastation and carnage caused by the explosion. The whole of the southwest corner was demolished. We discovered that the bombs in the basement had been timed to explode at 12.45 pm. Soldiers arrived very quickly and, together with members of the Palestine Police, started searching for personnel buried in the ruins. It was a dreadful time for them, especially during the days following when it was necessary for them to wear masks as it became obvious that there were many fatalities. The Post Master General was blown on to the wall opposite the hotel. Later, I discovered that my friend who went on to the roof was blown off into the gardens. I was told she was all right but I didn't see her again. The thought remains with me that I could have been with her.'

John Jeffery was, as he describes his role, a 'gofer' at HQ. He had been sent to post a parcel for the wife of the Brigadier in charge of administration. He believed it was a gift of a dressing gown. Gunner Les Ell accompanied him and on the way back from the Army Post Office they heard gunfire. An Arab Palestine Policeman was firing his Sten gun into the subway to the hotel's tradesmen's entrance. The passing local pedestrians lay down in the gutters and John and

Les took cover behind the gatepost of the YMCA and from there ran to the Military Police post outside the side entrance to the hotel.

Left: The King David Hotel 48 hours after the explosion, troops still searching for survivors. Right, Irene Lewis (R) with two friends at Allenby Barracks. Irene was in the hotel when it was dynamited. *Photos: Stan Hayward, Irene Lewis*

At that moment a bomb exploded nearby. John writes – 'having been admitted to the side door Les and I hurried upstairs, little knowing we were immediately above the explosives set to go off. We felt we deserved a 'cuppa' and disappeared swiftly up to the NAAFI, having collected Vera, an ATS girl who worked with us on the way.

We went up on the roof where the NAAFI was housed in a hut at the North end. Les Ell and I stayed there drinking our tea and Vera walked to the other end of the roof. There was an enormous bang and a great cloud of dust. The next thing I saw of Vera she was staggering along the road outside the YMCA. I never saw her again. I imagine she must have tobogganed down the roof as the walls collapsed.'

A Palestine policeman, Constable Trevor Kirby writes about his experiences in connection with the bombing. He remembers the two in the road outside the hotel at about 12 noon. After the main charge was detonated at 12.37 pm he was sent immediately to join

Police Sergeant Ken Price who had set up a casualty information desk at the top of the main entrance steps, which he and Trevor maintained over the following days and nights while Central Control Station recorded events and operated from a nearby military lorry! Initially there were hundreds of names but gradually they were eliminated by the persons themselves or relatives or friends and by identification of the bodies. Several persons were entombed alive, the last of whom to be rescued after 31 hours, was Mr. D C Thompson, an Assistant Secretary, but sadly he died a few days later.'

The servicemen, mainly from 6th Airborne Division toiled unceasingly to clear tangled wreckage and on July 29 the sappers demolished the central pillar to release the dangerously hanging wreckage, thereby enabling the clearance of the site. On August 2 the final death toll was fixed at 91 with 45 injured still in hospitals and 476 treated overall. One body still had to be identified and the rest of the missing were declared safe. Five British officers and soldiers were decorated for their part in the rescue, and two George Crosses were awarded – one to Sergeant T. Newman RASC and the other to Police Sergeant E A Smith. The Irgun Zvai Leumi led by Menachem Begin, claimed responsibility in a pamphlet stating – 'the attack was made by our soldiers courageously and with self-sacrifice. The British were to blame for disregarding the telephone warning.

The King David Hotel bombing was a significant event in a significant year. Palestine moved from being a political problem to becoming a serious terrorist problem requiring more decisive action.

Much of the Jewish population had changed their attitude from ingratiating to insulting. When their duties took them into Jewish settlements looking for terrorists and weapons British troops were openly greeted with slogans likening them to the Nazis with names like 'Gestapo,' 'Nazi sadist' or 'English bastard.'

Eighty-eight Britons had been killed in 1946 but it took the bombing of the King David Hotel to draw a firm course of action from the War Office. During that year not one single terrorist had been hanged and important voices were being heard, including those of Winston Churchill and *The Sunday Express.*

"Rule or Quit" read the *Sunday Express* headline and then went on to say that Colonial Secretary, Arthur Creech-Jones was not of the right calibre to be in charge. Security was still inefficient, armed clashes had led to 212 deaths including the eighty-eight Britons; sixty Arabs, forty-five British soldiers, thirty-seven unarmed Jews, twenty-nine British police, twenty-six armed Jews, fourteen British civilians and one other.

The deaths included those killed in the King David explosion. The signs foretold probably an even worse year ahead.

After more than nine months in custody the wounded Dov Gruner, captured during the raid on Ramat Gan Police station recovered and was tried, and on January 2 1947 was sentenced to death. The Zionist propaganda machine was working full time and Gruner was fast becoming a legend in his own lifetime. The British Embassy in Washington was bombarded with telephone calls and telegrams urging clemency.

During the war Gruner had served in the British Army and that was mentioned. Senator Robert Taft said Gruner was an electrician and was only on the scene because he was applying for a job. Lt.General Evelyn Barker, put the matter simply – 'Gruner had been caught red-handed, armed and shooting up British troops.'

Between 1939 and 1946 Britain had reprieved all Jewish terrorists but now there was a get-tough policy after the verdict.

In retaliation the Irgun were looking for hostages, easy targets for preference, and they found two, both civilians. No target could have been easier to capture than Herbert Collins, the Deputy Controller of Light Industries-Textiles. An ex-soldier born in 1896 and fought in the First World War from 1914 to 1918. In the Second World War he was evacuated from Dunkirk, fought in the North African Campaign and was at the Anzio Beach Head landings. In the forces he had been a major and his business card bore his title:– Major H.A.Collins. He was in Palestine to develop trade in the country.

On January 26 he was finishing his tea in his room in the Daroutis Hotel, Jerusalem when there was a knock on his door. A woman said she had a message for him but when he opened the door Jewish terrorists holding automatic weapons confronted him. Chloroform was poured over him; he was hit on the head, pushed into a sack and driven away. He was the first civilian to be taken hostage.

The second hostage was Judge Windham Laker he was taken next day.

January 28 was the date set for Gruner's execution. To everyone's surprise, except the Irgun, the execution was postponed for an appeal. An appeal that Gruner had not requested. On January 30 Major Collins was released, a sick man. As a result of the inhalation of excessive quantities of chloroform he developed chest troubles and was in and out of hospital until his death in 1960, at the age of 64. On release he was admitted to the Government Civilian Hospital Jerusalem and received a bill for £17, he received no compensation and his widow Mrs. Irene Collins received no pension. *8

With the advent of hostage taking it was necessary to evacuate certain vulnerable British subjects who may have been seized as hostages. Three thousand individuals, including officers' wives and ATS were taken back to the UK. Some Palestine police wives chose to stay and some ATS telephone operators were required to man the HQ telephone exchange. Because of her King David Hotel experience, Irene Lewis chose to return to the UK.

The events of 1946 and the belligerent attitude of the Jewish terrorist gangs, with the collaboration of the Palestinian Jews and Zionists worldwide alarmed King Ibn Saud Arabia. He was particularly concerned over the support given by America for Jewish terrorism and immigration. His views were expressed in a letter to President Truman on November 26 1946.

The King's courtesy concealed the strength of his feelings and his words were lost on a predisposed President. The feelings and rights of the existing population were brushed aside. The King's letter made these true statements and indisputable facts:-

'Great Britain adopted the Balfour Declaration and in its might embarked upon a policy of admitting Jews into Palestine, in spite of the decrees of its preponderantly Arab population and in contradiction to all democratic and human principles.' He took the opportunity to remind Truman that Britain stood alone against Nazism and told all Arabs that Britain would never betray these principles of humanity and democracy. He summarised the dilemma of the current situation with – 'It was the British Government which gave and still gives shelter to their (the Jews) leaders and accords them its benevolent kindness and care. In spite of this the British forces in Palestine are being seared by Zionist fire day and night, and the Jewish leaders have been unable to prevent their terrorist attacks. If therefore, the British Government (the benefactor of the Jews) with all the means at its disposal is unable to prevent the terrorism of the Jews, how can the Arabs feel safe with or trust the Jews either now or in the future.' *9

References

1. Unless otherwise stated most of the facts were taken from *Palestine Triangle,* Nicholas Bethell, Andre Deutsch Ltd. 1979

2. *C.O.733,461* cited in *Palestine Triangle*

3. *Palestine Post June 14 1944*

4. *Palestine Post April 23 1944*

5. *Palestine Post May 3 1944*

6. *Mandate Days*

7. *Cordon and Search,* Major R. Dare Wilson, Gale and Polden Ltd 1949

8. Correspondence from Mrs Irene Collins, 2001

9. *Arabia Unified*

5.

Not So Soft Targets

The troops arriving in Palestine from 1946 onwards were generally new recruits who had not seen war service and it was also, invariably, their first time out of the U.K.

Men of the RAOC and REME were not accustomed to the rigid disciplines of the infantry and airborne regiments. Their tours of overseas service were generally longer and they were in permanent bases with permanent living accommodation and worked in brick built depots and workshops alongside civilians.

The infantry and paratroops were likely to be in tents and likely to change locations more frequently.

There were two functions of the British Army in Palestine, one acted as peacekeepers and the other maintained the support services for all units and not necessarily for those confined to Palestine. In the immediate post-war years in many other regions were also fraught with tension.

There was the threat of a clash with Russia and members of the Communist Block. The depots that had been supplying ordnance to Russia via Iraq during the war would have been able to supply ordnance to the forces resisting an invasion of the Middle East by Russia.

Every conscript had six weeks basic training, a little of everything that one might expect a soldier to know and be able to do. It also served to sort the trainees out. Those best suited for infantry regiments were sent to infantry regiments. They would also be physically fit and show an aptitude for weapon training and accept army discipline. Those that went to the RAOC and REME were judged to possess aptitudes that were suitable for one of the variety of roles to which they would ultimately be appointed. Some consideration may have been given to their civilian employment. I, for example, had been an art student up to the age of seventeen, and then due to my forthcoming conscription, had taken a job in a menswear shop. It was a relief that they ignored my art training because I might have been given a painter's job camouflaging buildings and vehicles. Whereas clothing was one of the many items the RAOC issued. My corps training was at the RAOC Clerk and Storemans School at Portsmouth. The fact that I could rarely hit a target with a rifle and no matter how I tried, or as much as I was punished, I couldn't put my heart and soul into mock bayonet charges may have influenced the selector's decision. A few were posted to the RAOC because, medically or physically, they were not suitable for the infantry. Gus O'Brien a hut mate at 614 AOD could not see out of his right eye and Wally Salt only had one eye. The corps training lasted for four weeks and when completed one was either a clerk, storeman or on general duties.

The majority of RAOC troops were sent to the large depots and REME to base workshops, but some were posted to ordnance field parks and field workshops attached to peacekeeping regiments. They lived within camps, mostly tented, as the infantry troops did.

By and large it worked well. RAOC, REME and no doubt RASC (Royal Army Service Corps) had less military training than the fighting regiments whom, when not in action, were continuously training.

Our discipline was more relaxed and not so regimental.

Corporal Gus O'Brien gives a good example of the difference in the unpublished account of his life in the Army. He wrote about a stage in his journey home, whilst waiting at a transit camp at Fayid in Egypt. Being an ordnance corporal he was co-opted into a blanket distribution to a detachment of the Coldstream Guards.

'The first guardsman stamped up to my table and stood to attention and I asked him to write his name, rank and number on the clipboard and then sign for the blankets. "Yes corporal," he shouted. When he was given his blankets he picked them up stepped smartly backwards, turned smartly to the left and then marched off. He did everything but salute me. I'm sitting there saying to myself, "Hey! Hey! Hey! It's me, Gus O'Brien; you don't' do those kind of things to me." At the end of it I had quite a headache. The worst of it was going through it all again next day when they brought the bloody blankets back.'

Continuous infantry training not only improves discipline and military skills it also serves to maintain enthusiasm and confidence. John Hardwick proves the point with this incident.

Sometime following the announcement of Britain's intention to leave Palestine the Arab Supernumerary police force in 614 Depot was withdrawn. They were not part of the Arab Legion and the decision was taken as a security measure in light of the forthcoming inevitable clash between the Jews and the Arabs. Infantry troops responsible for daytime security were also recalled to their regiments and it was deemed necessary for a Depot Defence Force to be formed to replace them. Lieutenant Pauncefoot, an infantry officer, attached to the depot was put in charge. He chose Sergeant John Hardwick to be the platoon commander. John had received the same initial training that was given to all members of the RAOC; six weeks basic training and four weeks corps training, which in John's case was training in RAOC clerical systems. John did not welcome the idea and he protested. Lieutenant Pauncefoot brushed aside John's reluctance with 'We will cope!' Officers were prone to using the royal 'we' when they really meant 'you.'

His reason for choosing John was to be found in John's pre-service records, he had been in the OTC at grammar school. As the platoon was starting from scratch his duties were to help with the training and to have ready a mobile section. John viewed the prospect with apprehension;

'The section was equipped with an armoured car returned to the depot because it had an unusable two-pounder gun. The second vehicle was a 15cwt truck. The section was allocated between 15 and 20 men (John cannot remember the exact number) each with a rifle and ammunition.

I had access to a Sterling (sub-machine gun) should I need one.

We had 'training' on Wednesday afternoons, some weapon training, range work and basic drill procedures – parade ground stuff.

I hoped the 'enemy' would not attack because I felt there wasn't a real soldier amongst us. In fact we made the squad in "It ain't half hot Mum' look like the SAS.

My apprehension increased when later, as guard commander, one night I 'accidentally' read a restricted circular, addressed to the HQ giving details of the training procedures of the Haganah-Palmach and of their capabilities and the ruthlessness of the terrorist organisations, In fact we'd have been better trained by them.' Being platoon commander didn't excuse John from his guard duties every alternate night or his daily work in the Depot.

Despite the low level of regimental training and experience of the eighteen-year-old conscripts who worked in the depots and workshops they didn't present the terrorists with a soft target. Each installation contained many valuable and attractive military items that would be useful to terrorist gangs hoping to become a real army. The largest depot in Palestine was 614 Advanced Ordnance Depot, which until 1946 was a Base Ordnance Depot, 2 BOD. The establishment was reduced when the theatre of war moved away from the Middle East in 1943.

A manpower audit taken on September 17 1943 showed the total military personnel was 519 of which 325 were from the U.K. The U.K. military was made up as follows, 19 Officers, 91 NCO's (sergeants and above) 215 corporals and lance corporals, 190 privates and craftsmen. More chiefs than braves? Not necessarily, there were also 181 non-U.K. privates with only one sergeant and twelve corporals to make up the full complement of 519. There were also 223 civilians. That was probably at its lowest level and may have been slightly higher in 1946-47 and less non-British troops. The perimeter fence, which was patrolled at night, was approximately 3km long. There were seven gates into the depot, four of them for the rail service from sidings on the main Cairo to Haifa line that ran alongside the western boundary of the depot.

The three tracks within the depot were in total length almost 3km (98604ft). Arab civilian labour physically shunted the heavy wagons around the depot. Store sheds constructed of brick, covered an area of over 200,000 square feet, including the 5536 square foot armoury. An even bigger area consisted of concrete hard standing for outside storage.

Charles Edwards, former OC Khayat Beach Sub-depot returned to Haifa and 614 AOD in recent years to what had been Palestine but was now Israel. The depot was there and was still an important installation for the Israeli Army but not apparently kept in the same spotless condition, as it was when it was a British depot. Gone were the white painted stones, the bas-relief sign and the smartly attired gate police. Instead there was one capless, untidily dressed Israeli soldier lounging at the gate of a perimeter fence bearing the detritus of many take-away meals and drinks.

Left: Three very smart but youthful members of the Arab Legion who guarded the Khayat Beach Sub Depot. They were more resolute guards than we were (author). Right: Ken Parker and his dog Lance corporal Judy. *Photos: Eric Cook, Ken Parker*

Ken Parker arrived in January 1946 from Tel-el-Kebir, with about 30 others, when the depot was still 2 BOD.

Ken was already a Normandy veteran and he and five others were detailed for the motor pool, four armoured vehicles that had been returned as unfit for further military service. The OC however had decided they were useful enough for guarding the depot. Two were Humber Scout cars and two were South African Fords. Ken described the Fords in his memoirs as 'very heavy and ponderous beasts with a gate gear change and an acceleration of 0 to 60 in three weeks. It had a two-pounder gun that was just a bluff as the breach block had been removed. There was also a mounting for a Lewis machine gun, of which we had none, and had never been trained to use in any case. They did have one inch armour plating and a spotlight. Each working day one of the armoured Humbers and a Ford would escort the parade of about 250 troops down to the depot from Camp 153 on the other side of the coast road for work at 8.0 a.m.'

Ken preferred to drive the Humber Scout car. He writes: 'The Humber Scout cars were much more nimble, the quarter inch armour plate was adequate in this situation as the terrorists had no heavy weapons and the turret was fitted with a mounting for a Bren gun, for which we had ammunition and for which we were all trained. The cars also had a spotlight fitted on the roof.'

The two vehicles escorted the troops between camp and depot twice each way during the day. Lunch break took two hours of the day but it left the two drivers with nothing to do for seven hours. The arrival of the NAAFI truck at mid-morning was a welcome break and the troops were joined by the Arab labourers, who drank the tea and enjoyed the biscuits but refused the sausage rolls.

Two drivers who had been off duty all day would go on night patrol around the depot perimeter in one of the Humber Scout cars. One carried a Tommy gun. Another man, a member of the depot guard sat on the turret and operated the spotlight and Bren gun.

Three miles north of the main depot was the sub depot at Khayat Beach and it was part of the Duty Officer's round of night time guard inspections. Ken continues 'His route covered the guards at Camp 153, the main depot and the Khayat Beach Sub-depot. He would turn up at the main depot guardhouse to be driven around the perimeters of both the depot and the sub-depot. Early in 1946 the Arab Legion were performing the night guard duties at the sub depot. They were good soldiers and very conscientious guards.' All of them were volunteers who had been trained unhesitatingly to shoot if the need arose. Unlike the British conscripts who were inhibited by officialdom, and any case, it was doubtful if they could have been brought themselves to shoot. It was standard practice for the Duty Officer to be driven in the armoured car along the three miles of coast road and to be let into the Khayat Beach compound by the Arab guard and for the guard commander, an Arab sergeant, to come out and meet him. He would get onto the vehicle and accompany them round to the sentry posts. Each guard would let them pass when the night's password was given in Arabic. They had designed a well-disciplined system that worked well. When the RAOC personnel took over after the Arab Legion left they were nowhere as thorough.'

In Ken's memoirs he tells just how thorough the Arab Legion was when he was driving the Duty Officer on his rounds:-

'I drove to the depot as usual and stopped just inside the gate to wait for the guard commander. The officer, who was standing on the seat beside me with most of his body outside the vehicle asked me in a superior manner "why have we stopped?" Brushing aside my explanation he ordered me to drive on. I tried to explain the procedure but he would not listen, so I drove forward very slowly, keeping my eyes on the sentry in front of me. Over the noise of the engine I could not hear any challenges etc. but when I saw the sentry pull his gun up to the firing position I thought 'sod this for a game of soldiers' and stopped the armoured car (AC) just as the officer fell down on the seat beside me. At first I though he had been shot, then realised that he had also seen the sentry about to fire and had decided that discretion was the better part of valour. I myself was in no danger as I was surrounded by armour plate, but the officer and the machine gunner in the turret were very vulnerable.

However the sergeant of the guard appeared and climbed on to the bonnet of the armoured vehicle. We resumed our patrol in the regular manner and when completed returned to the depot with a subdued officer!'

In 1947 the men who worked in the depot in the daytime were also doing nightly guard duties. Each night a total of 32 men formed the main depot guard together with a guard commander, usually a sergeant. According to the daily routine orders the tour of guard duty was from 1830hrs to 0530hrs. Reveille was 0600hrs and breakfast from 0615 to 0700hrs with Morning parade at 0715hrs. Troops who had been on guard joined the parade at 0745hrs in time for the march from the Parade ground at Camp 153 down to the depot. *[1]

Camp 153 must have been one of the most pleasant army camps in Palestine. Built in 1942 when peace reigned supreme in Palestine, and like the depot, it was built for the army's permanent use. Its brick built living accommodation consisted of huts interspaced in an ancient olive grove on the gentle lower slopes of Mount Carmel. The camp spread over several acres and from the Spring of 1947 included an open-air cinema. There was also a casualty receiving station, a library and a row of shops. A local Arab had a small field of gherkin cucumbers and spent his day watering the vines by carrying water in jerry cans on his donkey to the top of the field and trickling water down the slope to the plants. Each olive tree had a mound of stones around the base of the tree. The stones attracted the heavy mists that so frequently occur at night time, it condensed and the water seeped down to the roots. The mounds were home to lizards, snakes, scorpions and a variety of other insects. The camp was not laid out or constructed to cope with the terrorists' treacherous malevolence in post war Palestine. Three expanded rolls of barbed wire bound the long perimeter fence; it was not really effective, as the troops proved by slipping in and out of camp at will. Twelve men and a guard commander plus a relieving NCO went on camp guard duty each night. Guards were placed at strategic points, one man on sentry duty at the gate and another in the Bren gun post a few yards inside the gate, two men on the armoury in the centre of the camp and one man on the perimeter point near the officer's lines. At times of high alert, as in April 1947,following the execution of Dov Gruner, an extra guard was formed comprising of ten men, a guard commander and a relieving NCO.

Extra guards would be deployed in a manner that matched the perceived threat. During the war years the troops who worked in the depot did very little guard duty. It was usually left to the Colonial forces like Indians and Basutos.

The Khayat Beach Sub-Depot was a small compact stores unit situated on the main coast road between the main depot and Haifa. That had a nine-man guard with a guard commander and a relieving NCO.

One man was placed at a main gate that was very high and kept locked and the others patrolled round the depot and the numerous stacks of baled stores on concrete bases. There were no weapons stored there; the only weapons in the sub-depot were brought in by the guards or the Regimental Police who were on duty during the day. The guardroom backed up to the perimeter wire fence and it was in the guardroom that the military personnel drew their pay. One Thursday they assembled for pay parade and those who had weapons placed them in a rack situated in the next room. Even for a small number of men an army pay parade is a long drawn out ceremony. Names are called out one by one and the recipients march up to the paying officer's table, salute and the Pay corporal states how much is due (minus any stoppages). The Officer counts the money out and hands it to the soldier, who steps back, salutes again, does a smart left turn and marches off.

On this occasion when those who had left their rifles went to collect them the weapons had gone. The chain that held the rifles in the rack had been cut; there was a hole in the back of the wall, and a hole through the wire. All this had happened within three or four yards of the paying officer's table. The Army Special Investigation Branch (SIB) were called but no one was ever caught although it was suspected that the guardroom bricks had been loosened from behind by a depot employee.

Throughout the 1945-48 conflict, Tel Aviv remained a hot spot of terrorist activities and much of the city was out of bounds but the Levant Fair workshops were never attacked. Captain Pat Waller served there throughout the war and when he was back in Britain the Army asked him if he would like to return for a short spell. He had so enjoyed the previous posting that he readily agreed, but he returned to a different Palestine, a Palestine of bombs and murder. He reasoned that the fact that the workshops were never attacked during the conflict was because of the efficient security measures in force.

Sarafand lies south east of Tel Aviv but it appears on very few maps, it was not a civilian town, it was a garrison town, no more than a complex built largely of timber by the army before and during the war. What in the early war years had been the main RAOC workshops were still operating after the war as 309 Workshops. Each military unit within the garrison was secure but there were parts that were vulnerable within the military area. Personnel from 614 AOD were on detachment to administer the stocks and supply spares and stores for the workshops. Within the garrison there was a cinema that had a particularly sad memory for Harold "Brummie" Draper. Jack Moss, Alan 'Eggy' Egerton and Brummie decided to go to the cinema to see an Al Jolson film. Eggy triggered an anti-personnel mine, which severely injured him. It was despicable atrocity by a totally ignominious individual that would serve no purpose to the Jewish cause.

Whilst Brummie was at Sarafand Sub-Depot he did no guard duties whatsoever. Members of the TransJordan Frontier Force, a division of the Arab Legion, carried out the guard duties. At the end of 1947 Brummie was posted back to 614 AOD and back on guard duty every other night.

Security in the RAOC depots and REME workshops in 1947 may have been excellent but that was due more to an efficient system than the individual military skills of the troops.

Leon Uris an anti British American author who has written books about the British Army in Palestine and Northern Ireland and in his book *"Exodus"* he described the situation in Palestine as 100,000 crack British troops held at bay by a handful of freedom fighters. By his choice of title and style of writing he was hoping to produce an epic that a thousand years from now might stand alongside the books of the Old Testament. It may have been good reading for the pro-Zionists but it was far from the truth.

A significant proportion of the British Army was there, not to chase terrorists or separate the warring factions. They were there to serve as storekeepers, repairers, distributors and collectors of weapons, hardware and equipment for the Army on the Mediterranean fringe.

A large portion of their effort went into returning surplus materials to the U.K.

Up to 1945 the level of security had been little different from that to be found in the U.K. military installations. But after 1945 security became so tight that Teddy Kollek, the Mayor of Jewish Jerusalem taunted John Briance a top policeman who had defended the Jews against the Arabs up to 1939,with 'Congratulations!' You have finally succeeded in rounding yourselves up.' *[2]

Many places were out of bounds and when they were in bounds troops went to the bars and cafes in fours and were armed. It was a hindrance to go into town with a rifle, for which, incidentally only five bullets were issued. Vehicles took to the roads in pairs with an armed escort sitting beside the drivers. Not surprisingly this was called 'riding shotgun' by the troops. The shotguns in this instance were generally Sten guns that were lightweight machine guns with a clip on magazine of twenty-eight bullets, and capable of firing all twenty-eight in less than one minute.

It was a gun that got its name from its inventors, Shepherd and Turpin. They were made, we were told, for seventeen shillings and sixpence but they were a low cost gun with a high accident rate.

In the centre of Camp 153 there was an armoury surrounded by a barbed wire fence. It was partly buried in the ground with a mound of earth on top. It may have even been an air raid shelter in the war years. One night I was paired off with 'Scouse' McCardle to guard it. Scouse was a rebellious soldier who had served several sentences in the detention barracks. He elected for us to do the 2200hrs to Midnight stag, he also decided that I would have the rifle and he would have the Sten gun. He was a man with whom you didn't argue. The man with the rifle stood guard at the entrance to the armoury compound and the guard with the Sten gun patrolled round the building.

Company Sergeant Major Cockram was known to come out of the sergeant's mess in his cups each night and doing a round of the camp trying to catch the guards out. McCardle was well aware of his strategy and said 'if he asks you to let him inspect your rifle, let him have it' by that I took it to mean give him the rifle, which was quite against regulations. McCardle was nowhere to be seen, but as predicted Cockram turned up. He was cordial and we exchanged pleasantries and then, as forecast, asked me to let him see my rifle. Hesitatingly I let him have it and Cockram's mood changed.

Jubilantly he said 'Now what would you do if I was a terrorist?' pointing the gun at me. Before I could answer McCardle came from nowhere and jabbed his Sten gun into the C.S.M's back and growled' You mean what the * * * * would you do? Cockram recognised the voice and in alarm said 'Put the gun down McCardle.' The matter ended there. Cockram went back to his berth and McCardle sat on the ground drinking from a bottle of beer and smoking a cigarette.

The main gate at Khayat Beach Sub Depot was kept locked throughout the night except for the visit of the utility van, that at 2200hrs, brought refreshments or the occasional visit of the Orderly Officer. However some nights a girl called Mary would come to the gate.

Mary, a Jewess, who lived in an Arab sector, was looked down upon by both Jew and Arab alike. Mostly known as 'Khayat Beach Mary' she was a prostitute. In a partially burnt out café across the way from the depot Mary would dance on the tables. Such as it was, the café still served food and drink. Mary provided customers with her irregular form of entertainment. She was known by several other names, some of which were far from complimentary, but she did respond to Alakeefik Mary. (Alakeefik was an Arab word used by the troops instead of 'couldn't care less').

One soldier reported sick with a sexually transmitted disease and claimed that he must have caught it from Mary. Staff Sergeant Alex Monaghan, the Chief Clerk at the Depot received a message to bring Mary in for a medical inspection. This was done but from whosoever the soldier had caught the disease it was not Mary.

One lunchtime early in 1948 she was found dead in a culvert that carried water from Mount Carmel under the main road near the depot. Alex was called to the scene. Her head had been smashed in with a lump of concrete and her crumpled body dumped in the culvert. The gory sight made the Arabs who found her vomit. Alex stopped a passing Palestine Police patrol and reported the discovery to them. In her short lifetime Mary was a legend and was known over an area from Acre to Athlit.

Bob Wells was a driver with the Ordnance Field Park attached to the 6th Airborne remembers one occasion when he drove a party of troops down to the sea at 614 AOD for a swim. Mary was down there and she asked for a lift to Haifa. She was lying down in the truck out of sight but when they reached the main road a military police jeep caught up with them. Knowing he was committing an offence, Bob drove on past Mary's destination until the jeep turned off. Mary was left with a long walk back. To those who did Main Gate guard duty at Khayat Beach she will be remembered as the girl who chatted to them through the wire during the lonely nights.

Sergeant John Hardwick was the Guard Commander at Khayat Beach Depot when he had a message on his receiver known as a 'Beetle' message, forecasting terrorist activity in the area. This was followed by a telephone call from Captain Mellor, that night's duty officer, to advise John to challenge once and shoot first. John tells what happened. 'Some time after midnight, well after curfew, I was at the main gate with the static sentry, having checked the two blokes on patrol when a vehicle approached, drifted to the gates and dipped lights. I challenged and the vehicle came even closer-no response!. I cocked the Sten gun I had been issued with. It would not fire so I immediately grabbed the sentry's rifle, cocked and fired one round, fortunately or unfortunately, only into the canopy of the utility truck.

There was a high pitched screaming – 'what the * * * * are you doing?' John recognized the voice as that of Captain Jenkins, the Adjutant. He was accompanied by Major Newman the OC.

I was told to consider myself under arrest but to continue duty. They then left for Camp 153.'

Newman and Jenkins were out of camp and off duty well after curfew time. John was due to be demobbed within the next four months and didn't want any trouble. He immediately reported the incident to Captain Mellor who wasn't at all happy about the behaviour of the two fellow officers. Newman and Jenkins along with CSM Cockram were rated as the most hated senior ranks in the establishment, by the NCO's, other ranks and even junior commissioned officers. Brain Rivers, then a subaltern, was the assistant adjutant summed up the two officers in one sentence: 'Alan Jenkins who was on secondment from the Green Howards, with a little more effort could have been almost as unpopular as Newman.'

CSM Freddie Cockram had two large dogs and often one of the would accompany him on his nightly patrol after the Sergeant and Warrant Officers mess had closed. On one occasion he climbed an olive tree to spy on the guard in the vehicle park, for it was from there that spare parts went missing and fuel tanks were drained. However his presence was revealed because his dog was standing on its hind legs, front paws on the trunk and looking upwards. Despite the guard placed at the entrance to the vehicle park, which was deep inside Camp 153, one morning the camp awoke to find the wheels missing from one of the lorries. They were found a short time later by the Depot Police. A lorry had broken down on the main road and three or four regimental policemen went over to investigate. The lorry owned by an Arab, had a broken clutch cable and the only way the gear could be changed was by pulling on a length of wire. Whilst some of the police were looking in the cab another looked over the tailboard and there were the wheels that had been stolen from the camp.

Prowling officers and warrant officers were not the only creatures of the night. Prowling round the camp and depot buildings were packs of piehards, feral dogs as common in Asia as the dingo is in Australia. Rarely seen during the day, their shadowy forms lurked around the buildings at night like the urban foxes today in Britain. The further they are removed, by successive breeding, from their original domestic size and shape, the more uniform they become. Lean, hungry looking and all of a nondescript shade, many small army dogs had been savaged by them and large army dogs had cohabited with them. Some even eloping with them as did one of Cockram's Alsatians when, answering the call of the wild, he abandoned his master and was later seen running with a pack of piehards.

Jeff Roper, attached to the 3rd Infantry Division at Qastina with No.3 Mobile Laundry and Bath Unit, can remember the numerous times when on guard duty they were harried by piehards that consistently set off the trip wire flares. Each time the guard had to turn out amid much swearing and cursing.

On March 21 1947 the Lehi turned the Haifa Oil refineries into a blazing inferno. Next door to the refineries was the RAOC Returned Stores Group at Kishon Camp. An extra guard was formed from Camp 153 under the leadership of a subaltern and sergeant to provide whatever guard duties were needed. Gus O'Brien was a member of that party and he was allocated a position near to the oil tanks. He described the situation, 'I was about one hundred yards from the perimeter fence which was about 15 feet high and consisted of concertinaed barbed wire. One hundred yards beyond the fence was a great silver grey oil tank, the only one that had not been blown up. Every other tank in the oil depot was either burning furiously or emitting volumes of thick black smoke. I wondered "Why were we there?" I could hardly be a deterrent.' If the last tank went up Gus was in a vulnerable position. After two hours he was relieved and when they each had done two hours duty they returned to Camp 153. Gus never did know the point of the exercise.

Manning the Bren gun in a pillbox a few yards inside the camp's main gate was the most boring duty one could be given. In the pillbox there was only one way to look and that was outwards to the gate through a narrow slit in the thick wall. It was safe but dull. It was far more interesting to be on patrol inside the camp where almost every night there was a magnificent sky to enjoy. The stars were so brilliant that even on a moonless night you could see things very distinctly and the buildings cast shadows. The sky at night was the midnight blue seen on a Christmas cards and when there was a moon it was not difficult to conjure up a scene from a Hollywood romance.

At eighteen years of age you did not give voice to your comrades of such romantic inclinations. Sentry duty at the camp was only slightly less boring. At Camp 153 the R.S.M's billet was only a few yards away, almost opposite the guardroom. R.S.M. Whitmell was a very military man; tall and lean with a leathery weather beaten neck. He personalised his billet doorway with a bead curtain made of Crown beer bottle tops squeezed on to strings. He arrived at 614

AOD and Camp 153 in the summer of 1947 and immediately made his presence felt in every way.

He was a thoroughly regimental soldier whilst he would not tolerate sloppiness he did inspire confidence. He was soon to sample the calibre of the conscripts under him.

It happened on a night when Dennis Nutt was in the pillbox with the Bren gun and a man with an effeminate sibilance in his voice nicknamed Nancy was in the sentry box. Probably to relieve the boredom, Dennis fiddled with the Bren gun taking out the magazine and replacing it and drawing a bead on various targets. He had drawn a bead on the sentry box at the very moment that Nancy stepped out of the box to march across the barrier. For no apparent reason Dennis pulled the trigger and a single shot went through the wall of the sentry box and out of the wall on the other side. Nancy thought terrorists were trying to kill him and fainted. Dennis thought he had shot Nancy and he fainted. The rest of the guards tumbled out of the guardroom. In retrospect it was seen as an amusing incident but it took the appearance of the R.S.M. coming out of his billet wearing a fancy dressing gown that created most amusement. Some men slept in underpants and singlet, others in their shirts and some naked, they certainly didn't have silk floral dressing gowns.

In the last days of the Mandate Bill Muncey was a sergeant at 531 Base Ammunition Depot in charge of the motor transport section and the fire service. He tells how they dealt with would be thieves caught at Wadi Sarar.

'The depot perimeter at Wadi Sarar was patrolled at night by the Arab Legion in armoured cars. Fairly frequently a volley of shots being discharged disturbed the camp. No intruder attempting to break into the depot was ever hit. It was obvious when seeing the tracers hurtling skywards that the Legion was not prepared to shoot at their Arab brothers.

On some occasions intruders were apprehended and locked in the guardroom for the night. Early the following morning the CSM, "Duff" Cooper would line them up against the rear wall of the guardroom, they were quite convinced they were about to be shot until I appeared, fire hose at the ready. Having received their 'early morning bath' they were then marched down to the main gate and sent on their way. We all had a lot of sympathy for the Arabs and the untenable position in which, we knew, they would shortly find themselves.

Whilst RAOC and REME installations were too formidable to be raided by the terrorist gangs they offered tempting prizes for entrepreneurial thieves especially in the closing months of the Mandate. The intended rule was to shoot intruders on sight but it was not an easy rule to follow because rearward service troops were not trained to kill and sometimes couldn't be sure of the reaction from senior ranks. In two separate incidents Colonel Gore, the Commanding Officer of 614 AOD displayed his inconsistency.

Staff Sergeant Andrew Howe was duty officer one night early in 1948 and doing the nightly patrol of the depot in the armoured car. The searchlight picked out two furtive looking characters in the vehicle park. He arrested them and took them to the guardroom for interrogation. Andrew wrote: 'the account of their presence in the vehicle park was almost unbelievable in its audacity. They were two Arab labourers who for the previous few nights had hidden in the depot instead of clocking out after work. They spent each night servicing a tank. The very next evening after their capture it was their intention to drive it out of the compound and proceed to an arranged rendezvous with the Higher Arab Executive. There, they were going to fill the tank with high explosives, drive it to Haifa and up Hadar-HaCarmel (the glory and splendour of Carmel) and there detonate it. One can only imagine the massive loss of life and destruction of property that would have resulted if they had succeeded in carrying out their intentions.'

Andrew called the Palestine Police and handed the culprits over to them and reported the incident to Colonel Gore. He was not surprised by the Colonel's reply 'Why didn't you kill them?'

Another night Leo Chambers was part of the depot guard when they caught three Jews in the Depot. The reason for shooting intruders on sight without exposing your position was a logical one; accomplices could be concealed in the stacks of stores and counter attack. But the rule was ignored and these men were taken to the guardroom. The guard commander rang the duty officer who in turn told Colonel Gore. The colonel came to the guardroom and listened to their extremely unlikely excuse. They claimed they had mistaken the time and were locked in. However, much to everyone's surprise he said 'Let them go.'

It seems every nationality, every corps and regiment had at some time or other guarded the depots and workshops, but when sailors came in to take some of the burden that was a surprise. Brian Cross wrote to *'Palestine Scrapbook'* wondering if anyone else could remember them and how they came to be there. Were they off a decommissioned ship or a spare crew kept at Haifa?

Brian wrote 'They caused a sensation on pay parade with their "how-de-do" salutes and 'present caps for pay.' Brian and his pals had met some sailors in a bar in Haifa and to go ashore the sailors had been issued with rifles. They were all drunk and because the sailors confessed they were not familiar with their weapons Brian's party escorted them back to the sea front. As they waited for their boat the soldiers offered them some weapon training and showed the sailors how to fire their rifles, out to sea of course.

The dock area became alive with activity and Brian and his pals rapidly escaped from the scene. Brian wrote 'You had to keep your head down when they were on guard!'

Gus O'Brien pointed out that sailors were entitled to extra pay of sixpence per day, a 'sleeping rough' allowance. He said 'what we thought of as a cushy billet they thought of as sixpence a day. If any of them grew a beard they would receive a further sixpence a day, whilst we would have got a rollicking from the RSM.

References

1. Unpublished memoirs of Pte. K. Parker
2. *Palestine Triangle*

6.

Palestine Realised

No matter what had been seen on cinema screens or what books had been read, no eighteen year old serviceman was prepared for the shock that awaited him when he first set foot in Egypt. It was not the romantic scenario that the *National Geographical Magazine* painted. It was an experience almost beyond belief. Long before the ship docks hordes of natives awaited its arrival at Port Said. They were looking forward to two or three thousand unsuspecting virgin prospects to exploit. They were waiting to offer worthless watches, cardboard handbags, fruit unfit for human consumption, dirty books and dirty postcards, the list is endless. They were there on the docks, at every stop of the train and every yard of the barbed wire perimeter of the transit camp.

Journeys by rail were always on slow moving trains and invariably made in the middle of the night. When Ray Machin, George Billings, myself and the rest of the RAOC contingent arrived at Almaza Transit Camp at Heliopolis we had been awake for twenty-four hours. After being in our uniforms almost every night since we left Southampton and with the loss of sleep beginning to tell, the thought of sleep out of uniform was uppermost in our minds. However it was not to be, instead we were divided into groups of eight and marched to the stores to draw one tent, sixteen six foot planks, sixteen trestles together with one blanket each. We marched back and were told where to pitch our tent, which we managed to do, even without instructions.

The beds were made using two trestles and two planks; the trestles raised the planks six inches off the sand. In Egypt temperatures drop rapidly at night and it was far from warm so we only took off our boots and wearily lay down to sleep.

Less than two hours later it was reveille, but surely that could not apply to us? But it did and an officer wearing tartan trews and a forage cap with ribbons trailing down to his collar turned us off our trestles. It transpired that he was an eccentric Scot and the CO This was the first day of what was to be our induction into army life in the Middle East. There was no washhouse, instead, there was a trickling tap at one end of a shallow sloping trough and men were struggling to wash, shave and clean their teeth in the same slender stream of water. No one expected water closets but they did expect the closets to have doors. Flies were a nuisance, but there was little an individual could do about them. To add to the frustration every newcomer was shown two films, one *"A Day In The Life Of A Fly"* served only to add to our impotence in dealing with the problem. This busy little fly seemingly spent its day between the cookhouse and the latrine. The second film, made in America, for the American army, graphically portrayed the effects of venereal disease. The men laughed when an image of a penis filled the screen but fell into sombre silence when the foreskin was pulled back to reveal a suppurating abscess.

One realised that this was to be the situation for however long we were at this camp and possibly at any camp to which we were eventually posted. It was of little use to contemplate what the future held. It was a question of 'resigning ourselves to the mysterious rhythm of our destiny,' as Winston Churchill so aptly put it, after Dunkirk.

From Heliopolis it was possible to take a tram into Cairo. However several times a day we were to hear warning messages over the camp tannoy system. We were told "Do not ride in a Garry, you may be taken to an out of bounds area, beaten and robbed."

A Garry was a horse drawn handsome cab of the type seen in Blackpool. There was a similar warning about the dangers of sex exhibitions and prostitutes and even warnings about having your boots cleaned by a shoeshine boy.

The moment you stepped out of the camp you were besieged. Small street urchins rushed to offer to 'Clean your boots Johnny?'

The warning advised us to say 'No.'

If anyone accepted the offer other bootblacks would also clamour and make the same proposition. They weren't offering their boot cleaning service; it was a simple form of begging.

Having favoured one and refusing the next could result in being sprayed with liquid bootblack. Other little boys far too old for their years offered to take you to their sisters or to a beautiful Greek girl. In Egypt there appeared to be no age of innocence.

Cairo tram which ran from Heliopolis into Cario with passengers clinging to the sides – and also the roof.

Trams rattled their way into the centre of Cairo with men and boys riding free by clinging to the sides of the vehicle. It was a familiar sight to see men urinating behind a stationary tram; apparently it was well within the law. It seemed that everyone could speak English except the police! When I needed to relieve my bladder I had difficulty in making one understand. I tried to tell him by gestures and he thought I was asking for a prostitute. A young boy who had been watching and listening came up, I think he wished to tell me but the policemen hit him with his thick cane. Eventually the policeman understood what I really wanted and pointed to the rear of the tram.

Inevitably several times we were offered to be taken to the sex exhibitions that we had been warned against. 'You want to see exhibish Johnny?' accompanied by a description of the event that left little to the imagination other than 'How does she do that?'

Every soldier that went into Cairo signed out in the guardroom and was signed back in again upon his return.

Every day there was a morning parade with frequent mass FFI (Free from infection) inspections. Men lined up in three ranks and the M.O. went along the ranks looking at the rows of genitals, occasionally lifting a penis with his cane, then going along the rear of the ranks inspecting each anus sometimes using torch. One very thorough MO even inspected armpits. It was not difficult to pick out the regular soldiers from the ranks as they had tattoos. Some remarkably imaginative tattoos on unusual parts of the body were to be seen.

Most of us carried tin mugs to take tea wherever we were, in numerous cookhouses, NAAFI wagons and Salvation Army canteens on railway stations. Like most other soldiers mine hung from a strap on my backpack. It was there as we left the SS Mooltan in Port Said but it had disappeared by the time I took my seat on the train. Those who didn't have a mug drank their tea out of a mug supplied by the cookhouse or NAAFI.

At Almaza, the mugs were rather unusual. They were made from beer bottles by the REME. Craftsman George Nicolas explained to me how they were made by pouring half a pint of hot oil into the bottle and then plunging the bottle into cold water. The bottle cracked neatly in half and then the tops were smoothed off.

In the Khamsin period when a hot wind blew in from the Sahara it carried with it very fine sand which found its way into everything. The improvised mug had a thick layer of silt at the bottom. Meals in the cookhouse were almost inedible.

Perched on the telegraph and electricity cable poles were the evil looking, bald headed Egyptian vultures. They were not quite as large as other vultures and were commonly known as shite hawks.

They perpetually scanned the sandy ground looking for the scraps of food that were often thrown away. They were as cheeky as the sparrows in a London park; some wouldn't wait for food to be thrown down. Walter Horrocks was carrying a plate of food to his tent when a vulture swooped off his pole and took it off the plate. Walter's comment was 'They had better stomachs for it than we had!'

By the time a posting came through we had no illusions about the Middle East and were ready for anything. Trains bound for Palestine stopped at El Kantara and El Arish for refreshments, which we ate and drank from our mess tins. Army mess tins were rectangular and made of steel with folding handles, a smaller tin fitting inside a larger one. Food was served into the larger tin and tea was poured into the smaller one. They came, when new, with a coating of manufacturer's protective grease. For those accustomed to using their own mugs, drinking tea from a rectangular mess tin was a problem. A drinking vessel still coated in grease meant the tea was barely drinkable and was stretching the soldier's love for tea a little too far.

After El Arish we were in Palestine and those bound for 615 AOD and 612 Command Vehicle Group detrained at Rafah. From that point everything began to change, the scenery, the climate and the people. There were still vendors at each railway station but they were different in attitude and dress. Egyptian vendors wore the fez or a white skullcap.

In Palestine the traditional Arabs wore a keffiyah, which was a large kerchief, sometimes pink and white check, or just plain white, and holding it to the wearers head was one or two heavy woollen coils. They sold the inevitable eggs and bread but also fresh fruit, oranges, melons, grapes and chocolate, luxuries that were not available in the UK at the time.

Most of us were tasting melon for the first time in our lives. The already slow trains were now even slower as they travelled northwards, with frequent stops as the guards looked out for the signs of terrorists. The orange groves were a perfect cover for terrorists, but the orange laden branches a few yards from a stationary train, was also a temptation for thirsty British soldiers. They would get off the train and bring back armfuls of oranges. From no oranges in Britain for six years, we could now see them by the tree full. Like guilty schoolboys scrumping we could help ourselves.

Stan Hayward was an RAOC driver and at one stage was attached to the 6th Airborne Division at Al Jiyah, South Palestine. He wrote about the armoured dingoes. These were armoured vehicles, normally used on the road, but converted to run on rails. Their wheels had been changed for flanged wheels as used on rail coaches. They would be driven along the track ahead of a train in the more dangerous areas.

The railway and the road followed the coastline and one caught the occasional glimpse of the sea. In places a tantalising beach with the odd date palm or two standing out against the blue sea seemed like a tropical film set. Such sightings aroused excited chatter from we young soldiers.

We were in the Gaza strip, the essentially Arab area. That same coastline that was built up with Jewish immigrant settlements and the native Palestinians could not get within five miles of the sea.

Changes in climate between southern and northern Palestine coupled with the variations of the terrain ensures an exciting and diverse wild life. It was another fascinating aspect that served to remind us that this was not Britain. Palestine's wild animal and the insect life stirred mixed emotions. Harold Draper remembered his delight at seeing baby tortoises popping out of the sand at Sarafand. On the other hand there was the alarming experience of finding small venomous snakes basking in the sunshine on the bales of stores in the depot. They were vipers similar to the British adder but smaller, deadlier and more prolific. They were not confined to the depot and were known to find their way into the quite cool corners of the billets. One morning as the men lined up for the 07.15 parade and roll call, a twelve-inch long snake was noticed in front of them. Despite it's diminutive size the men eyed it nervously although their boots and gaiters were designed for such a contingency.

R.S.M.Whitmell came forward to see what was creating this diversion and with a smart flick of his pacing stick threw it off the parade ground into the dry scrubby grass.

The ants were larger than the British ants and would find their way into everything. They were the silent illegal invaders able to find their way into lockers and kitbags especially if food had been left there.

However in Dave Alcock's experience they were looking for more than food, they were looking for a home. His first posting in Palestine when he arrived in 1946 was to 612 Vehicle Group. The camp was on the beach across the road from the Depot near Athlit. He recounted his experience with ants; 'One afternoon on time off I was awakened by the lads laughing. To my horror, coming into the tent were four lines of ants. Two lines carrying eggs and dumping them into the top of my kit bag and the other two lines heading off to the beach. It took me two hours to clean my kit and all of us another two hours to get rid of them.'

At night there was the constant croaking of bullfrogs which lay still and dormant in the daytime but on one occasion, during the day a frog limped its way across the office floor dragging it's injured leg with ants feeding on the wound and harassing it. Flies were everywhere and they found wounds irresistible. Danny Godfrey gave this account of his experience when he was working in the mine-filling factory at Wadi Sarar putting lids on field mines.

'During the time we were doing this I must have scratched myself and taken a few unnoticed knocks. Each night there was a terrible smell, which became stronger as I moved about trying to evade it. Eventually I found the source of the smell, the backs of my hands were swollen and bleeding. I reported sick and discovered that it was flies, attracted by my cuts, that had laid their eggs which had turned into maggots!'

Lizards ran up and down every olive tree and generally they were six to eight inches in length but on a quiet Sunday morning as I walked down the lane to catch a bus into Tirah I found myself confronted by one as large as a cat. It was recognisable as a chameleon, up to that point I regarded them as just lizards but now it was plain to see that the trees were home to baby chameleons.

Fred Page, the Fire Chief at 615 AOD was in an army all of his own. With his billet being well away from the rest of the camp, and the nature of his job he was outside many of the rules and regulations. The fact that he was able to keep a chameleon as a pet in a bunch of sticks in his billet surprised no one. The surprise was that the chameleon was happy living with Fred.

Six-inch long centipedes were prolific: they were capable of causing a poisonous reaction, if they left their thin legs in human flesh. Great care had to be taken when removing them if they were climbing up someone's leg. Ken Parker said a good stamping on them with an army boot would not kill them because the studs protected the centipedes flat bodies from being crushed by the sole of the a boot. It was more effective to hit them with a plimsoll. Foolish dogs would often find and molest unusual wild creatures. Lizards were easy to catch and kill. The dogs learned to treat snakes with care and bark in alarm.

When Ken moved from Al Jiya in the south to Ramat David in the north he encountered another remarkable creature.

'We had only been in Ramat David a couple of days when we met some of the local wild life. One of the REME lads had a dog and one afternoon we heard it yelping outside the hut as if in deep trouble. Going outside, we found that the dog had flushed out a large crab from under the hut, and the crab retaliated by nipping the dog on its nose with its claws. We had never seen a land crab before and this one was as big as a dinner plate and at least 30 miles from the sea!'

One was always aware of Palestine's natural world, large areas of the country were undisturbed and used solely for grazing sheep and goats. The Palestinian simple life style allowed nature to flourish. The Turks had regarded the native population as fitting custodians of the Bible Lands. We saw it as one might have imagined it to be in Christ's time, still retaining much of its virgin beauty. Mount Carmel for example, retained much of its ancient character. The western side of Carmel's long ridge is rocky and deeply furrowed by ravines with many caves and precipices. One could easily imagine how the wild goats lived on this bleaker side of the Carmel range. Each part of the country had its characteristic natural wonders to intrigue new arrivals from Britain. John White felt it was worthwhile noting in his diary a reference to the shoreline fishermen who cast their nets into the sea as they waded along the waterline. Their keen eyesight spotted fish that we could not see.

Eventually discovering Palestine's various species of wild life became commonplace and ceased to be worthy of a mention in diaries and letters. Army vehicle parks and depots in Britain were havens for wildlife protected by guards night and day, there were no farmers to shoot the rabbits or poachers to snare them so when Howard Allen beheld the rare sight of a rabbit in the 2 BOD Gun Park he felt it worth entering a reference to it in his dairy.

In the Spring of 1947 there was a plague of locusts and Gus O'Brien remembers a large flock of avaricious pelicans swooping on to the beach to feast on the locusts.

On another occasion I remember the sad sight of a large dead turtle washed up on the beach.

We were warned of the danger of snakes and reminded of a soldier who had died from a snakebite. Once off duty at the end of the working day we took a cooling shower and wore gym shoes, in most cases, without socks. The most direct route to the open air cinema was across dried grass, without the protection of boots and gaiters, fearing that there may be the little venomous vipers on the ground we though it safer to run. So prolific was Palestine's unusual insect life that Captain Styler, of the Wadi Sarar Ammunition Factory and Depot, took the opportunity to study entomology, reported the *'567 Times.'* The *'567 Times'* was a regular newssheet cranked out on a Gestetner and circulated within the Ammunition Depot at Wadi Sarar. For over sixty years Alec 'Waggy' Wagstaff has retained a few copies which gives an insight into the off duty activities of the troops. One item read: 'We hear that owing to the fact that Craftsman Johnson's pigeons had 'gravel rash' from their last record flight he is now looking for prospective buyers. This, Waggy told *Palestine Scrapbook*, is about Craftsman Johnson. Wadi's would be pigeon fancier, who bought half a dozen pigeons from an Arab. "Berry good, fast racing pigeons, Johnny," the Arab said. So they were taken some thirty miles away and released. Johnson said 'Let's get back to Wadi or they'll beat us.' But when they got back there was no sign of them. About four days later when we were all on parade the pigeons came walking up the hill. Even the Sergeant Major had to laugh.'

The further north we travelled the more verdant became the scenery. We were travelling up the coastal plain and Haifa was at the end of the journey and this is where the majority of the servicemen were bound. Numerous military installations. Depots and camps were clustered around Haifa and up the western slope of Mount Carmel. The port's development had been rapid and in less than twenty years a city had sprouted up.

After spending their formative years in embattled Britain the only yardstick that young soldiers had was their British experiences. Whilst our towns had been blitzed and Britain's infrastructure was in a state of decay, Haifa had been developing. It had an astonishingly modernistic art deco city centre with luxurious shops, cafes and bars to suit all tastes. There were sweets and chocolate in any quantity, beer in all the bars and the very latest fashion accessories, nylon stockings, generally only available in the UK for the women and girls who had American boyfriends.

Ken Parker went home on LIAP (Leave in addition to Python) in February 1947 and found the whole of Britain in the grip of the worst winter since the 19th century. Food couldn't reach the shops and fuel was scarce. Ken went to the cinema but despite his uniform, greatcoat and scarf he sat and shivered in an unheated cinema. Whilst he was on leave two demob groups were told not to return to Palestine. If the next higher group had been included Ken would also have not been going back. He regarded himself as lucky and despite the troubles was relieved he was going back and away from shortages, rationing and the icy weather. It was bitterly cold when he arrived in Britain and it was still bitterly cold when he left.

In pouring rain our train pulled into Haifa railway station and we were transported to Camp 153. Camp 153 had that refreshing English smell that comes on a summer's day after a shower has settled the dust.

Hidden amongst Camp 153's numerous olive trees was a carob tree, distinguished by the purple red pendant blossoms that were flowering when we arrived. By April or May those flowers had turned into fruit looking like blackened broad bean pods. Gus who had seen this transformation the previous year plucked a pod from the tree and bit into it to show that it was edible. Even in Biblical times it was considered the poor man's food but it was eaten by the Arab workers and was served with yoghurt as a dessert.

Our brick built huts had corrugated iron roofs and the pitter-patter of the first drops was to be welcomed after a hot dry spell in Egypt. From the moment I arrived in Hut 56 I was made welcome and for the first time since I was called up I felt I could tolerate army life. There was a lot of talk, questions about my home town, previous postings and the most current topic in February 1947 was the British winter.

The *Daily Mirror* published a weekly omnibus edition for troops overseas; it consisted of the six daily issues in simple cover. At that time it was Britain's biggest selling daily newspaper and stimulated much of the conversation.

I shared Hut 56 with nineteen other men and two dogs, Ludi a small terrier and Major a large mastiff cross. It was obvious the customary rigid barrack room rules and regulations that had been part of my three previous postings did not exist. My last U.K. posting was at Old Dalby in Leicestershire and its only asset was that I could get home every weekend. There we slept in Nissan huts and in winter condensation streamed down the roof arch and formed a wall-to-wall pool of water across the floor. Tired of the clerical work, tired of the weather and even tired of the mad dash home on a 36-hour weekend pass I volunteered for overseas service. I didn't tell my parents or my girl friend.

Early in 1947 there were opportunities to go into Haifa in off duty hours, but the camp itself was not without facilities. Once the evening meal was over the cookhouse became a cinema and occasionally a theatre. The trial and conviction of Dov Gruner put all military establishments on high alert but this coincided with the opening of the camp's open-air cinema for the balmy nights ahead. What a welcome break it was to sit at a table, eat, drink and watch a film in the days when films were pure escapism. Who cared if a gentle breeze blew the screen out of focus occasionally, such breezes were a refreshing contrast to hot sticky days. For a couple of hours one could forget the rigours of the day and the inevitable guard duty of the night before.

There was an opportunity to see a different film four times a week. Each film was shown for two consecutive nights except Sunday; those on duty that night missed that particular film. Camp 153 cinema was known by the Army Kinema Corporation (AKC) as White City, Tirah. The AKC was division of the RAOC and Camp 153 was one of twelve camp cinemas serviced in the North Palestine Circuit, circulating 35 films in a two-week period. White City wasn't exclusively for the use of 614 AOD troops. By arrangement other units and regiments would come to the cinema in trucks.

One night Brian Cross was on main gate duty when a lorry load of troops arrived and on their arrival Brian should have followed the normal procedure of checking each passenger as they turned out of the lorry and asking them to proceed on foot to the cinema.

Brian had evolved a simpler method for the airborne troops. He knew the driver so that night he waved a paratroopers lorry in. However as they passed he heard a lot of foreign chatter and to him it sounded like a gaggle of Hebrew voices. What had he done? – let a horde of terrorists into the camp?

Fearing the worst he reported the matter to Freddie Howells, the guard commander. Instantly all off duty guards were mustered, and taking a Bren gun and operator Freddie closed the cinema. Luckily the film had not started and all patrons had to leave the cinema. Visiting troops had to go and stand by their lorries whilst their documents were checked. The foreigners? – They were just a crowd of Danish paratroopers. Brian wasn't charged – probably it was all put down to a useful exercise.

Occasionally there was a variety show at the camp given by the Combined Services Entertainments Company (CSE) and they performed in the dining room on an improvised stage. Officers traditionally occupied the front rows and other ranks sat on the long dining room bench seats. The dining room had been used for live shows almost since it was built. There was an occasion when a party of wartime Australian troops occupied the front two rows and refused to move when the officers came in. The officers had no alternative but to surrender their seats to the Aussies and left without seeing the show.

Many shows were not memorable events, but one was, and several letters referred to it. John White wrote in his diary 'CSE show "Topliners of Variety" starring Judy Shirley, Kim Kendal and Bunny Doyle. Judy Shirley was smashing and very lovely.

Best show in the camp so far' Walter Horrocks wrote 'Kim Kendal sang a song, "Kiss me once, kiss me twice, and kiss me once again" whilst my mate, Eddie Cartwright was hanging through the dining hall window from the outside overlooking the stage. Officers were on the front row, of course, but she turned from the audience, held out her arms to Eddie and sang to him. If I hadn't held him he would have ended up on the stage. Great laughs and cheers came from the other ranks and weak smiles from the front row.'

Those sitting at the back saw a potentially alarming situation developing. The statuesque Kim Kendal stepped off the stage and walked down the aisle in the middle of the dining hall in a very tantalising manner.

But when she turned to go back she found the aisle blocked by the benches on which the exuberant men had been seated. Her consternation was but brief, the benches were returned to their rightful places and she received a deafening ovation. Kim Kendal was, in those days, one of two sisters who were not very well known. It was her sister, Kay, who was to rise to stardom to become a famous film star.

Every act in every show wasn't always a success and no attempt was made by the audience to politely tolerate it, let alone applaud it. Sometimes through no fault of the performer, the act wasn't suitable for the type of audience we were. There was one occasion when the majority were embarrassed by the reactions of a few, a young female violinist stamped off the stage in a rage because of the catcalls of a empty headed minority.

It soon became apparent that army life in Palestine bore no resemblance to that we experienced in Egypt. They were two different countries in almost every way. What one might have considered being the unhappy prospect of an unbearable situation for an indefinite period of time it was now proving to be more than bearable. However long it took to find a satisfactory solution to the Palestine problem we could now endure it with comfort. The concern felt in Britain for her young conscripts was needless. Had we not been weaned on a wartime footing far worse than that in which we now found ourselves? We were now sending parcels home to our loved ones and only rarely did an over anxious mum feel a need to send a parcel to her son.

At the most southerly tip of Palestine was 615 AOD at Rafah. Being that much further south it was that much hotter. It was situated on the coast and on the edge of the Sinai Desert and the men were in tented accommodation. The camp had the advantage of Provan Hall, a purpose built, and highly professional entertainment centre for CSE shows. It was complete down to its own permanent stage with rich curtains that opened and closed with every act. It was also used as a cinema and for meetings of various descriptions. When Fred Page, the corporal in charge of 615's fire station arrived there in 1945 he started the camp's own entertainment company, known as the Rafateers. Fred scoured the tents and unearthed all manner of talented people. Nearby 612 Command Vehicle Group (CVG) also came to see the CSE shows and also responded to his request for performers. Even Arab civilian workers wanted to participate and for Ali Sulieman, Bill Aziz and Shorty Baldwin who joined the team it was their moment of fame. Nothing was too much trouble for the show. REME workshops converted a normal bicycle into a one-wheeled unicycle. Sadly Ali couldn't get used to this improvised machine and he kept falling off and when the band started playing it all seemed to be part of the act.

Fred's first show in 1945 was called "The Army Takes Over," followed in 1946 by "Curtain Call" and the last show in 1947 called "Variety Christmas." The band that accompanied the Rafateers drew most of its musicians from 612 CVG. Other units were invited to the shows and the show's fame spread to units that could not travel to 615 AOD. For those units, REME workshops made a portable stage and the shows were then taken to them.

The fire fighting team at 615 AOD were a mix of troops and Arab civilians. Corporal Fred page, seated (centre) on the bonnet of the fire truck engine with military staff and two civilians.

The Arabs were amiable employees when they worked alongside the troops, even those who worked doing menial jobs around the camps or in the cookhouse. If they couldn't get a permanent job with the army they were happy to make a sort of living doing freelance tasks for little reward. Harold Draper and Jack Moss arrived at Sarafand on detachment from 614 AOD and they found life even more relaxed than at the main depot. They slept on hospital beds, and for the first time in their army life, between sheets and with pillowcases. To quote Harold 'We even had individual toilets with doors and the buckets were emptied every morning before the camp was awake.'

For just a few 'ackers' local Palestinians would do our dhobi, make beds and bring fresh fruit every day. Local Arabs could make 1,000 mils (£1) go a long way. As far as the British soldier was concerned the smallest coin was 5 mils and most transactions were in multiples of ten mils, but the Arabs would trade in coinage of a lower denomination when trading between themselves.

In Anglo/Arab relations Fred Page must have been the greatest exponent. With his duties as fire chief he had sufficient latitude to further his career as an impresario. He could trust his subordinates to carry on with very little supervision. Like so many functions within the RAOC there was a dependency on local civilian labour. Fred's fire station was no exception being manned by three Arab crews, one crew on duty, one on stand by and one off duty. They enjoyed the job and shared an affinity with the military staff. In short, they enjoyed the work and their soldier friends. They even helped with the popular "Fred's Follies." Fred says 'I was cut off from the rest of the camp. I lived with them, ate with them and even shared Ramadan with them. They were good lads and on one occasion we even beat the British Army Fire Service to a job at a place called Dimra.'

The father of one of the Arab firemen was the chief reis (foreman) at the Rafah depot. Because of his father's position the son was quick to assert himself as their leader, but with the best of intentions he took his quasi army career a little too far. It was quite acceptable and even thought to be very enterprising when he led the rest of the crew in daily PT sessions. Although some of the Arabs were reluctant, no one could deny it had a beneficial effect on their morale and they were decidedly fitter for it. Fred thought that all his men were beginning to enjoy it. Everything was going well until an irate Major Thorburn telephoned Fred commanding him to report to him immediately.

Fred had great difficulty in suppressing a smile as the Major revealed the cause of his anger.

Major Thorburn was making his way to the depot in his staff car when a capless, untidy body of men 'marched' into view. As they neared he could see they were the Arab firemen. His surprise turned into shock when the leading Arab gave him a salute and the ragged militia gave him an eyes left.

The Reis's son had had promoted himself to corporal, very acting, and certainly unpaid, by painting two red stripes on his overall sleeve. "We can't have this" exploded the indignant officer. It is a memory that Fred has often smiled about and wondered if the major didn't do the same.

Tirah village lay just behind Camp 153 and nestled in a cleft on the western slopes of Mount Carmel and was a major source of labour for the camp and depot.

The young men from Tirah called all homosexuals 'Nablus Wallads.' Initially I thought Nablus was perhaps the Biblical city of Sodom until I read that Sodom was near the Dead Sea and the expression was no more than youthful banter. In pre-Hebrew days Nablus was the three thousand year old city of Sechem. The Romans renamed it Neapolis, which the Arabs had difficulty in pronouncing and found Nablus easier to cope with. Since Ottoman times both Tirah and Nablus were strong Arab Nationalist communities. So nationalist they boycotted the national electricity supply because the contract had been granted, in the mid twenties, to the Jewish Rottenburg Project. Instead they carried on lighting their homes with naphtha lamps and cooking by primus stoves.

Nablus had the reputation of insubordination, disobedience, uprisings and great courage. It had been a source of trouble to the authorities ever since the true face of the British Mandate came to light and the secrets of the Zionist movement and of western imperialism were uncovered.

Tirah had the reputation of being hostile to strangers. Frequently at Camp 153 we could hear the echoing sound of gunfire coming from the village and we knew there was a traditional Arab wedding in progress. As in other Arab villages weapons were held illegally. Tirah was out of bounds but even if troops could be sent in it was doubtful if the cunningly concealed guns would ever be found.

Arab villages on the plains were often made of unfired clay but Tirah was built of stone on the slopes of the hill. The homes were simple and there was a village well that was the accepted meeting place for the women of the village. The men of the close-knit village met in a coffee shop and drank thick, sticky, strong black Turkish coffee and shared a pipe-full on the hookah.

There were two ways into the village, one way was along the Tirah track that ran behind our camp, and the other was by a lane that went eastwards off the main coastal road.

Many workers both in the camp and 614 AOD lived in the village and Jamel Mohammed Rayon; a camp worker was a special friend. I had an immediate affinity with him, he had a certain pride and strong loyalty to his village. He invited me to his home but the army rules were that we had to go out in fours and carry rifles. Obviously I couldn't turn up for lunch with three uninvited guests, all of us carrying weapons.

Convinced that the gate police had only been briefed on stopping anyone coming into the camp I decided to walk out through the gate and board the Tirah bus that stopped at the end of the lane. A Palestine lane is not like an English country lane; this lane was bordered with unfenced arable fields on either side. Not only did this lane go to Palestine's main North to South road, it went by a 6th Airborne camp and down to our depot.

The crowded bus looked as if it was returning to Tirah with most of the female population all heavily veiled and dressed in black, presumably returning from the Souk in Haifa. The British targeted Tirah in 1937 and as a result demolished houses still remained and I was told there was a lingering hostility towards us.

Trying to be less conspicuous, when the bus neared its destination I rolled up my cap and put it under my epaulet. Even with my tan I looked and felt singularly British amidst the crowd of Arabs. There was a faint whiff of hostility until, thankfully, Jamel came forward, seemingly from nowhere, said a few well-chosen words, and the crowd dispersed. We walked up the path past the cemetery, and alongside an open drain to Jamel's family house.

Jamel's father looked very distinguished in his long white galabia and headdress with the traditional black igaal, which contrasted with a very English looking worsted jacket and a belt round his waist that appeared to support nothing. He was the fourth most important man in the village. Despite telling him my name was Eric, Jamel's father preferred to call me George, otherwise I found he and his sons displayed exquisite courtesy and generous hospitality.

Lunch was served at a small low table; it was an honour to be at the first sitting with Jamel's father and his two older brothers. The next four brothers, of whom Jamel was the eldest, sat down after us. A chicken, roasted and stuffed with smaller bird – probably another smaller chicken-which was in turn stuffed with an even smaller bird was the centre dish. A variety of side dishes included poached eggs floating in a bowl of olive oil. It was a matter of using fingers and scooping the eggs out of the bowl with a piece of unleven bread.

After lunch I went into the hills with Jamel and his brother to explore the caves and look for porcupines. We didn't find a porcupine, but we did find some quills. Jamel's elder brother showed me his Luger pistol and said all of the men in the village were armed. They were expecting an eventual conflict but it all seemed pitifully inadequate. It was a pleasant day in a terrain not dissimilar to Derbyshire. I caught the bus back and walked up to the camp expecting to be challenged at the gate but wasn't.

My next trip to Tirah was with my friend Len Harris, but this time we wriggled through the camp perimeter wire and went along the Tirah track. We did encounter two youths who started to throw stones to deter us but we pacified them by taking their photograph. At Jamel's home we were given lunch, but less formally than on my previous visit. Some utensils, looking suspiciously like army utensils were provided. Again we went into the hills, this time with Jamel's brothers to make up quite an exploration party. We rounded off this interesting day by drinking strong Turkish coffee in the very small cups used at the simple coffee house. The standard of hygiene was dubious but we didn't want to offend our hosts or spoil a truly remarkable experience for two immature travellers on our first spell abroad.

The brother who had boldly shown me his pistol was a well-educated man who loved to quote from Homer's 'Iliad.' He was charismatic with a fondness for wearing military style khaki drill and exuded a swaggering confidence. Some days after the visit to Tirah I was called to see someone who had asked for me personally at the hatch where the visitors presented their requisition documents.

A highly irregular occurrence, even more so when I saw that it was Jamel's brother. He came solely to show me how easy it was for him, with no papers, to get into the depot. In a letter from Brian Rivers who went into Tirah following an attempt early in 1948 to enter Camp 153 which involved an exchange of gun fire. He wrote:

The author and his friend Len Harris were entertained by Jamel, his father and brothers at their Tirah village home. Top Left: Len and author in a cave behind the village. Top Right: Len and Jamel behind Jamel's younger brothers. Bottom: Jamel with (L to R) a younger brother, father and an older brother on the balcony of their home.

'On the question of stealing I am sure the Arabs of Tirah Village looked upon it as an 'Olympic Sport!' I well recall the evening when three or four of us were invited to the Mukta's house for coffee. Among the assembled throng was a young Arab with very good English. (I suspected that he was the Mukta's son.) Over coffee he asked, "Which of you tried to shoot me and my friends last night?" You were not very good shots because we all got away!" No animosity, just good sport!' Jamel's father wasn't the Mukta, he was one of the leading men in the village but the young Arab Brian described could easily be Jamel's older brother.

In the following weeks my friendship with both Len and Jamel strengthened but unfortunately, in September, an injury to my knee put me in the Casualty Receiving Station (CRS). I was there for ten days and then moved to Haifa Military Hospital, the first of a succession of hospitals that was to cause me lose contact with my friends. The last I saw of Len and Jamel was when I was in the CRS and they brought me gifts of chocolate and Azziz orange drink.

Washing and bathing facilities for the Army in Palestine were a considerable improvement on those in the transit camps in Egypt. It was possible to have a shower every day at Camp 153 and even though it was cold, it was at least refreshing. It could be classed as a luxury for those who came from one of the eleven million homes in Britain without a bathroom. Not every unit was as well placed for water on tap and a washroom, for them the RAOC ran the Mobile Laundry and Bath Units (MLBU). Kfar Bilu, south of Lydda was home to 52 MLBU. It was a good central location, strategically placed for taking hot shower facilities to the British Army all over Palestine right up to the Syrian border. The camp from which they operated was in a flat, windswept, sun-scorched area encompassing Ramleh and the air base, Wadi Sarar, with the ammunition depot and factory a suitably isolated spot for the making and storing of explosives. It was a wide, open, hedgeless space favoured by the elite Ramleh Hunt for hunting jackals in the heyday of the British Mandate.

The transport comprised of a least twelve vehicles including Matador tractors for pulling the laundry units and three tonners for the bath units. All regiments in the field, including colonial troops, called them in. Percy Birkett was a pipe fitter – cum – plumber and remembers one assignment above all others.

He writes-'In 1946 we took our mobile bath unit out near the Dead Sea, on the edge of the desert, to provide shower facilities for a unit that included West African soldiers. To our surprise the West Africans paraded in full kit, including boots and overcoats. I told their sergeant we had come to bathe them not their uniforms. He said "Never mind, just shower them as they are with all their clothes on" Could we convince him otherwise? Not likely! So we washed them as they stood and we laughed all the way back to camp; well almost all the way. Unfortunately as we turned to cross the desert our truck broke down and we had to spend the night in the 8th Airborne camp. Radio Palestine announced that 'twelve of our unit were missing, presumed killed! It was at a time when tension in the area was very high but our officer was overjoyed when he saw us roll up about a week later.'

Harold Draper obviously valued the privacy of a privy with a door for a natural but necessary bodily function. A common enough desire for most individuals but not always thought to be essential by the designers of latrines for the use of the British Army. In the big depots that employed civilians it was possible to find a row of closets all with doors, each bearing its own label – Civilians, Jewish Male and Civilians, Arab Male and similar closets for females. It became more complicated when it came to the military closets. They were segregated by rank and nationality, officers, senior NCOs and other ranks (OR's) then yet others for the various colonial troops. Each closet was equipped with a bucket and there were several sites all over the depot and the contents of the buckets were taken away at the crack of dawn.

Needless to say the man who undertook the job was an Arab. However in Camp 153 and other permanent camps there were the 'top of the range' communal latrines. They were brick built and offered a far superior service to the bucket system. Their construction, the work of an obvious specialist, was simply a circular concrete slab about 12 feet in diameter and a very convenient seventeen inches in thickness. These mighty slabs were placed over pits that must have been at least eight feet deep. Evenly spaced around the slab, were eight or ten holes the shape and size of the aperture being similar to the familiar British lavatory seat. The pit was emptied periodically by a Palestinian contractor with ropes and buckets, the contents of which were taken away on the 'honey cart,' an open lorry. The effluence was then spread on melon fields, which were, fortunately a few miles up the road. Occasionally there was a special bonus for the men who carried out the work when they found a pistol or a commando dagger that had been stolen and dumped when a hut search was rumoured.

Thoughtfully, to cater for a modicum of reservation, vertical concrete-dividing screens separated each occupier. These gave an opportunity to sit in semi-seclusion or even to read without disturbance. On the other hand, one didn't have to lean too far forward to have a chat with one's neighbour. However there were periods when demand was high and every seat was occupied and men were standing around whistling impatiently. On such occasions it was more considerate to talk or read elsewhere. The idea of communal latrines for the army may well have come from Henry VIII who called them 'houses of easement' which had twenty-four seats.

These brick built latrines, mostly for military use were positioned close to the perimeter and around the dormitory area. Unfortunately for those who might think it advisable to wash their hands, the washhouse was in the middle of this large camp, a discouraging walk away. At Bir Jacov Military Hospital there was a plump genial worker named Hassan. He came to work on a little donkey that was really too small to carry his weight. Every morning I would ask him the same question, 'How are you? and every morning he would answer 'Hassan berry sick man' and holding his back with one hand and a happy grin on his stubble covered face, he made a meaningful gesture with his free forearm. To me he looked sixty years of age but then maybe his four wives had made him look like that!

It was Hassan's job to empty the hospital's 'honey buckets' very early each morning. The toilet wing was at right angles to the centre of the timber built wards and the entire building was on stilts. I had one leg in bulky splints and bandages and was confined to bed. However, because I had no desire to use a bedpan, at first light I would make my way to one of the cubicles and with my bandaged leg resting on a 'borrowed' crutch I made use of the toilet. On one occasion as I was sitting uncomfortably the bucket was whipped from under me. I got to my feet in embarrassed consternation and looked down only to find Hassan looking up through the little door via which the buckets were removed.

'Sorry Johnny' said Hassan as he replaced the bucket. After that Hassan would give that wicked grin and say' Ingleezi berry tamman' (good) accompanied by his saucy forearm gesture.

You were never likely to hear of anyone 'going to the latrine' or even 'to the toilet.'

There were many different names for these communal latrines, some troops at 2 BOD called them 'the Houses of Parliament,' as Ted Burns did when the war in Europe ended and he drove his jeep round the 'Houses of Parliament' until it ran out of petrol.

At Camp 153 the dung lorry was called the 'Honey Cart' but 612 Vehicle Group called it the 'Hum Dinger.'

At 614 AOD some called the latrines 'desert roses' even though they were miles away from the desert. The real desert roses were urinals and were to be found in the camps of the desert regions, Gaza, Al Jiya and Rafah. They were so called because of the way they cropped up all over the camps. They were large tun dishes with a down pipe pushed well into the sand. When the sand became saturated and started attracting flies the 'roses' were moved to fresh locations. Sid Harold, 6th Airborne Ordnance Field Park at Jiya re-members a C.S.E. party of entertainers asking what these strange objects were. When they were enlightened they wanted to photo-graph one of them in use. These 'desert roses' had replaced the big white buckets that stood outside the huts, the NAAFI and the camp cinemas in Northern Palestine, the only difference being that these were kept well away from the lines of tents.

The war barely touched Palestine, a few bombs were dropped and the occasional aircraft limped back from Europe only to crash. Although it was strictly against King's Rules and Regulations, the

Army's law bible, an eyewitness recorded in his diary the fate of three Wellington bombers. He was called out on the night that the first one came down in the depot. None of the crew survived. The rear gunner, who had been badly burned was found lying dead behind some packing cases. When the second Wellington came into view, it was picked out in the beams of searchlights and guards saw it stall and nose dive into the sea.

Another Wellington bomber on its way back to base, crashed at 2 Base Ordnance depot. The guard was called out to look for survivors. None of the crew was found alive. The depot guard saw another as it crashed into the sea. A third came in on the searchlights beams when that too stalled, the engines cut out and it crashed into the side of Mount Carmel behind Camp 153.

The permanent military establishments remained in their wartime locations, 'peacetime' troops slept in the same huts and worked in the same sheds and workshops. The civilian workforce was largely the same. However there were significant differences in the lifestyles of the two generations of troops.

Wartime troops had almost unlimited freedom and there was no animosity towards them either from the average Jewish or Arab populations. If either community had a reason for hating the British it was the Arabs for the way in which their rebellion in 1938 had ruthlessly been put down and for promising their country to European Jews.

Charlie Kidd recounts some of his happy days in Palestine that were spent cycling and enjoying unparalleled freedom. He, along with Alec (Waggy) Wagstaff and Trevor Kirby of the Palestine Police were three friends who still meet every year at the Buckshee Wheelers Cycling Club's Annual Dinner. However time is taking its toll on the membership of those who formed the group over 60 years ago in the Middle East.

Their branch of the club was called the Alakeefic Wheelers and it had 20 members from 531 Base Ammunition Depot at Wadi Sarar. There were several other branches of the club in Palestine and they organised time trials and hill climbs. They held their time trials of twenty-five or thirty miles and hill climbs at Seven Sisters Hill just outside Jerusalem.

They mostly clubbed together and bought cycles but their collection included two converted army bikes and a Claude Butler model that was part of a consignment sent out by the Cycle Trade Federation. Friendly relations between soldiers and Jews during the war years were at a level never to be achieved again. Charlie Kidd and the appropriately named Alakeefic Wheelers (carefree wheelers) would cycle to almost anywhere the chose. Charlie Kidd was enjoying a week's cycle tour of Palestine when on October 31 1943 sixteen members of the Stern gang broke out of Latrun Detention Centre. As he cycled back to Wadi Sarar he thought the military and police activity was some sort of event or some parade.

Latrun Detention Centre had been set up during the Arab uprising six years earlier. Arab suspects were detained without a trial but in 1944 a large number of Jews were detained at Latrun and there was a worldwide outcry, evidence of the effective international Jewish propaganda machine. It was the same machine that went into overdrive after 1945 and still works feverishly today to justify Israel's treatment of the Palestinians.

It is obvious from correspondence submitted to 'Palestine Scrapbook' by wartime RAOC and REME that there was a marked difference in the attitude of the Jewish civilian employees. Fraternisation that had been acceptable in the war years was now non-existent. Hatred of the British became more evident, much of it created by the American press and Jewish journalists in particular.

Another of Charlie's pleasures was horse riding at Elia Gordon's Riding Stables in Tel Aviv. It was there that he met and befriended fellow RAOC Private Frank Bell from 2 BOD. Their friendship was renewed fifty years later through the *Palestine Scrapbook*. Both men were united in their praise for the Jewish stable owner. When Elia went for a holiday in the Lebanon Charlie took a week's leave to look after the stables and until Elia, a former Palestine policeman died. Elia regularly stayed on holiday with Frank in Devon.

The situation in February 1947 the month that my draft arrived in Haifa was alarming, but we were soon to find it was no more alarming than any of the months to follow. In the depot the nightly terrorist activity didn't affect us but two tragic accidents did. Brian Cross noted them in his diary;

February 6

RASC chap jumped from a lorry, banged Sten gun butt on the ground. Killed outright with shot through the mouth. This happened right in front of a Staff sergeant and myself.

February 17

'Pinky Crew accidentally shot a Pioneer corporal in the head while on guard at Khayat Beach. He was charged with negligently discharging his issued Sten gun.' Pinky was given 56 days detention and special arms training. Despite a bullet passing right through his head the corporal was still alive one week later. He was transferred to Jerusalem Military hospital. Nothing further was heard about him.

The reliability of the Sten gun had been the subject of discussions and complaints long before these two incidents. Many similar accidents were to occur before the British left Palestine. We never heard of enquiries being held, only Courts Martial for the misuse of weapons, and the brevity of these trials would astound a civilian court with its jury.

Two other entries for March, affected the working at 614 AOD and Brian in particular, they were;

March 2

'Martial Law declared in all major towns. Curfew 8 p.m. to 8 a.m. on all civilians.' This was quickly rescinded because the civilian staff were late for work.

March 22

'British Officers' Club in Haifa blown up. Several officers killed or injured. We were enjoying the hospitality of the Nelson Bar; the explosion brought us out of the bar in double quick time.'

The hastily and ill conceived curfew may well have been because on March 1 there had been an explosion at the Goldsmiths Officers Club in Jerusalem, which killed eleven and injured fourteen people. March ended with the Haifa oil terminal being blown up and the black smoke could be seen from Camp 153 and the depot, blackening the Mediterranean sky.

7.

A Way of Life

Army discipline was maintained by adherence to the KRR's (King's Rules and Regulations.) They guided every officer, non-commissioned officers and soldier's actions. It was through the KRR's that order within the ranks was maintained and behaviour towards the civilian population was controlled. When terrorist activity was testing the troops to the limit it was dealt with 'by the book.' Only once or twice did frustration cause those whose duty it was to keep the peace to boil over. It was that sense of duty and good order that kept the loss of British lives to a minimum and saved the Jews from the type of persecution that the Israelis are now inflicting on the Palestinians over fifty years later.

Camp life was governed by two sets of duplicated orders posted on notice boards and reading the orders was obligatory, ignoring them or claiming that you hadn't seen them was not accepted as an excuse. Some items didn't change on the Daily Routine Orders. As an example at the top of Orders for October 20 1947 and probably no different from the top of the Orders for any other day was daily timetable as follows:

Reveille	0600 hrs
Breakfast	0615-0700 hrs
Morning Parade	0715 hrs
Orderly Room	0730 hrs
Sick Parade	0800 hrs
Lunch	1215 – 1300 hrs
Dinner	1715 – 1800 hrs
Supper	1900 – 1930 hrs

Camp 153 and 614 AOD from the slopes of Mount Carmel. Sherwood Foresters and 6th Airborne were two of the infantry regiments occupying the tented camp on the left. The main coast road ran between the camp and the depot.

Personnel dismounting guard will parade at 0745 hrs on the Parade Ground.

That was the daily routine for 614 AOD and no doubt it was the same daily routine when it was 2 BOD or any other working depot. The only item that changed every day was the names of the sixty-seven men who were due for guard duty the next night. Guard was mounted at 1830 hrs and dismounted at 0530 hrs in time to be breakfasted, washed and dressed ready for normal duties at 0745 hrs. In addition, one man each night was nominated for early call duty and another for quartermaster duty storeman.

By October 21 1947 conditions had deteriorated and reached the stage that the troops marching to and from the depot to the camp needed protection and one platoon each day had to carry rifles and the platoon charged with this duty was Item 4 of the Daily Orders.

No detail was too small to be overlooked and if anyone missed seeing and not acting on a specific item relating to him he would be charged.

Item 5 dealt with private study and two men were told to report to the Education Office at 0745 hrs on the following morning. No reason was given why they were told to report to the Education Office but one assumed it was to improve their ability to read and write.

The Unit Library was open every day for off duty men to use as they would their local library at home. However there was a difference in the way overdue books were treated. The last item on Routine Orders for October 20 1947 was aimed solely at 374 Private Atha who was ordered to return an overdue book tonight Monday October 20 1947. If Private Atha should by any chance have not seen the instruction then the rest of the camp would have seen it and reminded him.

Whilst Daily Routine Orders ran to two pages the Regimental Orders (RO's) (Issue 250) of the same day ran to four pages and gave a better picture of the tedious disciplines of army life. Item 1 was the Welfare Messing Meeting dates.

Item 2 was punishments. Not a lot happened on that day in this well-ordered camp. Just two cases of punishment were recorded; the first was that of 763 Pte. Gray who on the 16 October 1947 was given 7 days CB (confined to barracks). This is what the whole of Camp 153 read when it was posted on the notice boards.

Sec 40 A.D-WOAS Conduct to the prejudice of good order and discipline, in that he failed to comply with Regtl. Part 1 Orders issue No. 247 Par 12 dated 16 October '47 i.e. failed to report to camp MI as detailed.

Broken appointments are the bane of today's National Health Service, they are a source of annoyance and expense and there is a case for imposing a penalty in the case of such missed appointments. What in 1947 happened if we simply forgot to collect our repaired footwear from the camp cobblers on the agreed date? It did happen to 322 Pte. Osborne when not only was he named and shamed but was also given 3 days CB because he forgot to collect his repaired boots from the Quartermaster's Store as detailed.

Both the Daily Routine Orders and the Regimental Orders were the combined efforts of the Adjutant, Captain Jenkins, and the

Officer Commanding, Major Newman, two extremely unpopular officers. Newman was prone to placing men under open arrest and then often, fortunately for the victims, and probably due to his excessive imbibing forgetting all about them.

Item 10 of Regimental Orders 250 under the heading Welfare Food Parcels was a one off opportunity that most would not want to miss. It read:

Seventy Welfare Food Parcels have been allotted to this unit. These parcels will reach the UK during the first days of December.

Cost of a parcel is 250 mils, and any parcel going astray is replaced free of charge.

Personnel wishing to send a parcel, will hand in their No., Rank, Name and Address of the person to whom they wish the parcel to be sent, to HQ by 0900hrs. Wednesday 22 October 1947.

Seventy out of the hundreds of men in the camp turned it into a lottery.

Two hundred and fifty mils sounds a lot of money but it represented only five shillings or about one sixth of a private soldier's weekly army pay.

Item 11. 'Bounds. Twenty-six establishments in Haifa and nine in Tiberius were placed out of bounds to all troops. The item read:

A number of cases of serious illness have been caused recently by the consumption of mineral waters, ice cream, fruit and confectionery from unauthorised sources, hawkers are the source. The dangers involved, if this practice continues, cannot be overstressed. All ranks will take note of all "Out of Bounds" establishments published below.

This notice was then followed by a list of restaurants, cafes and hotels with both Jewish and Arab proprietors.'

Top of the list was Spinney's Restaurant, a popular dining place since the First World War. Spinney was a former British soldier who retired to Palestine and opened several food businesses. He was by World War 2 the largest caterer and purveyor of foods in Palestine. A substantial portion of his trade came from the British forces and their families that were resident in the country until 1947.

One bar owner, George Beer, sent a 'long and touching' letter to the High Commissioner complaining that the GOC had placed his bar 'out of bounds' and his family was on the verge of starvation. In his three-page letter he pleaded for justice; soldiers should be allowed to return to his establishment, The Nelson Bar at 67 Jaffa Road. *1

Beer received a curt reply, to the effect that the High Commissioner could not intervene. George Beer, the proprietor, had been a judge in Germany and had taken all his savings with him to Palestine. By 1947 he had resorted to running this shabby little bar with two 'hostesses' who would chat to the soldiers and police-men for the price of a couple of drinks. If those drinks hadn't been the coloured water that they were, the hostesses would have been well and truly drunk half way through the evening.

Brian Cross and three of his hut mates drank there so frequently that George Beer would often give free egg and chips to encourage them to stay a little longer. Brian didn't know the proprietors full name until he read about George's letter in *'One Palestine Complete'* by Tom Segev.

"I well remember a little fat waiter called George, this must have been George Beer keeping his eye on the girls, Joyce and Olive' wrote Brian, the girls being the 'hostesses' at the Nelson Bar.

The very last Item on Regimental Orders was a miscellany of no-tices some of them being personal announcements, including lost and found notices like for example the black fountain pen found in the Corporals Club. One also wonders if the person advertis-ing for the return of his lost wallet containing 4500 mils (£4.10s) was ever returned. It was lost between the camp and the bathing beach.

Once out of the camp gates the route to the beach, although mainly used by the military, was a public highway, the route includ-ing part of the main coastal road. The neighbouring camp was home to a 6th Airborne Unit whose troops also used the route.

Notice No: 5 was a reminder to inform all ranks to remind their correspondents in the UK of the new postal rates, (poor publicity was given in the UK to the new rates).

The new Air Mail rates were 2½d. for letters to Forces overseas, letters not exceeding 1½ ounces 6d and for each additional half ounce 6d. Postcards 3d.

What's on at the open-air cinema was the last and most well read notice. On Monday 20 October 1947 the film showing was Ralph Richardson in 'School for Secrets.'

After a few weeks of the routine, the in-camp facilities, the climate, the beach and the little luxuries that were not available in the UK, and above all the comradeship, life became a lot more than just tolerable.

In 1947 two RAOC men, Jules Neujean and Jack Pascoe of the Army Kinematographic Corporation (AKC) were seconded to the Middle East School of Artillery (MESA) with the specific task of establishing a training film unit for gunners. Their first job was to turn a dilapidated barrack room into a small cinema using furniture and materials that they managed to scrounge. It involved a considerable amount of improvisation. Jules highlighted the non-training use of the unit.

'Not only did we show training films, but also occasionally we would borrow a feature film from the AKC depot on Mount Carmel and give the lads a show. We had a few scratched records that we played before the film, so we improvised by connecting our home made radio to the amplifier and relayed their records from Haifa Radio station, remembering to cut out the presenter's voice.

The school also had a large Camp Cinema operated by camp staff for showing films supplied by the AKC. Northern Circuit Depot. When there was a problem Jules or Jack were on hand to fix it or even operate the projector on the rare occasion that it was necessary. Being experts in a small cinema brought them the odd request to show private films. Jules remembers one unusual request. 'One day three officers came to see if we could run a film they had taken on board a ship. When they saw it on the screen they reacted with surprise and alarm. One of the officers wanted to know what our equipment had done to his film! Jules explained that they were looking at the negative and not the print.

One other vivid memory was of the quiet Sunday afternoon when they were having a nap in their two-man billet at the end of their cinema. They were awakened by the Irgun's explosion at Acre Jail. The MESA was close to the jail and they went outside and saw the resultant smoke but no activity.

When the time came to return home there was little point of being in warmer climes if one didn't look as if one had been in warmer climes. Everyone, with few exceptions, wanted to go home with a tan and most took every opportunity to go to the beach to get it. We had to go in groups of not less than four and carry rifles. Some had to guard the weapons whilst some swam. I remember the sense of freedom on our first stroll to the beach on the last Saturday in February, a nice warm day. Fellow draftees, George Billings, Ray Machin, Keith Hughes and myself were shown the way by 'Yorkie' Backhouse who had been at 614 AOD for almost a year and was our guide to camp life. He was, incidentally, also the man who took us to the Venus Bar in Haifa, my one and only leisure trip into the town. We ambled down the lane past the Airborne Camp and between the stony fields on either side. Who owned those fields? One night a herd of camels rested there on the way south to Egypt. Gus O'Brien was on guard duty at the camp gate that night and the camels were noisily snorting and rumbling all night, sounding very disgruntled. However it was apparently quite the reverse, such noises were a sign of contentment from well-fed and watered camels. The main road ran alongside the Depot, silent on Saturdays, the civilian staff were in their homes, it was the Jewish Sabbath and the troops were re-laxing in the camp or at the beach. Our route to the beach took us down a second lane and at the corner of the lane an Arab had pitched his tent with a mountain of oranges stacked beside it. He sold his oranges 10 for 10 mils (2½d). We couldn't believe the price, 1000 for a £1. Over the weeks that he was there the pile slowly disap-peared and the vendor and his tent eventually left the site.

We had just finished our first week's work in the office, Britain was still locked in the coldest winter in living memory and we were walking to the beach down a lane that was lined with flowering shrubs. A fringe of Tamarisk trees, known to the nomadic tribes as the willow of the desert, screened the cleanest, gentlest beach imaginable.

Clean sands and clear sea made 614 AOD an ideal recreation spot for Camp 153 and other camps in the Mount Carmel area. The author is sitting on a raft in front of the watchtower, changing rooms and toilets erected in 1947. Note the black flag flying means "No Swimming Today". For one week the author was the lifeguard.

Why was it so clean when there was no tide to sweep away the debris twice a day?

During 1947 the Army built changing rooms, a watchtower and a toilet enclosure to hide the big buckets used as urinals. The sand was soft and fine and above the water line and most of the year it was too hot to walk on in bare feet. Because of this most men changed on the beach leaving their boots just out of reach of the sea. They made 'teepees' out of their weapons and clothing. Some men bathed in swimming trunks, some in their PT shorts and some swam naked. The number of men swimming in the nude increased dramatically when a party of Queen Alexandra's nurses invaded our all male domain. Proud naked men ran into the sea but even on the hottest day the water was cold enough for them to emerge like little boys.

On April 12 following a command in the Daily Routine Orders the military personnel at 614 AOD started wearing their khaki drill uniforms. On April 14 the weather turned very much colder and on April 17 John White thought it was cold enough to return to the standard battle dress. Poor John, he was in deep trouble but although no charge was made against, him he learned that the Army will decide when it is cold enough to change the dress order. He ended his diary entry with the words 'dropped a clanger' a considerable understatement.

Despite this unexpected cold spell in mid April by May temperatures were rising and with the rise came the danger of mosquitoes. We were issued with mosquito nets and advised to sleep under them. They were welcome because they were seen to offer a degree of privacy – quite a fallacious assumption.

Letters up to a certain weight were sent to the UK free of postal charges and once a month there was an opportunity to send home, free of charge, a well-packed parcel, the contents of which, at the time, were regarded in the UK as luxury items.

In Shed 14 there was a band of skilled civilian workers called sail makers and it was their job to pack and send all manner of stores in neat and tidy packages to the British Army wherever it might be stationed. It was the sail makers who packed the parcels we sent home. In my parcel I enclosed tins of fruit, chocolates, small gifts and my free issue of cigarettes. The items were packed incredibly neatly in specially made boxes wrapped tightly in hessian. A linen label was sewn on to each parcel bearing the recipients name and address. The cigarettes were "Players" and they came in airtight round cans of 50 and were distributed every week.

During the war years Lance-Corporal Joe Neate was in charge of the sail makers and they were loyal hard workers but on one occasion they were absent from work for several days in succession. Then one man did arrive, having walked from his village, Fareidis about 15 miles to the South. Normally they travelled to work in a fellow villager's lorry. Apparently the military police had forbidden civilian lorries to travel along the roads unless on official business in order to save precious petrol.

Rather than take the time consuming course of going through official channels, Joe, faced with a growing pile of stores for dispatch, used his initiative. He typed his own 'warrant' and signed it making Lance Corporal look as close as possible to Lieutenant! The Arab went back to his village with six copies and the happy sail makers returned to work next day.

Ray and May Machin were sweethearts before Ray embarked on

the SS Mooltan and she said that Ray used to send her nylon stockings, which it would seem could be bought anywhere in the world except Britain.

To keep within the weight restriction on free mail to the UK Ray would put a stocking in one letter and the other in the next letter. Full advantage was taken of the Forces free mail service; it brought to our lives, pleasure, profit and even romance. Those who had wives or girl friends wrote to them practically every day and to parents occasionally. Two popular magazines in the post war years were Picturegoer and Pictureshow. One of these magazines, probably, Picturegoer, had an extensive pen pal section with an especially large number of requests from servicemen. Dennis Nutt, an RASC man seconded to 614 AOD, sent in his letter, appealing for a pen pal, to the magazine and received a sack full of replies. Apart from his beautiful copperplate handwriting Dennis had a way with words and a creative imagination. From his brick built billet on the gentle slopes of Mount Carmel, pleasantly situated amidst the olive trees, he composed a magic letter. It is impossible to recall the brief but appealing message, but it was the tear-jerking phrase 'A lonely soldier stationed in a desert outpost' that must have done it.'

He received more letters than he could cope with so most of the men took their share of the burden of replies. Naturally those that included ten bob notes, usually from older ladies, Dennis replied to personally. His hut mates didn't mind because for a man who didn't drink and only went into Haifa three times in 1947, he was surprisingly perpetually broke. In midweek he would get a loan from someone and promptly pay it back on payday. All his money went on sweets and cigarettes, one or the other, or even both, were always in his mouth. His fifty free cigarettes went nowhere.

The correspondence for those that shared their burden of replying developed into some interesting postal relationships. The volunteers who brought in the hut mail would look at the back of the envelope intensely before calling out the recipient's name. The early correspondence came with SWALK or HOLLAND printed on the back. One could measure the romance level by some of the place names: ITALY-'I Trust And Love You' was a little rash for two people who had never met. Even worse was NORWICH, and all that can be said of the forward man that wrote that is that he didn't even know how to spell 'knickers.'

Ken Parker received a letter from a former ATS girl's mother. Ken had found the girl's name and address on a spark plug carton. The reply from the girl's mother explained that her daughter was now married with two children and the address on the carton must have been written three years previously as the girl had been demobbed at least two years before. This reply caused great hilarity amongst the lads in the hut said Ken

Until they arrived in Palestine very few conscripts could claim that they had an exciting life. When asked fifty years later, most said that they would like to relive those days again. The sense of excitement not only outweighed the risks but also enhanced the feeling of adventure. Clerks and storemen envied the drivers and general duty men who acted as their escorts, they saw more of the country than those who were in the depots and workshops all the working day.

Any soldier serving overseas whose demob group was close was called back to the UK and on to York to be kitted out for civilian life with a suit, shoes, shirt, raincoat and trilby hat.

After a pint or two in one of York's English pubs it was on to the train with a cardboard box containing a full demob outfit. In fact it was the 'Full Monty' so called because Montague Burton was the forces clothing outfitter, and that is how the expression 'the full Monty' came into use. York was the Army's main demob centre, or to give it it's correct name, Military Dispersal Unit (MDU).

During the war years many Jews and Arabs volunteered for the British Army and the RAOC attracted many to the corps. They had arrived in the country in the pre-war years. For both the Jewish and Arab soldiers benefit, and for the Arabs all ready in the British Forces there was an MDU at Rehovet near Tel Aviv.

Private Joseph Mannion was on the staff there and Joe writes;

'I was transferred from Haifa about June or July in 1946 to the MDU. I don't know when the unit was opened but we were pretty busy supplying Western clothes to ex members of the Jewish Brigade and Arab clothes to the Arabs. There were six military staff, 5 RAOC and a corporal from the King's Regiment, plus a few civilians. The corporal could speak Yiddish, which proved very helpful on a number of occasions. After documentation the ex soldiers came through for their civvy suits etc. The corporal took care of the suits and the rest of us varied between shirts, shoes and hats. At first the unit was situated outside Rehovet and the South Staffordshire Regiment provided the guard. Eventually the demobees dwindled to a trickle and the unit was then transferred into Rehovet town and was manned by three of us namely, the corporal, a lance corporal and myself. There was also a small detachment of the South Staffs who did guard duties but we also had to do guard duties between 6 p.m. and 6 a.m. I was mainly responsible for the issue of shoes. There was a choice of black or brown in four styles. I can remember three of them, Oxford PC (punched cap) Apron fronted and Oxford plain.'

Joe made no mention of sandals, the most popular footwear of the Arabs or of those who preferred the Oxford style with brown punched caps and the rest of the shoe in white leather. Many of the Jewish soldiers who served at 614 AOD were demobbed and took jobs in Palestine. One of the men who went through the MDU was John Adler, the second in command to Frank Mitchell, the CO of the RAOC Palestinian Store Company at Rafah. In a letter to John Tarran, Frank told how he, John Adler and the store company returned to the main depot at Haifa John Adler later became editor of the *Palestine Post*, for how long it is not known because he died, in Israel, at the age of 50.

On July 8, for the first time since joining the, army we slept between sheets. After a year of sleeping between the standard issue of coarse army blankets, without pyjamas, this was a hygienic change for the better.

Each day the Routine Orders nominated a barrack room orderly and periodically it was the orderly's job to debug the billet. In Hut 56 at Camp 153 I was never aware of any bugs, even so the beds and corners of the billet were dusted liberally with DDT. I'm sure the blankets we slept under were laundered occasionally but I do not recall anything other than sleeping between unwashed blankets which, when shook, emitted clouds of DDT. An outbreak of the bubonic plague in Haifa may have been the reason for the distribution of sheets because the two events happened on the same day.

The implications of the outbreak went wider than our billets and our beds. Our bodies were dusted with DDT every day and being soldiers we accepted it. However before civilians could enter military establishments they had to pass through the DDT procedure. Arab employees accepted it and male Jews reluctantly accepted it but Jewish females were alarmed. Carefully selected troops were chosen for the task and Gus O'Brien, a corporal and a mature soldier (he was a year older than most of us), was one of the decontaminators. Gus later wrote to *Palestine Scrapbook*, when in 1998 British television showed how barbaric British soldiers had humiliated Jewish women by spraying their bodies with DDT. "We did think at the time though, as the bubonic plague was rampant and DDT powder was not readily available we were doing them a favour." Gus went on to explain the procedure that he and his six 'better class' privates used.

"Our instructions were that each private should kneel in front of the female, place the nozzle of the spray under the hemline of her dress and whilst averting his gaze, pump three helpings of DDT up her dress. The private was then to stand and ask the female to raise her arms and give her three more helpings of powder under her armpits. Whilst in an upright position the private was then to pump a further three helpings on to the crown of the female's head. Finally the private was to ask her to pull away the top of her dress and, whilst once more averting his gaze, pump three more good helpings down her chest. You can see now why the better class of private was assigned to this task.

It was decided that the service should be offered, free of charge, to the civilian population and a marquee was erected on a traffic island in Kingsway, Haifa, but there was no obligation to take up the offer. The marquee was immediately behind the docks where, it was believed, the source of the plague lay, after being carried into the country by black rats. *2

When new arrivals first went swimming few had bathing trunks but in the camp there was a little shop within a row of shops that did a lively trade. It was the business of Mr. Woolf, a Jewish trader, established for several years, selling books jewellery, pens and newspapers to wartime and post war troops. We bought our swimming trunks from him even though they were all the same style and colour. John White bought a ball point Biro pen, at that time it was a new innovation and his diary entry read 'Bought pen from Woolf's, 380 mils a swindle but it will do.'

When posters were appearing in camps throughout Palestine stating that any officer caught by the IZL would be whipped, Mr. Woolf' despite his long standing business relationship with Camp 153 was one of the Jewish workers within the camp and was suspected of placing the Irgun poster and as a result he was suspended from the camp.

There was a poster within Camp 153 and one in the Sherwood Forrester's Camp adjacent to Camp 153. An unknown Forrester wrote on their poster 'Don't forget the RSM!' The next shop to Woolf's was a photographic supplies business. Apart from selling cameras and films it had a developing and printing service. The proprietor of this shop wasn't averse to making an extra acker or two by selling extra prints from photographs with universal appeal, like the oil depot fire and beached immigrant ships. Over 50 years later Jack Hibbs was showing me photographs I had taken during the outward-bound journey to Palestine.

Paperback books with attractively designed lightweight glossy card covers were available from one of the shops. Penguin and Pelican books were typical of the war economy paperbacks in Britain, a cartridge paper cover printed in black and one other colour and bearing no more than the title, author and the publishers logo.

Every camp normally had a civilian barber and Camp 153 was no exception. He was a barber who listened to his clients' requests rather than the Regimental Sergeant Major's demands for short back and sides.

Periodically the conversation in the billets would turn to our favourite things back home. For many it was fish and chips out of newspaper, but for others the range was almost endless, even mentioning rain in the back streets of their home town, cheering their local football teams on Saturday from crowded stands. Enthusiasm for football in the camps before, during and after the war was universal all over Palestine.

This passion was not confined to the Army, the Palestine Police were even more enthusiastic and occasionally a police team would play a regimental team. Inter-regimental fixtures always created an intense loyalty by the supporters of their team but it could never reach the level of intensity that it did for professional football in Britain. Every Saturday evening half the British population sat in front of the wireless to listen to the results and every Sunday morning those same results were pinned up in all the camps throughout Palestine.

Malcolm Astley the corporal in charge of 614 AOD Telephone Exchange remembers the results coming in on the teleprinter. It was also possible for troops to 'do the pools.' Coupons were available through a network of outlets in Palestine.Vernons Pools of Liverpool had main agents in Tel-Aviv and Haifa but there were also sub-agents at the Universal Book shop in Kingsway, Haifa, The Wireless Shop in the shopping centre,Sarafand and the Photo Shop in the shopping centre at Julis. It is quite possible that 614's punters obtained their coupons from Woolf's shop in Camp 153.

Some of the books that circulated around the camp were not purchased within the camp but almost certainly bought in Egypt. They were badly printed and full of misspelt words but to own one of these books would have been against the KRR's.

Two that were banned were 'Lady Chatterley's Lover' by D.H. Lawrence and 'My Life and Loves' by Frank Harris. In those days these two books were classed as obscene and banned from sale to the British public. Not everyone wanted to read them and some only wanted to hear or read the spicy paragraphs. Inevitably someone would read out those sections to much ribald laughter throughout the billet. Many young conscripts were reluctant to admit they were virgins and it is doubtful if those who were not had indulged in the type of sexual experiences related by those two authors. Disbelief no doubt, accounted for some of the laughter.

Wartime soldier, Ken Brown's wife was the daughter of the owners of a chain of fish and chip shops and that made Ken a connoisseur, but he was disappointed in trying to find the perfect fish and chip meal in Palestine. There was a fish and chip bar halfway up Mount Carmel in Haifa but the fare wasn't the same. The fish wasn't cod, the batter wasn't crispy and the chips weren't fried in lard. In the NAAFI, and in the cafes and bars the accepted alternative was egg and chips. It was cheap and it went down well with Gold Star beer.

Len Harris was so tired of the hot spicy food passed off by the cookhouse as curry that he spent most of his pay on egg and chips in the NAAFI. He claimed that the greatest benefit of being promoted to corporal was that he had more money to spend on food.

We seemed to be perpetually hungry but we ate all that was slopped onto our plates even though cookhouse food was far from appetising. We lined up to get it, men with shirts sticking to their backs, perspiration dripping from them and forming pools on the stone floor at their feet. Arabs served the food from a steaming cauldron with large ladles and their perspiration droplets falling into the spicy stew. When the Duty Officer came into the cookhouse pausing at each table and asking 'Any complaints?' he was greeted either with a disinterested silence or the odd feeble 'No Sir.' Anyone who dared to say there was not enough were told to report back to the cookhouse at 7.p.m., which we did, and were told to take some bread from a tea chest and a piece of hard cheese. As demand grew the cheese was melted by the cooks and poured onto a slice of bread, with a cup of cocoa. that was supper.

Throughout Palestine troops were preparing extra food for themselves in midnight feasts and al fresco suppers. The ingredients were easily obtainable, members of the Royal Army Service Corps and the Army Catering Corps would trade corned beef, spam, bacon and bread for blankets, soap, shirts and socks, and if absolutely necessary, money.

More than one tent was burned to the ground as the result of an illicit barbecue. Drivers were the prime movers in the self-catering business not only because they were equipped to cook on long distance journeys but also they were able to buy eggs from almost anywhere. Every house had chickens running loose all over the villages and a little money bought a lot of eggs. A blanket bought a lot more.

We often talked about our future in Civvy Street but most had no clear frame of mind; our career forming years were slipping away. Fellow hut mate Peter Green knew exactly what he wanted and left me in no doubt that he would achieve his ambition. His demeanour convinced me, he was the tidiest man in the billet with a quiet disposition. One could tell he would soldier on, complete his service and get back to the land as did the yeomen of old England. True enough, he returned to the Lincolnshire farm to carry on his work where he had left off, he had done his duty and that was that. It was not difficult to find him fifty years later; a free announcement on the Lincolnshire radio brought an immediate call from him. He had returned to the farm that took him on as a boy at fourteen years of age and he stayed there until his retirement, eventually achieving the position as farm manager.

Fellow clerk Tubby Mason was set on being, like his father, a Fleet Street journalist. Tracing old comrades in cosmopolitan London is far more difficult than in the provinces. When we thought about returning to civilian life we would often wonder how we might fill our non-working hours – what would we do in the evenings? In camp, if there was no guard duty, then there was the cinema with a different film each night. There was the social atmosphere of the NAAFI with its singsongs around the piano.

The songs were often bawdy ballads with army versions of popular tunes; the repertoire included Irish rebel songs and also *Lily Marlene.* It was an army tradition to sing songs that were written by the enemy to boost the morale of their troops, or to lower ours. Eddie Cartwright was one of the popular pianists and to ensure full audience participation, whether they were standing around the piano or sitting at the tables, his melodies always started with *Daisy, Daisy give me your answer, do* followed by *Two lovely black eyes* and others. He was successful at steering clear of songs with a ribald army lyric until he discovered that there was even an alternative version to *After the Ball was over.* To please Lancastrians he would play *She's a Lassie from Lancashire* and *I Belong to Glasgow* for the Scots. But

Eddie's own choice was for the songs of the day including *Beautiful Dreamer, Souvenirs, Getting Sentimental Over You, If I had my Way* and many more.

In the billet there was always social chitchat and someone with whom to share personal problems. Stan Pope remembers one such occasion at 615 AOD, Rafah. One of his pals received a letter from his girl friend telling him she was now with another. Sympathy was immediately on hand, one bright spark went round the billet and collected photographs of girls from his comrades and passing them on to the broken-hearted man, said 'Here, send these to her; tell her to pick out her photograph and send the rest back.'

Every hut had at least one troublemaker and Alan 'Steve' Stevenson was the one in Hut 56. He was always in fights in the bars, with members from other huts and even with his own hut mates. There could be no quieter gentler man than Len Harris but he had his nose broken by Alan and Len ended up in hospital. One night a group of Scots were having a demob party and Steve went along to join in the fun. Whatever he did at the party it was enough to make them to pursue him back to the hut. A fight followed and Steve was stabbed with a carving fork. The clash was hushed up and the Casualty Receiving Station orderly dressed the wound and neither Steve, the Scots, or the witnesses ever mentioned it again. On another occasion Steve fired a single bullet from his Sten gun that went through the corrugated iron roof and the resulting hole let in the rain.

It is difficult to imagine an army camp better situated than Camp 153. It was located well clear of the port of Haifa, but close enough to the sea and at the foot of Mount Carmel. One day Len and I set out to explore the higher reaches of this hill where Elijah slew the prophets of Baal. We climbed Carmel in a North-easterly direction hoping to reach the summit somewhere behind Khayat Beach. A little way behind the camp, on the hillside, we passed the blackened site where a week or two earlier had stood a shack beside a fig tree. It had been the home of a poor Arab family. The Arab had built his primitive home from jerry cans flattened into shingles and these were nailed to a frame of scrap timber. Early one morning in the spring of 1947 it was completely destroyed by fire. We watched help-lessly from behind the camp fence.

A surprise was in store for us when we reached what may have been the top where we were greeted by the smell of freshly mixed concrete. New houses were being built and the builders' were as surprised at our presence as we were of theirs. But we were strictly out of bounds and we beat a hasty retreat.

Allenby had revered the Holy places in Palestine and he was alarmed at the use of corrugated iron as roofing material in Jerusalem and forbade it use. The little jerry can building now gone, was incongruous but these concrete dwellings were also out of place on a grand scale. Looking at a map afterwards we had reached The Herbert Samuel Way that ran across the top of Mount Carmel.

The cement came from a local source, the massive Nesher Lajour Cement Works at Jalama. It was quarried, ground and baked on the lower slopes of Mount Carmel, north east of Haifa.

Khayat was a name familiar to all who served in Palestine. There was the Khayat Bus Company, the Khayat Beach Military Cemetery and there was even a judge in Jerusalem in the 1940's with that name.

How did Khayat Beach get its name? Who owned the Khayat Beach Bus Company?

The beach was named after the Khayat family who also owned the bus company and a considerable proportion of the property in the Haifa district. Their splendid dwelling was on the western slopes of Mount Carmel overlooking Haifa Bay. Brian Rivers and his fellow officers were often guests of 'Ma' (Brian's word) Khayat and together they sang Hoagy Carmichael songs on the veranda of the Khayat residence. Brian said 'Ma' was a Hoagy Carmichael fan and spent a large part of every year in America.

References

  1. *One Palestine Complete,* Tom Segev
  2. Unpublished memoirs of Cpl. 'Gus' O'Brien

8.

Time Out

There were circumstances that could take a soldier out of his everyday duties, and leave was the most popular reason for absence from duty. Leave in addition to Python (LIAP) was leave that was looked forward to with the greatest joyful anticipation. There was also regional leave to Mediterranean leave centres. It was even possible to take leave within the camp but it was a poor second. A spell in one of the detention barracks could also take a delinquent out of the daily grind, but for most, not an acceptable proposition. Finally there was the cosseted life in hospital if you could cope with injury or sickness.

Regional leave was particularly attractive. In wartime the Holy Land of Milk and Honey had been the premium Mediterranean leave centre. Its popularity began to wilt in peacetime and had petered out altogether after the King David Hotel explosion. After that the milk was sour and the honey bitter it was now the land of murder and mayhem. Leave centres were to be found in Lebanon, Cyprus and Egypt and by far the favourite was Cyprus, the most unusual was to be found in the Lebanon in winter.

For Jack Harris, whose wartime service included spells from Normandy to Belsen, his first leave since after arriving in Palestine in September 1945 was in February 1946. He was offered the choice of one weeks leave in Cyprus or two weeks at a ski centre in the Lebanon. Jack and friend David Chapman elected to go to the ski centre.

'I still haven't had a better holiday in the 60 years that have elapsed since then. We set off in a jeep along the coast, such a beautiful coast with mountains dropping directly into the sea. Eventually we reached Beirut, occupied by the French for so long that the nightlife was Paris by the sea. However we were not allowed to stay more than one night. What mattered to us was getting to the Cedars of Lebanon, an area frequented by rich Arabs as their holiday resort. Everywhere was covered in thick crispy snow and the sun shone from the crack of dawn till nightfall. We were 10,000 ft above sea level and able to look across the mountains to the Mediterranean. We soon got cracking learning to ski. There were no ski lifts or other aids but being young and fit we soon became skilled skiers. How could such a holiday end? In fact it didn't end on time. The day before we were due to leave there was a terrible snowstorm that completely blocked the road from the Cedars down to the coast. It was impossible to use the road and a snow plough was sent from Beirut broke down.

'What should have been a two week break ran into a whole month of good food beer and sunshine. Above all, there was a rest centre for nurses in one of the hotels, so we were dancing every night – Oh! What a lovely war.'

The sixty to seventy mile stretch of clear blue water between Palestine and Cyprus gave the island a significant advantage over the alternative leave centres on the Mediterranean fringe. The leave ship Tripolitania left the heavily guarded quayside at Haifa two or even three times a week. Each time, just before departure to Famagusta the hull was inspected by frogmen for possible terrorist mines. Not wishing to take any infection to Cyprus there was an FFI parade for the 400 or so male passengers before the Tripolitania sailed. On their return there was another FFI parade to make sure they were bringing nothing back. The holiday island offered troops from strife torn Palestine the opportunity to go unfettered by the ubiquitous weapons and to freely wander through towns, villages and beaches at will.

They could escape their uniforms and the barbed wire to mix with civilians. For those wishing to exchange the heat of Palestine for the cool pine clad mountains they could take their leave at Troodos 5,500 ft above sea level at the Pine Tree Holiday Camp. The camp was just 2 miles away from Mount Olympus and offered a leave with a difference. Accommodation for servicemen was in tents but there were many features including a ballroom-cum-cinema, sports facilities and a tavern with a country pub atmosphere and an extensive range of drinks not to be found in Britain or Palestine.

Troops who chose Troodos came back greatly refreshed by the facilities offered and from the company they enjoyed. Hundreds of civilians, wives and families of men serving throughout the Middle East also took their holidays there and troops came back talking of the people that they had met and the female company they had enjoyed. The Women's Voluntary Services provided home comforts and that included the care of sports kit. Young single soldiers were more attracted to Famagusta, the main port of Cyprus, for its nightlife and numerous bars, and in the daytime, sunny sandy beaches. There was a choice of two centres, Welfare's 181 camp and the other 2 miles out of town, The Golden Sands Holiday Camp run by the NAAFI. Both centres provided many amenities for those who had been so restricted and unable to leave depots and camps.

The men from 614 AOD and other camps with a cinema were likely to be disappointed with the cinemas of Famagusta and Nicosia which screened films much older than those provided by the AKC. Cyprus is crowded with places of historical interest and for four pence ha'penny (less than 2p in today's UK currency) a cycle could be hired to tour places within cycling distance. Sightseeing further afield was made possible by organised bus outings, some of them under the auspices of the WVS.

In central Cyprus the Garrison Club provided another leave centre and to make up for the absence of the sea and beach it had a swimming pool. If you didn't mind the heat it was the ideal camp for a city holiday and gift shopping. When soldiers serving in Britain went home on leave they were given a living-out allowance to cover their board and keep. In Cyprus leave camps the Army paid the living out allowance directly to the NAAFI. And a soldier paid 3s. 2d of the 8s.6d per day that the NAAFI required. Officers were charged eleven shillings. The journey by ship to Cyprus was free of charge and in Britain rail passes were issued to leave takers, in both instances the Army saw it as their responsibility to get a soldier to a leave destination without cost. After stoppages a private soldier's pay averaged 3s.6d.a day.

The accommodation was simple. At Golden Sands for example it was tents on the beach and food was served in a large marquee. It was by far the most popular choice but for those who preferred a seaside holiday there was a cooler resort, Kyrenia.

Jeff Buck said he and his pals, Jim Knapp and Stan Cox spent most of their leave on the beach at Golden Sands with the occasional ride on the narrow gauge railway into Famagusta

Ian Christie and two pals enjoyed their week at the YMCA in Kyrenia taking only bed and breakfast. It was a base for sightseeing in Northern Cyprus and they had to use taxis to get to many places. Both Jeff and Ian found it frustrating to be in a land of freedom with plenty to see and do and with so little money.

A lucky few had jobs that were nearly as good as a holiday, one such man was Staff Sergeant Ray Yellop who went very frequently to the Base Depot at Tel-el-Kebir to organise convoys of urgently needed spare parts. He described his visits to Tel-el-Kebir . 'Tek was really a holiday, breakfast at 8.30am then down to the depot to check on the mail from Haifa before going to the NAAFI for coffee; back then to check on the different departments to make sure all orders were being dealt with. After lunch we would hire an army truck for one shilling to take us to Ismalia for a swim in the Great Bitter Lake, returning in time for afternoon tea before checking that the convoy was being loaded. We dressed each evening for dinner in the mess that was always followed by a film show. Someone in the mess was in charge of the projector and we saw all the latest films.'

Early in 1948 when the evacuation of Palestine was well under way, stores were being shipped out of Haifa and convoys of men and materials were journeying south by dusty roads across the desert to Egypt. It was at this time that the RAOC moved 52 Mobile Laundry and Bath Unit to Rafah to refresh the rearguard units with hot showers and laundry facilities. One of the men involved in that operation was Denis Burns. He had been at Rafah just a few weeks when he developed septic tonsillitis a complaint that needed professional attention and there was no suitable medical capacity at Rafah and the military hospitals North of there were either closed or closing. It meant a trek across the Sinai by ambulance to the Military Hospital at Fayid. He arrived there at night. 'Next morning I awoke to find I had been placed in the VD ward. However it was only temporary measure and I was soon taken to the surgery ward' 'After the operation I was on a diet of ice-cream and jelly for about a week and then moved to Deversoir Convalescent Depot for two weeks' rest and recuperation. It was like a holiday' said Dennis.

It was a pleasant change to lay aside the inevitable weapons and escape the feverish activity of the withdrawal from the much trouble Holy Land. He was able to go swimming and on a number of occasions swam across the Suez Canal.

Denis knew that this pleasurable break could not last forever but was not dismayed when he was posted to Transit Camp 156 at Port Said. It was recognised as a comparatively pleasant camp staffed by German prisoners of war who did all the chores. It was the camp that those who were leaving Palestine for the journey home assembled and were accommodated. Denis found life in Port Said preferable to life back at Rafah and with a bit of luck he might even be placed on a ship along with other Palestine veterans on his way back to the UK. But he was wrong. Denis had to return to Rafah.

Before and during the war the school leaving age was fixed at fourteen and by 1945 many of those that were of military age were in reserved occupations and excluded from conscription. It was a sore point with the conscripts that were not in reserved occupations, as whilst they were receiving a derisory pay their reserved occupation contemporaries, were by comparison, receiving high wages in employment, with a certain future. Although we may not have realised it at the age of eighteen our general education hadn't ended when we left school. Army life fulfilled some of the advantages that university life might have done. There was political and social discussion in education centres, in the billets and on field trips within the lands in which we were stationed. In the camps education hut Sergeant Ian Christie taught those that needed it the three R's.

The British Army made a considerable effort to ensure that there was an opportunity to continue learning and even to swat for a post service career. John Tarran for example was given the necessary books and materials to continue his intended career in accountancy. At Rafah he studied during his off duty hours by the light of a Tilley lamp in his tent. Palestine was a unique opportunity to take an interest in history by visiting sites of historic and religious importance such as the ruins of the Crusaders castle, the ancient mosques and the places that Christ visited.

When Bill Howard arrived in Palestine in 1936 he was given a 32-page booklet that had been printed and published by the Government Printer in Jerusalem. It was a useful publication that was issued to all British troops arriving in Palestine in 1936. Written by the Rev. H. G. Williamson, MA. and entitled *Palestine Past and Present.* Its purpose, wrote Lt General J.G. Dill, Commanding British Forces in Palestine and Transjordan, is that those who serve in Palestine should 'learn all they can of the places and buildings of biblical and historical interest in this Holy Land.

It was a good historical reference into Palestine's places of interest for example Jaffa, which has had many names. It was Joppa in the scriptures, the Jews called it Yafo and the Arabs Yafa but in Hieroglyphic it was Yapu and in Greek Iope. It is one of the oldest cities in the world, going back in history to a time between 2000 and 3000 years BC. In the Egyptian period of Ramses II it was famous for its gardens.

Jaffa was the scene of Jonah and the big fish. The Cedars of Lebanon felled for the building of Solomon's Temple were floated to the port of Jaffa. St. Peter lodged in the house of Simon the Tanner and was there when the messengers came from Cornelius. It was in Jaffa that St. Peter restored Tabitha (Dorcas) back to life and here; too, he had the vision of the clean and unclean beasts.

When Britain was at war with Germany the strength of Britain's Army increased many fold and the YMCA facilities had to expand to meet the increased demands on its services. The YMCA played an important role in Bill Howard's progress from Lance Corporal to Major. He made use of the library, reading room, the sports facilities and the excursions. From within his box of souvenirs Bill produced a copy of the monthly YMCA newsletter, the *Red Triangle* Issue No. 5. Vol.III dated May 1938. It was an enlightening little four-page publication that revealed the remarkable breadth of the role of the YMCA. At the height of the Arab rebellion, surprisingly it was possible to lead a reasonable off duty life. Both Jews and Arabs took advantage of the YMCA's services.

Bill's favourite pastime was to play squash on their courts. He also went on one of the many excursions they organised. It was advertised as a 'One day trip to the Arnon River and the hot springs of the Dead Sea, on Saturday May 21 leaving at 6.30.am.

Bill remembers that the temperature was extremely high at the Dead Sea and the trip was not exclusively for service personnel. The party was largely civilians of mixed religions on the day when Jews, Muslims and Christians waded into the River Arnon together. They went by bus from the YMCA to the River and the rest of the day went as intended according to the notice: 'We will take the boat from Mr. Deeb's place and will go to the Arnon River. In the afternoon we will proceed to the Hot Springs (Kallirhoe) where we will have a dip in that useful mineral water. Bring your swimsuit and old tennis shoes to enable you to wade on the pebbles on the bed of the River Arnon. Experienced life savers will take good care of the party during the swimming. Do not forget to bring your lunch. Ladies may join the outing.'

The fees for the bus and boat transportation were; Members 450 mils. Non-members 500 mils (nine shillings and ten shillings respectively in 1938 British money or 45p and 50p in today's currency).

The YMCA had a school and library and in January 1938 three students passed the London University Matriculation examinations. The successful students were Mr. J. Strauss, Mr. W. Feilchenfeld and Mr. S. Laufer. They and their teachers were congratulated in the newsletter.

Considering the ruthless manner in which the Arab revolt was being put down and the numbers of Arabs being hanged in 1938 it was quite remarkable how the YMCA carried on unaffected.

A trip Bill remembers fondly was in August 1937and he recalls 'The Assistant Chaplain General, Colonel Webb hired a local bus and driver to take a party of junior NCO's, including myself, on a holiday to Syria travelling from Jerusalem via Nazareth, Tiberius, Damascus, Baalbeck, Bayrouth and then up to the Cedars of Lebanon. We returned by the same route.'

How different it was from the hostile post war period when the freedom to visit historic places was much more difficult. Leave could sometimes be taken within the camp but it required determination and imagination for it to be a relaxing break. It was necessary for example, to ignore the activity in the camp, and in particular the billet. There was no change in the mealtimes, including breakfast, which were fixed with no flexibility for off duty personnel. As army camps go, Camp 153 was a beautiful camp but it fell well short of being a holiday camp even though it was, as many a seaside landlady claimed, only ten minutes from the sea and its wonderful beach. Through the entire Mandate years the Army seemed determined that the troops should be given the opportunity to visit the key scriptural sites, particularly those with strong Christian connections. Jerusalem, Bethlehem and Nazareth. As they were predominantly Arab areas they were safer destinations. Those who went to the Church of The Holy Sepulcher in Jerusalem could leave with a certificate of their pilgrimage, signed by the Archbishop.

At the Garden of Gethsemane one could purchase greeting cards adorned with dried Gethsemane flowers. Charles Eyles thought the vendors went too far when on his way to the Church of the Holy Sepulcher he and his companions were met by a guide carrying a tray of rosaries. razor blades, crucifixes and contraceptives.

One of the most popular annual events was to go to the Shepherds Field at Bethlehem on Christmas Eve. It was an event that Bill Howard attended before the war but even after the war thousands of troops made the same pilgrimage every Christmas Eve during, and regardless of, the terrorist activity.

For the last three Christmases of the Mandate so many wished to be present that they had to apply for tickets. In 1946 the BBC Radio made its first post war Christmas worldwide broadcast of the pilgrimage. Malcolm Astley spoke for the thousands who were at the 1947 Christmas in the fields.' It was memorable as we were able to celebrate Christmas Eve in the fields at a Watch Night service, a very moving event.' He summarized his period in Palestine with 'We were able to visit, at the Government's expense, Jerusalem, Tiberius, The Dead Sea, Nazareth and Bethlehem in the days when Palestine was not looked upon as a tourist attraction and at a time when these places were unspoiled and still in an 'uncommercialised ambience.'

Arthur Hammond with 58 ML &BU at Qastina discovered that being ill wasn't without its compensations when he developed an ulcer on his leg that would not heal and was admitted to the hospital at Sarafand. He was in a ward for minor surgery when he, and a guardsman, who was making a good recovery, decided one night to go to the cinema. On the way back the guardsman deliberately kicked, with all the force he could muster, one of the white rocks that lined the path. When Arthur asked him why, the guardsman said he wanted his wound to burst open again so that he could prolong his stay in hospital.

After my uncomfortable and painful spell in the camp CRS with an injured knee I viewed going into hospital with some trepidation. It had been bandaged to a bent splint causing the knee to be locked and wasted giving a skeletal appearance. Haifa British Military Hospital was a haven of peace and comparative tranquility. The attention and care give by the Queen Alexandra nursing sisters, who were in charge, was a refreshing contrast to life in the camp and depot. We had time to read a book a day if one felt so inclined. In the next bed was a man whose hernia had just been repaired and he would insist on showing me the scar. The soldier on the other side of me was waiting to have a bullet taken out of his leg. His last words to me as he was wheeled away for the operation in a drowsy pre-med haze were 'Make sure they return the bullet.' I was to find out later that all wounded men wanted to keep the bullet or shrapnel as a souvenir. Back in the ward his first words were "Where's my bullet?" Thinking that this poor fellow must have been caught up in an ambush I asked him how it happened. He said, "My gun went off accidentally, but fortunately it was pointing downwards. I wonder if the simple unvarnished truth survived in the re-telling of the events in later life.

Injured American soldiers were given a medal 'The Purple Heart'; British soldiers were allowed to keep the bullet or the shrapnel.

A week or so later I was transferred south to Palestine's largest Military Hospital at Bir Yacov and admitted to one of the surgical wards. On entering the ward I was greeted by the sight of a one-legged amputee sitting on his bed and cheerfully playing a mouth organ. Was he really happy or was it bravado to dispel his fears?. Until my injury I had never been in a hospital before and now I was in a ward of men like me, young and fit but now enduring disabling physical injuries some inflicted by terrorist activity and others because of accidents. For much of the day we were left alone, except for an orderly or the nursing sisters. The orderly attended to mundane needs, principally, urine bottles or the bedpan and screens. Apart from changing dressings and administering medication the sister on duty would change sheets, tidy beds and give bed baths.

It was the long hot summer in Palestine in 1947 and the high temperatures continuing well into October that contributed to the discomfort of having my leg heavily bandaged to splints. A minor fear was that one of the ants that occasionally climbed the walls of the ward might manage to get into my dressing. It was so hot that the staff wore very little clothing. On one occasion it was necessary for the surgeon to re-break a leg because the original fracture was not healing properly. Screens were put round the patient and the anesthetist came into the ward wearing his cap and gown. As he walked down the ward those whose beds he passed could see that his gown did not meet at the back and were privileged to see his naked buttocks. We lay in bed covered by only the obligatory linen sheet which the nurses came and straightened several times a day. They too, wore very little clothing. Their white dresses had press studs at the side but the studs had been flattened by constant laundering and when the nurses were bending and tending to the beds there was a gap at the side and sufficient flesh was exposed to stir a man's imagination. It wasn't a very wide gap and gave no more than a glimpse of bare nubile flesh but that coupled with a delicate feminine fragrance was sufficient to evoke a memory of the female companionship that was missing from our masculine lives.

Bir Yacov had patients drawn from all sections of the Army. In the next bed was a patient whose broken leg had been repaired with a narrow stainless steel plate secured with what looked suspiciously like two wood screws. Initially his leg was in plaster but now he was an up patient and getting about the ward helped by a walking frame proudly displaying an X-ray of his repaired bone. He left the hospital with his X-rays bound for the Nathanya Convalescent Camp taking his X-rays as a souvenir. Another man in that bed was from Connah's Quay. I will, for the sake of the story, call him 'Taff' although his accent was more Liverpudlian than Welsh.

He was brought in from Gaza Detention Barracks, the Army prison with the reputation of breaking the most defiant spirit. Taff had multiple fractures in one of his legs. It happened when he was on a high stepladder whitewashing a ceiling when the Regimental Sergeant Major stepped immediately below him. He couldn't resist tipping the contents of the bucket over the unsuspecting R.S.M. Feigning an accident was preferable to the unimaginable punishment that was in store for him so he fell from the ladder, following his bucket. To mend Taff's fractures it was decided to use one of his lower ribs instead of the customary steel plate and screws. He said he was a friend of Emlyn Williams and my scepticism was dispelled when he received a letter from the famous playwright.

One morning Taff had gone. Some days later he was brought back with blood oozing from his plaster. He was then placed in Ward 6 under lock and key. His freedom had ended at the Lebanese border where tired and in pain he gave himself up.

His companions also escapees from Gaza Detention barracks got over the border, they had apparently come to collect Taff during the night. At Chester Military Hospital I met Taff again he invited me to go to his home at Connah's Quay when I was back from disembarkation leave. He was on the run again when I called..

Every night there was a singsong and free beer ration: a one litre bottle of Gold Star Beer shared by two patients or for those patients with jaundice a bottle of Guinness.

Eventually I became an up patient and doing my share of ward duties, this included joining a team of four who distributed the nightly ration of beer and stout. A surprising perk went with the job. Some patients didn't want their half litre of Gold Star and even more of the jaundice patients didn't want their Guinness. After the distribution was finished we met in the ward kitchen to drink the unwanted beer by tipping it all into a white enamel pail and dipping our drinking mugs into the mixture. It was a Jewish-Irish type of Black and Tan and I went to bed feeling slightly giddy.

In the ward rank was immaterial, patients used first names. A sergeant in the guards now occupied Taff's vacated bed. His armoured vehicle had been overturned by a mine pinning him underneath and causing several injuries. He was brought in rambling and in pain with fractures in both thighs. His legs were fixed in splints with pins and each leg stretched and elevated by traction. He was confused for several days, frequently wetting the bed until he learned to ask for the urine bottle. Early one morning he called for the bottle but he placed it in the wrong postion, fortunately the unflappable Sister Surtees spotted it and repositioned his penis into the bottle. On another occasion and still confused he screamed each time he reached up to change his body position using the handle suspended above his bed. It was thought that his pain was caused only by his leg injuries but on this occasion a fractured bone was sticking out of his forearm. For at least a week this injury to his arm had gone unnoticed. We had the utmost sympathy for him and helped him in whatever way we could.

The collecting of mail for the ward was taken in turn. When it was my turn I said, 'One for you Sarge.' 'Sergeant to you Private Lowe he barked,' clearly he was on the mend and we realised that he never used anyone's first name. He addressed us all by rank and, or second name, he was thoroughly regimentalised, but for all that and with affection we still called him 'Sarge.' His attitude could not diminish the benevolence we accorded him.

Conscript soldiers needed to be eighteen and a half years old to be sent to Palestine but the rule didn't apply to boy soldiers. In the ward there was a junior bandsman. He and I would stroll to the perimeter wire and chat to the passing Arabs walking along the track beyond the wire. Two little Arab girls about nine or ten came along and offered us oranges 'baksheesh' (free). In turn, we gave them 'baksheesh,' a ten-mil coin. Within ten minutes they were back with an armful of more 'baksheesh' oranges. Next day they came back with yet another armful of oranges and I gave them another ten mils. It then became a daily arrangement, both girls laden with oranges and both of us giving ten mils each time. The fruit had been stolen and was still on the branches. Everyone in the ward was enjoying fresh oranges until the one day the little girls failed to appear. Maybe they had been caught, maybe their father stopped them coming or maybe their family were driven out of the area because this was a predominately Jewish region and the intimidation of the Arab population was in progress. I was transferred to Nathanya Convalescent Camp for extra physiotherapy but my knee was not improving. Early in January, after spending Christmas at Nathanya and getting out into central Palestine on an exciting escort duty I returned to the same ward at Bir Yacov but there had been changes. The evacuation was under way and many patients had left on hospital ships sailing from Haifa. A Christian Arab, Sulieman.from Nablus was now in the ward, he had sustained an injury for which the Army felt responsible. Communicating with him was difficult, he could speak no English and my Arabic was very limited. He showed me his crucifix to let me know he was a Christian Arab and in return I drew him a picture of Christ on the Cross and we became friends. His wife and two of his children, a boy and a girl, visited him and he proudly showed them my sketch. With typical Arabic generosity they gave me some dates.

Infantrymen and paratroopers did a wonderful job keeping the peace in the world's most violent post war hot spot. It was a job that clerks, storemen and mechanics were not trained to do nor did they possess the necessary disposition to do it. The infantry and paratroopers hunted terrorists, manned roadblocks, searched houses and were involved in gun battles, as no other army has ever done so patiently and effectively. We, on the other hand, worked alongside civilians and the bond we formed with them influenced our attitude, our thinking and the language we used.

The peacekeeping forces could not afford the same affinity with civilians. At times this difference in outlook manifested itself and made me feel very uncomfortable. Never more so than one Sunday evening when a patient from the far end of the ward appeared dressed as a clergyman and set up a mock pulpit to perform his highly irreligious act. It was an act that involved taking well-known lines from the Bible and suffixing them with his own obscene expressions. I had seen this act before and was alarmed when, as the man set up his props, I saw how delighted Sulieman was with the prospect of a Christian service. Sulieman couldn't understand what the 'clergyman' was saying and was perplexed at the raucous laughter. I felt embarrassed and ashamed.

There was another Arab in the ward, a young Arab Legion soldier and he too couldn't speak any English, but he could pick up the Arabic words that had found their way into a soldier's vocabulary. One of those words was 'macnoon' a word that was used far too liberally. Its lighthearted use by soldiers had replaced the word 'crazy.' Arabs used it in a very serious context and never as flippantly as we used the word 'crazy.'

Unfortunately the young Arab assumed we were talking about him and he went into an almost uncontrollable rage. To make matters worse the young soldier's rage only served to make most of the rest of the patients laugh.

In normal circumstances not much ails fit young men of military age and many illnesses and some of the injuries were successfully treated at the Camp CRS.

Dysentery and sand fly fever were commonplace amongst the troops in the Middle East-but anthrax, surely not! But it was. It happened to Rex Fursland when he was attached to the Sixth Airborne at Rafah.

Anthrax may show itself in three ways, affecting either the skin, the lungs or the intestines. In Rex's case it was the skin and in particular his face. Had it been either of the other two forms it would have proved fatal. The rapidity with which the disease can spread is illustrated by Rex's story.

It began with a shaving brush bought from the camp NAAFI in which the spores of the disease had lain dormant, an occurrence that should not be possible in a brush made in a reputable factory. Rex washed and shaved prior to going on guard duty. Within a couple of hours his face began to swell but Rex resolutely did his stint of guard duty. By the time his watch stood down, to quote Rex, his face had 'swollen like a balloon' Rex was photographed for a medical journal and then a few weeks later the core was removed and it smelt dreadful. It was so big that it left a hole in his face which when he brushed his teeth caused the water to spurt out. To this day Rex has a scar even though the wound has thoroughly healed.

Meanwhile back at camp at Rafah the outbreak had created panic. Drastic preventive measures were taken, which, sadly, included destroying all the dogs.

Rex thought he had a boil (in fact anthrax is a Greek word meaning carbuncle). On sick parade the Medical Officer diagnosed anthrax. He was sent to Haifa Military Hospital and put into isolation. All who entered the ward had to observe strict hygienic rules that included wearing masks. If the same spores that had affected Rex's skin found their way into his, or anyone else's intestines the disease could have been fatal and even could have led to an epidemic.

Rex recounts: 'I was give penicillin that was injected into my buttocks every three hours throughout the day and night. The treatment started at 100,000 units and progressed to 500,000 units with each injection. By this time my eyes had shut through the immense swelling on my face. One nurse refused to enter the ward but apart from that the staff were wonderful.'

Rex will never forget the MO Captain G.M. Mann. whose kindness and prompt action had saved his life and prevented the spread of the disease. Rex's one regret was that he never saw the MO again and was unable to thank him.

One certain way that soldier could escape from the treadmill of the routine in which he felt trapped was to commit a misdemeanor of such magnitude as to warrant a Court Martial and be sent to a detention barracks. In the last days of the British Mandate so many were found guilty that at times there was no room for them in the detention barracks.

When this occurred the sentence had to be served in the camp and this meant sleeping in the cells, on the spot soul destroying rigorous exercise on the parade ground and fatigues in the cookhouse and around the camp. Theft and desertion were two of the offences frequently cited for the surge in military crime. Some deserted and were never caught and others deserted with the sole intention of making a trip to sell some stolen goods. Life in a detention barracks was not an enjoyable experience and it is hard to imagine it occurring in wartime Palestine particularly for desertion. However the only account of life in a detention barracks comes from Danny Godfrey, a wartime soldier serving at 2 Base Ammunition Depot, Wadi Sarar and it wasn't for desertion. His 'crime' was, if not debatable, certainly minor. This is Danny's account of his 'crime' and the time spent in detention.

Danny went on strike because his accumulated pay entitlement showed a debit instead of a credit despite having made several weeks voluntary pay reductions. He requested to have payment of £3 to buy his wife a present but there had been a clerical error. Determined to show his anger and the following day by staying in bed instead of going for breakfast or to work. It wasn't long before Sgt. Major Box came in to Danny's hut and asked what was wrong. The Sergeant Major told him that if he got out of bed and went to work he wouldn't report the matter. Defiant Danny went to the NAAFI for a bite to eat and a cup of tea. He was asked again to go to work and again Danny refused. He was placed under close arrest. Danny's own words best explain the subsequent events.

'In front of Major Domenico I pleaded guilty to refusing to obey an order from a superior officer and was given 28 days detention in the Glasshouse at Jerusalem. I remember my trip to Jerusalem with two mates as escort plus the driver of the open jeep. All the way there we were cracking jokes and singing until we stopped outside the gates of a large building. I was just holding one of the escort's rifles whilst he lit a cigarette when there was a deafening bellow from a building on the other side of the street. "Who's the prisoner?" My mates let the big fellow know by throwing my kit out and shouting

'So long Danny' and shooting off back to Wadi Sarar at top speed.

The Staff Sergeant shouted 'Pick up your * * * * * * * kit and stand to attention. Left right, Left right, left at the double and pick your * * * * * * * feet up. I doubled into the compound and was made to double up and down the length of the building before doubling into the building. I was told to strip off and double naked to a table where a Captain was sitting. After listening to the Riot Act I was taken, still at the double to my cell, carrying my gear, full pack, and the lot.

There were two other occupants in my cell, a young chap about my age and a friendly 52-year-old Irishman. He'd been caught stealing potatoes from the docks at Haifa and selling them. When sentenced he lost his rank of Sergeant and was given six months detention of which he had only done six weeks. He told me that if he could get into hospital he would serve most of his remaining time there in there. He asked me to break his wrist for him, even to the extent of showing me how to do it. There was no way that I was going to do it but I went through the motions for him, saying I wasn't strong enough, just to appease him. His wrist became a trifle swollen so I gave it up, as my heart wasn't in it.

Life was one long grind every day. We were split into work parties and given jobs. The most hated job was teasing coir in the coir factory. The coir, when teased, was to fill the 'biscuits' which soldiers slept on. Coir was messy and the dust in the air was thick.'

Life improved when Danny was transferred to work in the Sergeant's Mess. It was a job he wanted to keep. He wrote 'I kept the place spotless and leftovers included huge slices of bacon, uneaten sausages, loads of bread and other delicacies that I took back to the lads. Half smoked cigarettes were left which were taken to the other side, where smoking was a punishable offence, and rerolled, made countless cigarettes.

Our keepers were loud of mouth, doing what they had been selected to do, intimidate. There was one exception, and he was a Samaritan. We went with him to pick up stores and both there and back he allowed us to smoke. He also had a bag of sweets that he shared with us.'

9.

Clifty Wallahs

Theft, driven by poverty, was rife throughout the Middle East but stealing from the British Army took on a greater significance. Conscripts who had lived through the hard times saw the unbelievable extravagance of war. Palestine was one huge arsenal packed with the tempting war material in the middle of a burgeoning war zone. There were attractive rewards for the successful thief. But it wasn't only civilians that were the predators; there were thieves within the camps, the depots and workshops. Neither was theft confined to the other ranks. At 614 AOD a colonel and a major were stealing weapons on a grand scale and two sergeants, in the guards, stole two tanks and sold them in Tel Aviv.

For all the security measures and the certainty of the severe punishment there was one crime so prevalent that no detention barracks could hold all the offenders if they were caught.

Some called it 'buncing' and others called it 'liberating' but by whatever name, it was stealing. The men who were meant to prevent it, the guards, did most of it at night. Many of the stores were piled in bales on concrete bases out in the open. The most accessible were to be found at the Khayat Beach Sub Depot. I found a bale of Bergen framed rucksacks, my one unaffordable desire when rambling and youth hostelling as a civilian. On the same guard duty at Khayat Beach I also found a large superb vacuum flask. It was not a problem getting them back to camp on the truck along with other troops who all had spoils of one kind or another. The guard commander always sat in the cab with the driver. When we reached camp I concealed the rucksack in the branches of an olive tree and buried the thermos flask in a soldier's tin box, in the garden of Hut 56. I intended to sort out the problem of getting the items back to Derbyshire when that blissful time came. Quite unexpectedly I went into hospital and never saw 614 AOD or my rucksack and thermos flask again.

Leo Chambers had the happy knack of finding some very desirable acquisitions, particularly at Khayat Beach. Brian Cross wrote 'Leo liberated a bale of beautiful soft, white Turkish bath towels, generals for the use of. He gave me six which I concealed in the food parcels we were allowed to send home once a month, post-free.' He also wrote of another cheeky theft.

'Towards the end of 1947 my pal Staff sergeant Jock Sinton had a wedding dress made from parachute nylon taken from a bale in the Sub Depot. His fiancé, Muriel sent him the vital measurements and Jock had the dress made by a Christian Arab woman.' Shortly afterwards Jock returned to the U.K. and married.'

Because the army was dispersed throughout Palestine the RAOC had depots and vehicle parks throughout the country. 612 Command Vehicle Group at Rafah was the largest vehicle group in Palestine. It was strategically placed on the Palestine side of the Egyptian border and the Sinai desert, for long distance lorry journeys.

Dennis Harding was stationed at 612 and he gives this account of a vehicle theft that had all the hallmarks of Jewish organization.

'In the latter part of 1946 ten 3-ton Dodge lorries were awaiting collection at the delivery park. During the morning the civilian drivers turned up with apparently the correct paperwork and drove the trucks away. Later that morning another party of drivers arrived to collect the vehicles. It was obvious that the first party was bogus and the trucks had been stolen. The Palestine Police and the SIB became involved and two days later I accompanied Col. Guy to the Jaffa Police H.Q. and from there we were escorted through the back streets of Jaffa to a large workshop where we found one of the trucks repainted in civilian colours, a deep maroon.'

However Jaffa was an Arab city and finding one of the stolen trucks there only served to make the case more puzzling. Dennis continues 'only the chassis of one more truck was found. It had been dumped in Tel Aviv outside the H.Q of the Orange Growers' Association premises.' Two Arabs from Khan Yunis, about ten miles north of Rafah and the site from where the theft took place, were later arrested and convicted. No evidence was found to suggest that any British or other ranks were involved. The evidence pointed to a criminal gang of both Jews and Arabs.

Bedouin Arabs were a nomadic people, they roamed the whole of the Arabian Peninsula and North Africa making a living by whatever means possible.

Every year they harvested olives, growing on trees within the camp. Both Gus O'Brien and Brian Cross were at Camp 153 for the harvests of 1946 and 1947 and both had stories about the Bedouin harvesters, about the overloaded donkeys and overworked womenfolk. During the olive picking a mounted guard patrolled the camp on the lookout for petty thieves who may be tempted to slip into billets and steal personal possessions. Most huts also had a faithful guard dog able to determine who was a soldier and who wasn't, even if the soldier was not in uniform. Bedouins were Arabia's seasonal casual agricultural workers but as T.E. Lawrence so graphically wrote in *"Seven Pillars of Wisdom"* they were not averse to a spot of looting.

With the ebb and flow of the war in the Western Desert they were there picking up abandoned weapons. In 1943 trials were held in Jerusalem for British military and Jewish civilians regarding illegal weapon dealing. The Palestine Police and British Army found a cache of arms in a secret Jewish training camp at Ramat Hakovesh. The Bedouins had transported them from the North African desert and by 1944 the Irgun was using stolen weapons against the British.

James Russell who was with OFP attached to the 61st Infantry Brigade, was on guard duty one night at one of the gates at the 61st Infantry Brigade camp when he saw a shadow pass the nearby cooks' tent that was close to the guard's tent.

Not entirely sure what he had seen his fellow guard went to investigate and found that a rifle had been stolen from one of the sleeping duty guards. Although off duty, guards had to sleep with their weapons attached by straps to their bodies or their beds, a strap had been cut and the rifle had gone. The following morning a hole was discovered in the rolled barbed wire perimeter fence. The hole was not repaired immediately and a watch was kept for the next few days and nights but the thief was too smart to use that hole again.

Small scale thieving by stealth was the trademark of an Arab raid.

When the P & O troopship Strathnaver, on it's way to the UK docked at Port Said, Henry Smith, a Brigade Ordnance Warrant Officer with about six months service to do before demob disembarked, He was on his way to 614 AOD, Haifa. There was no role for a Brigade Ordnance Warrant Officer but Colonel Gore wanted a stock take of the blanket store. It wasn't difficult to imagine that there would be a discrepancy, after all in the Middle East if a soldier needed a quick quid he only had to sell a blanket but Henry's stock-taking exercise came up with a startling result. Henry wrote-'It was not long before I discovered that the actual stock and the figures in the accounts did not balance. I had to report a deficiency of approximately 20,000 blankets. This must have been about the same time as the arms were being sold from the depot at Haifa. So not only were we arming the terrorists we were also keeping them warm with blankets. The S.I.B were called in to investigate and they did arrest a corporal in the RASC who had been driving into the depot and removing blankets by the lorry load. He had to face a Court Martial and, although I did not have to give verbal evidence, my demob was delayed until after the trial and I served an extra three months in Palestine, finally sailing home on the troopship Georgic.'

I stole a blanket for the journey from Bir Yacov to Port Said and swapped it at El Kantara railway station for a pigskin holdall, it was beautiful real leather but when we docked at Liverpool the bag filled with some of my gear fell apart, the leather was fine but the stitching was weak. The 61st Infantry Brigade was encamped in the south of the country at Al Jiya, just north of Gaza. It was a predominantly Arab area and prone to surprises from the cunning local thieves. James Russell saw an audacious attempt to steal, in broad daylight, the rails from the railway sidings near the camp. The incident was seen from the camp and the culprits were handed over to the Palestine Police and their donkey was released in the hope it would find its own way home. Audacious and dangerous is how one would describe a theft at the Ballad-es-Sheik British army fuel depot and filling station on the western side of Mount Carmel. It was a large installation, so large that a pipeline direct from the oil refinery at Haifa kept it supplied with petrol. It had a weekly 'evaporation allowance' of 5000 gallons that gives some idea of the size of the depot. Former Palestine Police Sergeant Martin Duchense recalled an incident in some detail in their Old Comrades Newsletter (214). Suspicion was aroused when the 5000-gallon allowance reached 25,000 gallons a week. The Special Investigation Branch (SIB) was called in but no major irregularities were found. One day a police armoured scout car was in the main square of Ballad-es-Sheik and the driver noticed that many vehicles were pulling up and filling cans at a standpipe located in a shack.

Successive crews watched the procession of vehicles of every description going to the shack; even men with panniers on their donkeys were filling up. Eventually Constable Pat Devlin's curiosity got the better of him and he found that it wasn't water they were taking away but petrol, and some were even smoking while drawing off the fuel.

An investigation team equipped with a mine detector traced a pipe running from the shack back to the main pipeline. The main pipe had been drilled and the 'water' pipe inserted and the joint sealed with clay.

Far more precious than petrol, in a land with large areas of desert, was water. Only in the larger cities was water on tap. Many of the rural communities still drew their water from wells as they had done in the time of Christ. For troops stationed in those dry areas without showers or washing facilities the Army's mobile bath units were essential. In some cases it meant laying a temporary water supply pipe from a single source or from a water tanker. Percy Birkett the Mobile Laundry and Bath Unit pipe fitter remembers the occasion when he fitted a supply to the unit and turned on the tap, only to find there was no water. Going back along the pipeline he found it had been diverted by Bedouins to fill their water tanks. Taking another person's water is stealing and in bygone times many Arab lives were lost over disputed ownership of wells.

Within the larger camps there was usually some licensed traders and one was the 'dhobi' in Camp 153. It was a family business in one small shop run by six Arabs who also lived on the tiny premises. As a sideline they bought stolen items. One of Len Harris's last duties before Camp 153 was closed was to empty the sand filled fire buckets and secreted in one of the buckets he found ten rifle bolts. He took them to the 'dhobi wallah' and much to Len's amazement he was give £10 for them. The bolts would then probably have been taken to the souk in Haifa and resold. Weapons of all descriptions, including live hand grenades, were on sale in the markets and souks, and most of the items were of British origin.

10.

The Gun Runners

Regular soldiers, who have served for a long time, have an exemplary record and a considerable amount of luck might find themselves in one of those rare RAOC jobs well out of the danger zone. In 1951 the much travelled Warrant Officer First Class Bill Muncey found himself in a job that was the envy of other senior NCO's, he was the second in command to Captain Lucas of the BAOR Officers' shop at Bad Oeyuhausen, Germany. The captain informed him that a senior RAOC officer was requiring a new dress uniform. Bill arranged for Bruno the master tailor to be there on the following day. When the senior officer arrived to discuss his requirements it was non other than Bill's former C.O. Colonel Thomas Gerard Gore, OBE, DSO. He was duly measured by Bruno and a date was arranged for the first fitting, but a few days later Captain Lucas was informed that the Colonel would not be requiring his uniform.

In 1950 Brian Cross had a visit from the Army's Special Investigation Branch for a statement about his time as the corporal in charge of 614 AOD's armoury. The visit was a surprise for Brian who had been demobbed two years earlier. In his statement he said that he had been in charge of the armoury up until March 1948. During that time he made several trips out to sea to dump unused weapons, mostly surplus Tommy guns. Then Major Newman replaced him with Sergeant Dennis Michael Ivers.

Brian was particularly upset because he was a good soldier and had signed on for an extra six months to be with his pals up until the end of the Mandate.

In December 1951 Bill was to know why the order for the dress suit had been cancelled and Brian to know why the SIB wanted his statement. In fact the whole of Britain knew about Colonel Gore and his misdemeanours when reports of his Court Martial was carried in all the national newspapers.

When *Palestine Scrapbook* published the story in 1999 memories of the colonel began to come in from those who knew him. Some of the stories about the colonel border on legendary like the one about the sentry who presented arms when the colonel passed his sentry box and was instantly promoted to lance corporal. What is apparent from the letters and comments is that his leadership and consideration for the welfare of his men soon won him respect.

Colonel Gore had an accomplice and he was Major Ralph Herbert Newman who had been accused and found guilty a year earlier. Newman served six months and was cashiered. No one ever spoke well of Newman, he was disliked seemingly by all ranks. Most felt sure that it had to be Newman that put temptation in the way of Gore.

Major Bill Howard was in the Middle East from September 1936 to October 1943 most of the time at the HQ Palestine and TransJordan in Jerusalem. Bill was, by 1941, a sub conductor, which carries the rank of WO II, and was Chief Clerk to the Deputy Director, Ordnance Services, Line of Communication (East) Colonel R.A.Weir in Haifa.

'I was instructed to prepare an office for Major Gore, who was to join us as Deputy Assistant Director Ordnance Services.'

'At the same time I was told to get out the policy files and flag up important documents for Major Gore to familiarise himself on what we were doing.

Major Gore duly arrived, a formidable figure with revolvers strapped to both legs-every inch a fighting soldier. When I brought in the files for him to read he said "Mr Howard, this is no place for me. I must get a job where there is action!" Within a couple of days he was posted to Tobruk.'

I met him again in Normandy when he was commanding the Advance Ordnance Depot.'

Many correspondents echoed Bill Howard's description of Gore as a 'fighting soldier.' Those who met him spoke of his height and the two revolvers strapped to his legs but by the time he reached 614 AOD in 1948 and toured the depot his personal armoury had grown. He now had two hand grenades hanging from his belt and carried a Bren gun and had a large dog at his side. He certainly impressed the impressionable young soldiers and junior officers. Brian Rivers, a subaltern who later became a Lieutenant Colonel, no doubt saw a role model in Gore when he summarised the general feeling in his letter.

Lt. Col. Thomas Gerard Gore (centre, right) former Chief Ordnance Officer at 614 AOD, with Lt. Col. 'Pip' Watson (Border Regiment) Junior Commander Feeney (ATS) and Penny, daughter of Brig. B.D. Jones, at a garden party in Tel El Kabir, Egypt, 1948 after the evacuation of Palestine. *Photo: Lt. Col. Brian Rivers*

'Colonel Gerry Gore was the sort of officer you would follow to hell and back knowing full well that you would survive. He nicknamed me "Young clanger," I suppose I deserved it but I was the one who would be woken up late at night by one of the Mess staff with orders to "go to the armoury and load his favourite weapon, arm yourself and pick him up in the jeep in half an hour-you're going out on patrol" The objective was to patrol the depot areas to deter thieves, be they Arab or Jew.

Gore's charisma went beyond those who served under him; he was one of a few soldiers in post war Palestine who had the opportunity to fraternise with civilian women. The most talked and written about was the precocious Mrs Fisch, the civilian Welfare Officer in the Depot. Colonel Frank Mitchell was one man who managed to avert Mrs. Fisch's approaches during the war years. Recounting his days in Palestine during the war years in a letter to John Tarran in 1982 he wrote; 'She came to see me twice a week on some pretext or other with clearly indicated intentions which I was able to fail to recognise.'

In the pre-war years the Jews established various under cover surveillance units and in 1942 they merged into one network under the Haganah with the name The Shia. One of The Shia's activities was to enrol female civilians to gather information by whatever means. Extra carbon copies were made of typed documents, some were even photographed. Some of the veterans suggested that this was one of the reasons for Mrs Fisch's relationship with Gore. Others thought surely he wouldn't want the aging Mrs Fisch when he had the lovely young Suzy Zulficar.

Frank 'Chopper' Wood, the pay corporal, wrote 'My main way of averting the tedium of the pay office was to go as armed escort with the ambulance, or with the commanding officer in his staff car. After Colonel Gore joined us I went the length and breadth of Palestine with him, so long as I was in the pay office on payday. I remember going as escort with Colonel Gore once or twice to a nightclub in Haifa. He was a great chap; he sent bottles of beer out to the driver and myself while he enjoyed himself inside. He had the most beautiful girl friend there, she would travel in the back of the staff car with Gore. Her name was Suzy Zulficar. What I wouldn't have given for a night with her, but colonels get first choice, don't they?

We did pick up a lot of different people as we travelled on our journeys to Jerusalem, Nablus, Sarafand, Nazareth, Tiberius, Acre and so on. Whether any of them were in on the arms deal which led to Colonel Gore's downfall. I have no idea. All I know is that he was a lovely man, unlike Major Newman whom I detested.'

It should be said that not all Jewish girls were in espionage, many married British soldiers during the war years. Mostly they chose officers or senior N.C.O's and they were happy to come to Britain with their husbands to settle down in this country. After the war the armed forces were discouraged from marrying civilians in Palestine.

Ken Lloyd remembered Colonel Gore as the CO of 17 Vehicle Company and as one of a group of officers who formed an advance party on Beach Gold, Normandy on D-Day to command a group of which Ken was a member. The Colonel and Private Jack Whithead were the only survivors when their ship was sunk, but he was on the beach to meet Ken's party when they landed.

The dramatic circumstances in which Leslie Morgan, a young recruit on his way to 614 AOD, caught sight of his new C.O were as memorable as Colonel Gore himself.

Leslie was on the Cairo-Haifa Express that was mined on the 29th February 1948. Both Leslie and Gore were on the train bound for the same destination. After almost three years of peacetime soldiering the explosion gave Gore the opportunity to display his legendary qualities of leadership.

Leslie wrote 'I recollect that we were not allowed to get off the train until the corpses and the wounded had been taken to various places for treatment. Colonel Gore with a red band around his cap and gorget patches on his jacket has remained in my mind as a colossus. We were walking along the railway track in full service marching order (FSMO) and Colonel Gore was standing on the embankment which only added to his stature.'

It was at Tobruk, as CO 500 AOD at Derna Camp that Gore earned the DSO for organising resistance even after the order had been given to lay down arms.

Howard Allen remembered Colonel Gore when he was posted

from Sarafand to Tobruk.

'In June 1942 I was at the Derna Camp of 500 AOD and recommended for promotion from Corporal to Lance-sergeant. Colonel Gore came to the camp and I had to march in to present myself before him. Before doing so I had to do saluting drill (arm and hand the longest way-up shortest way down). I have a lasting memory of standing erect before him as he sat, with a big black moustache and red tabs, at a trestle table.

He bellowed out to me "To be a sergeant you must be a competent soldier. If you are not I shall come back and tear your stripes down." After a perfect salute I smartly stepped back into the tent pole.

A few days later, the bugler sounded the general alarm and we hastily assembled to learn that Jerry was up the road. As it was the case of longest in I was fortunate to get out and reach Alexandria. In the few weeks before the evacuation we had a regimental drill before work in the depot, square bashing, saluting drill and even marching about wearing gas masks. Jerry must have been laughing. Obviously these were the orders of Colonel Gore.

I said cheerio to my dugout mate Edgar Tremaine who was taken in the 'bag'(captured). He has since died but I saw him after demob. He told me how they all went down to the main depot and Colonel Gore was going about with a revolver threatening to shoot anyone who got into the slit trenches.

Lieutenant Colonel Malcolm Stone and Gore's paths crossed on several occasions. The first occasion was in 1946 when he was a captain attached to the Ordnance Directorate in Cairo and Gore was serving with the British Military Mission to the Egyptian Army.

Later both men were posted, Malcolm Stone to H.Q.Palestine in Jerusalem and Gerry Gore to command 614 AOD in Haifa. Stone also knew Major Newman, 'a wartime officer and a most unattractive person,' was the Regimental Officer.

Malcolm Stone was the Staff Captain to the Deputy Director of Ordnance Services (DDOS), Brigadier C.H.E. (Kit) Lowther to whom Gerard Gore was responsible.

Lowther had known Gore before the war as both were regular officers, and always spoke of him with considerable affection. Brigadier Lowther had been awarded the Military Cross in WW1. 'There were rumours that Gore and Newman had been involved in the sale of arms that had been captured by the Palestine Police and handed into the depot for sea dumping.' Said Stone.;

'When Gore was arrested and then Court Martialled he was confined in the Officers' Mess at Feltham. I was then in the War Office and my superior Lt. Col. D.W.Heath had to take turns on escort duties-strangely he had been my superior in Cairo – and was often visited by Gore and therefore found these duties a distressing experience. This of course, demonstrated that Gore had reverted to his substantive rank of Lt. Colonel.'

(Lt. Colonel Malcolm Stone was answering a query that had puzzled many who had served in his units. From Tobruk to Germany, eight years he had been a Colonel but apparently not the full substantive rank of Colonel' Was this perhaps one of the reasons for his behaviour?)

Major General J.G. Denniston who was the Director of Ordnance at the time of the invasion of Normandy told the Court Martial of Gore's invaluable service at the Allied landings. He said that 'Colonel Gore had excellent powers of leadership but in peacetime it was difficult for him to find the 'right job.'

Being the CO of a large ordnance depot didn't offer a 'fighting soldier' a lot of opportunity to exercise Gore's type of leadership. He was after all part of a rearward service. He found a little satisfaction when the regimental police of the camp and depot responded to his motivational efforts. He improved their image by improving their appearance, their weaponry and their morale. They in turn christened him 'Trigger Gore of 614' due to his fetish for personal firearms and continually exhorting them to shoot civilians found breaking into the store sheds. No one was shot in the depot but two separate shootings did kill Arabs breaking into the camp NAAFI.

A regimental policeman shot one and he was sent home to the UK. On another occasion the NAAFI was a target for petty thieves, young men from the nearby village of Tirah. Drink and cigarettes were the main attractions, neither easily available for Muslim youths.

They would either cut or wriggle their way through the concertinaed perimeter fence. When their point of entry had been found it was left undisturbed. This was the case when the second shooting occurred. Colonel Gore instructed a guard to lie in the NAAFI and wait, and sure enough, like a wasp to a jam jar another came to try his luck. The guard fired and killed the intruder as soon as his head appeared at the rear window. He then waited for the guard to turn out upon hearing the shot. When the guards didn't come, without disclosing his position, he twisted round a fired through the glass in the door to attract their attention. Killing a civilian, for whatever reason was considered a traumatic experience and the unfortunate soldier was repatriated. If the intruder was a Jew then the soldier would be sent home in case of reprisal.

The court martial of Lieutenant Colonel Gerrard Gore D.S.O., O.B.E exposed the significant difference between a Crown Prosecution trial and a military court martial.

It was shorter; there was no long period of adjournment for the jury to reach a decision because there was no jury. The Court closed for 45 minutes and announced its findings. But that was not the only difference, the evidence by the prosecutor, Colonel R.C.Halse of the Army Legal department was largely the same as that heard in the earlier case of R.H.Newman, who true to form, had made money by selling his story to a Sunday newspaper.

Those who had endured Newman in the army and knew him as an irrational egotist were not surprised to read that in his story he had described himself as 'the King of the Middle East Gun Runners!' It also came as no surprise to read that he had been described by his previous commanding officer as 'unreliable and a heavy drinker.'

What we were left wondering was which CO had given him that undesirable reference. Was it Colonel Stamp who left 614 AOD in October 1947 to retire or was it Lt. Colonel George Mayes who filled in the gap until March 1948 when Gore took over?

Newman, the most likely instigator of the illegal arms deal, received a two-year prison sentence at his earlier trial for his part and received a dishonourable discharge and Gore received a six-year sentence, and was dishonourably discharged.

In addition to the stiffer custodial sentence Gore had the further humiliation of being stripped of his rank, his decorations and his pension rights.

It is no accident that the accounts of Lt. Colonel Gore's court martial and his ignominious discharge were struck from the records. His name does not appear in the official RAOC history book despite his spectacular wartime exploits. Throughout his court martial he kept a dignified silence, which may have accounted for the disproportionately amount of column inches given to the unnecessarily protracted eight charges made by the prosecution.

It was admitted by Colonel R.C.Halse, prosecuting, that evidence given by Major Newman would be tainted, but there would be other evidence with independent testimony. Even so, Newman's testimony makes interesting reading.

Newman described himself as the former deputy Commander at 614 AOD in 1947 under the command of Colonel Gore. He had regular discussions with Gore about the security of the depot and as a result of earlier discussions he contacted Haganah.

Selling arms to an enemy was a serious offence; in this case the enemy was the Haganah.

There were negotiations with Haganah and he acted in direct conjunction with them. At one discussion, in April or May 1948 about surplus arms that were to be dumped, Gore was present together with representatives of Haganah.

Gore then told Newman what surplus arms could be sold to the Haganah.

The weapons were mostly Browning machine guns, and there may have been some obsolete weapons including Piats (Projector Infantry Anti Tank). These were among a large quantity of lease-lend arms at the depot, which had to be dumped in the Mediterranean Sea before the British evacuated Palestine. A large quantity of Tommy-guns and other small arms were dumped into the sea and there remained a balance of Browning machine guns that were diverted to Haganah.

Newman then agreed with the Haganah the sum of money that was to be paid (and no doubt, how it should be paid).

Also implicated in the illegal arms deal were Staff Sergeant Grieves and a former staff sergeant, Dennis Michael Ivers who gave evidence at the earlier trial of Major Newman and they were present when Colonel Gore and Major Newman were discussing the sale. It was arranged that Grieves would load the weapons into a white scout car and take them to a former British vehicle camp that had been sold to the Jews, and was near their own camp.

The British vehicle camp in question was the former 611 Vehicle Group south of 614 AOD and near Athlit.

All three RAOC installations, 614 AOD, Camp 153 and 611 vehicle Group had been sold to the Jews prior to being vacated. Gore's Chevrolet car may also have been included in the sale because it was photographed by Eric Long at Camp 153 whilst the camp was deserted. About six shipments were made and Newman reported to Gore on each occasion. If the arms deliveries were made in April or May then that part of the northern coastal plain was in Jewish hands. Many villagers in the area had fled before the massacres of Tantura and Fareidis south of Athlit. Menachem Begin said panic overwhelmed the Arabs and they began to flee in terror following the massacre at Der Yassin.

Dennis Michael Ivers of Marston Green, Birmingham in his statement at the earlier trial of Major Newman said he joined the army as a national serviceman in May 1946 and was posted to 614 AOD and promoted to staff sergeant. Early in 1948 he received instructions about an escort duty. He was armed with a Sten gun and told to get into a truck. They went to a camp that had been taken over by the Jews about 12 miles from Haifa. There some Jewish civilians unloaded arms from the truck. Later, between three and six further journeys were made to the camp.

Ivers said he had never received any specific instructions about the arms from Major Newman 'I gathered they were something to do with MI5' he said. 'Major Newman conveyed that impression.' He also gathered by inference that if he said anything to anyone, measures would be taken against him.'

Weapons and ammunition were being dumped into the sea months before Colonel Gore arrived at 614 AOD. To some it would seem like burning £1 notes. The only obstacle to any theft was likely to be the acting CO who was a long serving regular soldier and the NCO in charge of the armoury. The existing NCO Corporal Brian Cross was replaced by the more malleable newly promoted Staff Sergeant Dennis Ivers. A Court Martial doesn't require every 'i' to be dotted nor every 't' to be crossed, there is no jury to be satisfied. Gore offered no defence. When the adventurous, but gullible, Colonel Gore became CO Newman's scheming became feasible.

The British Army's past Haganah connection would make the MI5's alleged involvement a plausible story, but Staff Sergeant Grieves version of the events is the most likely story. He was the quartermaster sergeant at 614 AOD and in April 1948 he was with Major Newman and Colonel Gore who were discussing selling arms to the Jews.

Asked whether any mention was ever made about money, he replied 'The money from the arms was to be divided equally among the four of us-about £25,000.'

Major Newman was present at every loading, which was about six and sometimes Colonel Gore was also present. The arms consisted of Bren guns, Vickers and Piat antitank weapons. Sergeant Grieves said that on another occasion, Mr. Silver, a Jewish civilian tore a £1 note in half and gave one half to Major Newman. He said the money would be paid to him when he presented his half of the £1 note in England.

Sergeant Grieves said that he returned to England in February 1949 and after about six or seven weeks he received a telegram from Major Newman. They met in Edgware and went to Dewsbury and there they met another Mr. Silver – not the Mr. Silver they had seen in Palestine. Major Newman produced his half of the £1 note and Mr. Silver handed him a suitcase. The suitcase was not opened there, but Mr. Silver said there was about £25,000 in it. Sergeant Grieves said the suitcase was full of £5 and £1 notes. Major Newman said 'That is finished now. Everything is right.'

Bernard Isadore Silver of Dewsbury said that in 1948 he received a package to hand to Major Newman, who had half of a £1 note that was his introduction to him. When Major Newman took the package he said that there should be between £15,000 and £18,000 but Silver did not discuss the matter.

When asked where the suitcase came from Silver replied 'from an acquaintance of mine.' Asked who the acquaintance was, Silver said 'I am not prepared to answer that.'

He was then asked 'Was it a Jew?' and he again replied 'I am not prepared to answer that.' After being told that he could be committed for contempt of court, Silver replied 'It was a Jew.'

In a statement to Major R.C.Lambert of the Special Investigation Branch on August 24 1951, Newman said that about February 1948, Colonel Gore, who discussed the possibility of selling arms and ammunition to Arab countries, approached him. Colonel Gore gave him a list of arms in the armoury. He understood that these were to be offered to the Arabs.

The statement then described visits to Cairo, Damascus and Beirut where, Newman said he was told that the price to be paid for the arms was £25,000. But he decided later that there might be a plot to kill Colonel Gore and himself, so he abandoned the plan. Later, Colonel Gore suggested the possibility of selling arms to the Jews. Newman said. 'Very foolishly, and I regret it deeply now, I agreed to his proposals. I took Grieves and Staff Sergeant Ivers partly into my confidence. A quantity of Brownings and other obsolete arms that were due for dumping or destruction were delivered to a Jewish camp at Athlit. For this we received a payment of approximately £18,000; £7000 of this was paid in Egypt to an acquaintance of Gore's. On our return to England a man who had Jewish connections paid me the money. His name was Silver. I made several payments to Colonel Gore amounting to approximately £1,500 and, in addition, it was agreed he had a 30 percent interest in any investments we made.

So it was clear from this statement that Newman was laying the blame for the spearheading of the arms deal on Colonel Gore.

Over 50 years later those who served at 614 AOD firmly believe Newman was the mastermind behind the illicit arms deals. An opinion, perhaps, coloured by the man's lack of charm and compassion. He had the contacts with the Haganah and took trips into Haifa after curfew.

In the eyes of those who were serving in Palestine at the time, no arms of any kind should have been passed to those who were, right up to the end of the Mandate, terrorists killing British soldiers and policemen. Between December 1 1947 up to the end of the evacuation 222 more British troops were killed.

Although the end of the Mandate was May 15 there were still troops and supplies in the Haifa zone, including Marines, and Royal Dragoon Guards were protecting the area.

Referring to Newman's statement that Gore was involved in any meeting with the Haganah, Mr. Melford S. Stevenson, KC, representing Colonel Gore cross questioned Major Newman. 'I put it to you that Lieutenant Colonel Gore was never present on any occasion when negotiations took place between you and Haganah.'

Newman replied 'That is correct.' Staff Sergeant Grieves and Mr D.M.Ivers gave much the same evidence at Colonel Gore's Court Martial as at Major Newman's.

Mr. Bernard Isadore Silver said that he handed Newman a suitcase at Euston on the instructions of a dear friend. He understood it contained money. Grieves said he did not go to Euston to collect a suitcase containing money. Where the money was collected was not seen to be important, but Silver's version differs from that of Newman and Grieves on that point.

A detail that no doubt would have been more fully explored in a civilian court.

When cross-examined Silver agreed that he had a brother in Haifa. He did not know of any arrangements by members of his faith for the employment of Newman after his present troubles. So from being reluctant to say who handed him the suitcase and whether that person was Jewish we know that it was Bernard Isadore Silver's brother.

Colonel Gore pleaded not guilty simply because five of the charges – those of which he was subsequently acquitted-were not supported by any evidence and had for all practical purposes, although not technically, admitted the charges of which he had been found guilty.

Mr. Stevenson, in making his case for the defence said,' Up to the time of these events Colonel Gore had enjoyed the shelter of army life, which protected him, to a great extent, from meeting the kind of people who were to be met with in company abroad.

Was it not clear that the spearhead of this enterprise of selling arms to the Jews was Newman?'

The court had seen him in the witness box and had seen in the person of Mr. Bernard Silver at least one of the family with whom Newman chose to associate.'

Thousands of Jews in Palestine were determined to use every device at their disposal to get hold of arms. They were a people who had thousands of years of business in their blood. What could the wretched Gore do if they were determined to get him?

Once such a man was prevailed upon to accept a few pounds, he was finished. In spite of his magnificent record, the accused had become a moral casualty. He was defiled by the scum with whom he came into contact.

The report in *The Times* left those who knew him pondering on many aspects of his court martial. Few could believe that Newman and Gore hadn't sold more. The quantity couldn't be verified. Lieutenant Colonel George Mayes. the officer who was the caretaker CO at 614 AOD between Colonel Stamp's departure and Gore's arrival, told the court the records had been lost in Haifa Bay prior to the court martial.

There were rumours about Gore's involvement, one popular theory was that the weapons in question were captured from Haganah by the Palestine Police and handed into the depot.

Many, including myself, thought that Gore had sympathies with the Zionists. He hadn't been in Palestine as long as most of the military who had become wary of the Jewish population because of the actions of Jewish terrorists and their ability to fade into the Jewish community after atrocities. At the same time the troops had become more sympathetic to the Arabs of Palestine. Furthermore Gore had more opportunities to negotiate with the Jews. There was, for instance, the visit of Ben Gurion to the depot.

There was a close relationship by Gore with Mrs Fisch who had the 'ear of the Colonel.'

"*Palestine Scrapbook*" in its first edition sparked fresh interest when it reprinted *The Times* report. Stories came in regarding Gore's leniency towards the Jewish intruders caught in the depot when he ordered their release. On the other hand he was dismayed when Arab intruders were not shot on sight but were handed over to the police against his orders.

Those whose job it was to take surplus weapons to Haifa for dumping agreed that if two senior officers were giving the order there would be no difficulty in diverting them elsewhere.

Although *The Times* gave a fuller report than other newspapers it included items that provoked interesting questions but not the answers. Newman returned to England early in 1949. he met Gore at Farnborough later in that year and gave him £1000 in banknotes. Newman bought four properties for £200 in the name of Margaret Gore, Gore's sister, but they were in trust for Newman's benefit. Gore's sister understood from her brother that if Gore needed money whilst he was abroad she would be able to sell them. Miss Gore and Hector Barcilon, a barrister and former member of the Judge Advocate General's Middle East staff were prosecution witnesses. Barcilon had lent Gore £770 (in 1947 a large sum of money.) Newman repaid the debt after receiving money from Silver.

Throughout, *The Times* report, 614 AOD was mistakenly referred to as 614 Advanced Ammunitions Depot.

The last few months of the Mandate were a hurried and unsatisfactory end to the British administration in Palestine, and only those who served there know the climate that existed at that time. There were many instances of weapons being stolen; some of the instances being suspiciously like inside jobs.

Getting out was a scramble, not without precedent. Staff Sergeant Freeman working in Shed 11 in 1947 was a Dunkirk veteran and told those who worked with him how they got out of France. They were instructed to pack and crate the stores ready for removal but the call to leave came and they left in a hurry. The enemy inherited a large quantity of boxed essential ordnance. With every advance or retreat by one side or the other there was sufficient confusion for 'liberating' (a euphuism for pilfering) desirable and valuable items. Although the retreat from Palestine was not quite so hurried as wartime retreats it was sufficiently chaotic for theft to rise above normal levels.

Getting 'liberated' W.D. property back into Britain by the troops was difficult to say the least so they were most likely to take something that could be turned into instant cash. Gore and Newman chose to sell their weapons to Jews rather than the Arabs because they feared the Arabs may have killed them, having once taken delivery of the arms.

A more likely explanation is that the Haganah had the perfect receiving depot in the former 611 Command Vehicle Group and the finance and the organisation in England to hand over the cash.

No Swiss bank, in fact, no bank at all – and no cheques.

Gore and Newman's arms deal was not the last treacherous privateering acts on the part of unprincipled members of Britain's army in Palestine. An audacious theft occurred on June 29 1948 twenty-four days after Gore and Newman sailed out of Haifa on the Georgic II. Three tanks were stolen from Haifa airfield at 01.30 hrs by two British sergeants of the Royal dragoon Guards and a member of the Haganah. The sergeants, Michael Flanagan and Harry MacDonald had been stealing fuel and various items of equipment and selling them to the Haganah for some time. According to Dan Kurzmann, author of 'Genesis 1948' they were paid £28,000 for the two tanks they managed to drive from Haifa to Tel Aviv. The third tank, driven by a member of the Haganah, an inexperienced driver slid into a ditch.

Flanagan and MacDonald's iniquitous deed meant that if they returned to Great Britain they would face a Court Martial and a long term of detention. Instead of returning home they had little alternative but to stay in the State of Israel and serve in the Israeli army. Kurzmann described their life after service in the army as one of contentment, with Jewish wives, in a Kibbutz.

Peter Marsh, former corporal was with the Royal Dragoon Guards when they left Haifa on July 1 1948. He remembers the incident well and drew my attention to the book 'A Captain's Mandate' by Philip

Brutton. In the book Captain Brutton quotes from the official report of the theft by Major Pat Robertson, which corroborates the theft. The post crime life of the two sergeants came from 'Genesis 48.'

References

Court Martial proceedings from *The Times*, December 1951

Other material from correspondence to *Palestine Scrapbook*

11.

An Atrocity Too Far

There was a sequence of events in 1947 that was to crystallise the hearts and minds of British politicians and stir the wrath of the British public. Since Bevin had become Foreign Minister he had been besieged with conflicting pressures, largely from America, but some from politicians in this country and not least from the Zionists within his own Parliamentary Labour Party.

The King David Hotel bombing may have been the seminal event of 1946 that drove Churchill, a disenchanted Zionist, to demand positive action with his 'Rule or Quit' statement.

We didn't get news of every atrocity and the news we did get was lacking in detail, and even the Jewish owned *Palestine Post* didn't record them all. We were almost certain to learn of atrocities that occurred in North Palestine, not through newspapers or official bulletins but through the transport network. Men and lorries from all regiments mostly with RASC (Royal Army Service Corp) drivers were in and out of the depot all day during the hours of daylight. Our own drivers, with escorts, were travelling between the docks, sub depots and workshops. The depot was a hive of information. Just days after we started work in the depot, Barclays Bank in Haifa was bombed. The following day John White hitched a lift into Haifa in a jeep and heard more explosions. From his diary we learn that on May 15 1947 a train bringing Arab workers to 614 AOD was blown up and as a result the Jewish workers were not allowed into the depot. What we regarded as a round of tedious terrorist activity was the subject of a gloating letter written to the *New York Herald Tribune* that coincidentally was printed on the same day as the rail explosion. It was written in the form of an advertisement and paid for by Ben Hecht, a Hollywood scriptwriter. Its contents were a grotesque incitement to further violence.

'The Jews of America are with you. You are their champion. You are the grin they wear. You are the feather in their hats. Every time you blow up a British arsenal, or wreck a British jail, or send a British railroad sky high, or rob a British bank, or let go with your guns and bombs at the British betrayers and invaders of your homeland, the Jews of America make a little holiday in their hearts.'

The wrecking of the jail, which for Hecht was having a holiday in his heart, took place on May 4 1947 when the Irgun Zvai Leumi attacked the jail at Acre. It was a daring daylight raid by a group that normally preferred to use the hours of darkness, but on this occasion the nighttime curfew imposed following the hanging of Dov Grumer was in operation. First there was a diversionary attack on a nearby camp.

The terrorists arrived at the jail disguised as British troops and in a British lorry. Explosives had been smuggled into the prison sometime before and the wall was breached by explosions from both inside and outside the jail. During the short period of time that the wall was breached two hundred and fourteen Arab convicts escaped in addition to the forty-one Jews that the plot had been intended to release.

John Cosgrove recollects the incident because a group of his REME comrades from

3 Base Workshops at Qyrat Motzkin, north of Haifa, went to an Arab wedding. They were having a lift in a truck with airborne troops who had been swimming, and as usual all were carrying arms. Alarmed by the noise of the explosions and the sounds of battle they rushed to the main road to set up a roadblock. The escaping terrorists ran into the road block and eight were killed and five arrested. Three of those captured were hanged on July 29 and this brought an immediate reaction from the terrorists.

On July 8 when their death sentence was pronounced a retaliatory plan was triggered.

At 1 a.m. on July 12 two sergeants, Mervyn Paice and Clifford

Martin, in the company of a Jewish clerk were kidnapped from a cafe near Nathanya. Both men were in the Intelligence Corps and Martin had been a boy soldier in the REME until September 1946. On August 1 through a *Daily Express* headline the horror of Jewish terrorism was taken to every readers breakfast table, it read "HANGED BRITONS: Picture that will shock the world" under a six column picture showing two bodies hanging from eucalyptus saplings. The gruesome story was carried in all the national newspapers in a manner that befitted their editorial style and politics. Only the *Daily Express* had the photograph that was distressing for the murdered men's families.

In 1947 communications at the time were such that probably the newspaper was the way by which the victims' parents learned of their son's deaths.

The Times carried the story and the reactions to it in greater detail. The sergeants hadn't been hanged as in a British judicial execution, they had been strangled and their bodies hung from the trees. As one of the bodies was cut down and hit the ground a mine exploded, blowing the body to bits and hurling the other body twenty yards.

At the time Mrs Meyerson; later known as Golda Meir, the representative head of the all powerful Jewish Agency was told by the British Government that unless the Jewish organisations cooperate, in the sense the Government means by that word, everyone is likely to suffer.

A formal announcement of powers to demolish buildings was made on July 31.

The dead sergeants bodies were found wearing the clothes in which they had been kidnapped. Pinned to them were notices from the Irgun stating that the sergeants had been held in underground captivity since July 12 and they had been tried and found guilty of "criminal anti-Hebrew activities namely, Illegal entry into the Hebrew homeland, membership of the British criminal terrorist organisations (the British Army) and illegal possession of firearms. The note concluded by stating that this action was not a reprisal for the recent executions of the three Jews.

When Mr. Creech-Jones, the Secretary of State for the Colonies announced the outrage in the House of Commons it was received with cries of 'Shame.' He went on to say "His Majesty's Government also pay tribute to the services in Palestine for their courage and good bearing in conditions of risk and arduous responsibility"(cheers). He received loud cheers when he said, " it must surely mean the final condemnation of the terrorists in the eyes of all their own people. We can only hope that this latest act will stir the Jewish community to root out this evil in their midst"(more cheers)

Interesting comments came from the pro-Zionist members of the Government, many of whom had called for 'Justice in Palestine,' which was a euphemism for favouring the Zionist cause at the expense of the non-Jewish indigenous population. Mr. Edelman (Coventry W) described the murders as 'terrible acts' and asked for 'unrelenting steps to see that both the authors and inspirers are brought to justice.'

Mr. S Silverman (MP Nelson and Colne, Lab) said 'as one who has taken a share in trying to awaken public sympathy for what I regard as a just cause should have been so stained with blood.'

Even Barnett Janner the Jewish Labour M.P. for Leicester West, probably the most vociferous advocate for unrestricted settlement in Palestine by European Jews, whilst seemingly oblivious of the humanitarian problems that it would create for the resident non-Jewish population voiced his sympathy. 'May I' he said, 'as one who also frequently advocates the justice of the cause (Zionism) in Palestine, express my own very deep horror and regret and sympathy with the relatives, and say that there is no question at all but that the whole Jewish community, the Agency and the Zionist Federation regard this dastardly deed with horror.'

Though the death toll was only two compared with the ninety one killed in the King David Hotel, the murder of the two sergeants made a far greater impact on troops in Palestine and on the general population in Britain.

For some young troops and policemen the murders were one atrocity too many. They had contended with unwarranted vilification, coped with danger and lived with increasing tension but their normal restraint cracked and some went on the rampage.

Five Jews were killed, Jewish shop windows were smashed and vehicles overturned. Anti-Semite riots also broke out in Britain. Jewish traders had bricks thrown through their shop windows, and in Derby, a synagogue suffered an arson attack.

A Jewish Agency spokesman and the Jewish National Council announced through their information departments in London 'they had no words to express their execration at the dastardly murder of the two innocent men by a set of criminals who are impervious to the voice of conscience and arrogate unto themselves power to decide upon matters of life and death.' *[1]

The message went on to call upon the Jewish community to fight this ghastly act of terrorism.

It is doubtful if any member of the armed forces or police in Palestine expected the sentiments of the politicians or the piety of the Jewish Agency would bring about a lessening of terrorist activity.

It certainly didn't lure us into any sense of unawareness. The Jewish population did not expose the murderers. Irgun member Amihai Paglin who was responsible for the kidnapping and killing of the two sergeants went about his business unhindered. He was the explosive expert behind the King David Hotel atrocity the previous year yet no one denounced him. Despite the notices pinned to the victims bodies stating that it was not a reprisal for the hanging of the three terrorists on July 29, Begin in his book wrote, 'The grim act of retaliation forced upon us in Nathanya not only saved scores of Jewish young men from the gallows but broke the back of British rule.' *[2]

This amounted to a U-turn on the reason for the outrage and was one of the rare unambiguous statements that he wrote in his own one-sided story. It was only partially true. Monetary problems more than any single atrocity led to the relinquishing of the Mandate. In Britain the economic situation was tightening it's grip. A further loan from America was badly needed and Britain was already struggling to repay to America a war loan. The same newspapers that announced the murders also announced further cuts in the rations, the butter ration was reduced to three ounces per person, and the bread ration was reduced by 25% and petrol by a further one third. Because of the petrol shortage a glut of vegetables and other produce in the West Country could not be distributed to other parts of the country. The only bit of good news was an advertisement on the front page of the *Daily Express* telling the readers that Heinz own label baked beans were now again available.

Sergeants Clifford Martin and Mervyn Paice were buried in Ramleh Military Cemetery located between Jaffa and Jerusalem, in all probability on the day following the discovery of the bodies.

Sergeant Derek Kent a friend of Mervyn Paice, and one of the last persons to see him alive, went to Israel to see the graves at Ramleh (now spelt Ramla).

The day the news broke, the Friday preceding August Bank Holiday, I was in Geniefa, Egypt for an interview and tests for the post of an art instructor at the Army Education Corps Rehabilitation Centre. There was a three-day break in the selection process, because of the Bank Holiday weekend and the news of the murders did not reach me until I returned to the Depot in Palestine. It was an exceptionally hot weekend both in Palestine and Egypt. The depot had closed for the weekend and re-opened on August 4 by which time much of the men's' wrath had been vented before they met the civilian workers and life in the Depot had almost returned to normal. We didn't talk to any civilians about our feelings on the murders, but we did talk about them between ourselves. By that time, half way through this bloody year, nothing fazed us, but for me, and most others it dispelled and vestige of sympathy we may have had for the Jewish immigrants in Palestine. Myself and Private Mason, who worked alongside me on the wall of stock record cards, were discussing the general situation and referred to 'the bloody Jews,' a symptom of our withering sympathy for them. An overweight Jewish clerk, about our age, overheard me and said I was anti-Semitic.

For the Army and Palestine Police the Martin and Paice incident was one more atrocity in a catalogue of atrocities and within a day or two after the shock and reactions they settled down to carry out their duties. Their hands were still tied and their understandable desire to punish the culprits, and those communities that harboured them was suppressed.

In the UK the population were not so easily pacified and one editor found himself in court for seditious libel.

He was James Caunt the owner/editor of the *Morecambe and Heysham Visitor* an independent weekly newspaper with a circulation of 17,600 copies.

That week's edition had been received the day before the *Daily Express* published the photograph and story of the murder of the two sergeants. Even so, a week later, on August 6 a lengthy, angry and unduly provocative article appeared in 'Mustard' the *Visitors* opinion column under the headline 'REJOICE GREATLY.'

'On the morning of the announcement of another catalogue of pains and penalties hardships and shortages there is very little about which to rejoice greatly except the pleasant fact that only a handful of Jews bespoil the population of our Borough!'

The foregoing sentence may be regarded as an outburst of anti-Semitism. It is intended to be and we make no apology, neither do we shirk any responsibility nor repercussions.

The time has come for plain speaking. The *"Visitor"* expresses the hope that Morecambe and Heysham will be spared the residence of any more of the Jewish community.'

Although no Morecambe and Heysham troops had been killed in Palestine the article stated 'There are parents who, in these so-called "peace days" are torn with anxiety and quoted the death of 21 year old Albert Dean of Edgeway Road, Marton who had been shot from behind by Jews whilst on recreation.

Caunt described the horrified protests of British Jewry in the national press as 'merely face saving propaganda.' He extended his anger by claiming British Jews had been proved to be the worst black market offenders and should 'disgorge' their ill-gotten wealth 'to dissuade the United States Jews from pouring out dollars to facilitate the entrance into Palestine of European Jewish scum, a proportion of whom will swell the ranks of the terrorist organisation' He also claimed 'there are more Jewish MP's than at any time in English history.'

That should have been the last article on the traumatic incident and probably would have been if the *Reynolds News*, the Co-op Sunday newspaper hadn't come out with a vitriolic attack on the article on August 9.

So what started as a local story in a small weekly newspaper became national news and on Monday the *Daily Herald* asked would he be prepared to defend his article in court.

On August 13 Tom Driberg (Lab. Maldon) asked the Attorney general, Sir Hartley Shawcross if his attention had been called to the article – "which was professedly anti-Semitic"

The Attorney general said he had decided to forward it to the Director of Public Prosecutions.

But on the same day another inflammatory article by the unrepentant editor appeared in the *Visitor* containing the following statement—

"In order to nail to the mast our reason for last week's article, we cannot do better than repeat this sentence! 'It is not sufficient for British Jews to rush into print with howls of horror at what their brothers are doing in Palestine and laying wreaths at the Cenotaph. They should take more active steps to stop the money without which this terrorism would peter out."

So the die was cast and James Caunt appeared before Mr. Justice Bickell at Liverpool Assizes on November 17 1947. Caunt pleaded "Not Guilty."

The trial lasted from 10.30 a.m to 4.30 p.m. and the accused was unanimously found "Not Guilty" It was a clear-cut decision; the jury took just 12 minutes to reach their verdict.

The result may have surprised some politicians and journalists, the *Reynolds News* in particular; whose response to the article had been the most violent.

To emphasise their irascibility they headlined the article by describing it as a Jew baiting article and including a photograph of Julius Streicher, a renowned Nazi Jew baiter who was executed as a war criminal.

It must have disappointed Mr. W. Gallagher, the communist M.P.

for West Fife, who said anti-Semitism in essence was an incitement to murder and should be treated as a crime.

It was a time in our history when it would have been wiser for those who disagreed with Mr. Caunt to stay silent. The appalling murder of Sergeants Martin and Paice brought to a head the festering anger that war weary Britain felt over the Palestine debacle. *Reynolds News* and Driberg had fanned the flames of aggravation by turning a local incident into a national contretemps.

Throughout his cross examination by Mr. Denis Gerrard, K.C. and Mr.Glyn Blackledge, James Caunt stood firmly behind his written words with forthright answers. He said he was voicing opinions that he had formed on contact with people. Most Britons were concerned for the 100,000 troops, most of them young conscripts in Palestine. Sympathy for the plight of displaced Jews had been considerably diluted by the activities of Jewish terrorists and the moral and financial support they were receiving from British Jews.

Mr. G.O. Slade for the defence clarified an impression that may have occurred during the cross examination by stating that the number of Jews within the *Visitor's* circulation area was between twenty and thirty. He asked, "Had you any idea in your mind that twenty or thirty would attack the remaining 17,700 or the remaining `17,700 would attack the thirty?"

Mr. Caunt answered "Certainly not" and that put the case into context.

Mr. Slade's summing up for the defence lasted 62 minutes and hinged on the freedom of the press.

President Harry S. Truman's support for the Jews was seemingly beyond doubt when he recognised the provisional government within eleven minutes of the State of Israel being illegally declared, eight hours before the end of the Mandate. Early in his Presidency he proved himself to be less of a diplomat when he exposed the details of confidential discussions over the quota of immigrants that should be allowed into Palestine.

Caunt's article and trial proved there still existed in Britain a cultural suspicion of Jews. In 2003 evidence came to light that the same suspicion existed in America even at presidential level. How sincere was Truman's concern for the Jews? Entries in a secret diary written by him in July 1947, when Jewish terrorism had reached it's most sadistic level and thousands of displaced persons (DP's) were looking for somewhere to settle revealed his anger and frustration. Those who, for whatever reason, cannot speak out often confide in a diary, as they might to a friend. Truman privately expressed his distrust of the Jews unequivocally, when he wrote, "The Jews, I find, are very very selfish. They care not how many Estonians, Latvians, Finns, Poles Yugoslavs or Greeks get murdered or mistreated as DP's so long as the Jews get special treatment." He continued " Yet when they have power, physical, financial or political neither Hitler nor Stalin has anything on them for cruelty or mistreatment to the underdog.

References

1. *The Times,* August 1 1947
2. *The Revolt,* Menachem Begin, W.H. Allen, 1951

12.

The End is in Sight

By October 1947 activity by the terrorist gangs including the British trained Haganah was a nightly occurrence. In September 1947 alone, twelve policemen were killed, four of them in a raid on Barclay's Bank and three in the Haifa Police Headquarters. British troops were confined to camp for most of their off-duty hours. Whatever army job they performed in the daytime they were called upon to do guard duties every other night. Pressure on the Government to leave Palestine was growing from every quarter. Even Major General Bernard Montgomery called for a withdrawal. His message to the Prime Minister was "There are 100,000 troops stationed in Palestine with their hands tied and two of them are being killed each day!" According to the world's press the morale of Britain's troops in Palestine was at low ebb. In reality though, anger was being mistaken for low morale. They were underestimating the guts and determination of those youthful soldiers. The reason for anger was understandable; they were restrained by a policy that would not allow a more vigorous response. This was evident by the casualty figures that showed three times as many British forces personnel were killed, as Jewish terrorists. Despite their restraint the Jews called British troops "Nazis," a cry that was echoed in the American press. The British Army in Palestine comprising largely of young conscripts was well disciplined and to liken them to Nazis devalued an appellation that should be exclusively reserved for members of the German Nationalist Socialist Party. These conscripts were also victims of Nazi aggression.

They were children during the war in Europe; they were accustomed to siege, shortages and hardship. They were boys well on the way to being men, before the Army called them up. Having seen the distressing conditions that European Jews and other inmates of the Nazi concentration camps had endured they went to Palestine with every sympathy for the Jews. That sympathy was totally eclipsed by the injustice of the situation and the inequality that favoured the Jews. The terrorist atrocities turned away any affection they may have had for the Jews whilst their friendliness towards the Arabs flourished.

As largely working-class conscripts from a country impoverished by six years of total war they saw in the kinship of the Arab community an element not dissimilar from the comradeship to be found in the British Army. Drivers, mechanics and storemen formed bonds with the civilian Arabs they worked alongside. There was a repartee similar to that which existed between the military and civilians in the depots in Britain.

The Palestinians were relaxed and displayed the confidence one might expect from a people well rooted in their own country, as their fathers and forefathers had been for centuries before.

They could not, in 1947, have visualised the fate that was about to befall them.

Jewish civilian workers in the military depots and camps held the better jobs and were consequently more highly paid but even when the jobs were equal the Jews were still paid more.

They had the Histadrut (Jewish Trade Union) that demanded and obtained higher wages for the Jews. These were European immigrants with nationalistic aspirations and an odd combination of socialist and capitalist tendencies akin to those displayed by European fascists in the 1930s. They were tense with an obvious determination to succeed. They had organisations, some of them covert, capable of marshalling an army and establishing a nation. They had an administration in waiting.

Britain in all its thirty years of occupation had done nothing to prepare the indigenous Muslim and Christian population for self-rule. The Mufti, Haj Amin al-Hussein a man capable of organising the population for self-rule had been exiled in the 1930's for his resistance to Jewish immigration.

For over four hundred years Palestine lived under Turkish rule, a rule that could not have been described as oppressive. The Turks were Muslims and tended to have a reverence due to the occupants of a Holy Land and allowed a good deal of independence. But for the next thirty years the country was ruled by Britain that allowed a tide of European Jewish immigrants to flood in and centuries of peace ended.

October and November 1947 were months of intense debate not only in Britain, but also within UNSCOP (the United Nations Special Committee on Palestine.) Partitioning the country was the solution suggested by Britain, it was not a new idea, it had been around almost since the Mandate started. Neither Jew nor Arab wanted it. British politicians had talked of transferring the Arabs to neighbouring states. Secret talks between a British delegation and the Mufti had taken place in September and when the subject of partition was raised his answer was simple, and to the British delegation, undeniably logical. " Put yourself in the Arabs' place. Remember yourselves in 1940, did you ever think of offering the Germans part of Britain on condition that they left you alone in the rest? Of course not, and you never would. To start with you would have preferred to die defending it, and you know that they would never have kept their word to remain in the one part. The Jews did not want part of Palestine; they wanted it all and more besides. [1]

Arthur Greenwood, amongst others, had raised their expectations in 1944 when, as leader of the Parliamentary Labour Party, and a Jew, said at the Labour Party's May Day rally "Our intention is to establish a Jewish national home and let Jews go there until they become a majority." He went on to say Arabs should be transferred to neighbouring countries. [2]

On December 4 1947, Britain's withdrawal dates were decided. May 14 1948 for the end of the Mandate and the total withdrawal to be completed by August 1 1948 it was a decision received with mixed feelings by the troops, most of whom were glad to be going home, but they were surprised to be leaving without finishing the job. Some felt frustration at the excessive restraint under which they had soldiered, anger at the callous, cowardly terrorists who had avoided justice, and sadness for their comrades who had died, seemingly, for nothing.

Some felt so angry that they deserted to carry on fighting with irregular Arab brigades who welcomed the experience they brought with them. Each of these brigades was made up of young, hot-blooded, wild talking men without military training and lacking in discipline. Their leaders modelled themselves on Lawrence of Arabia and were very fond of displaying their prowess on the back of a horse. It was apparent to the British soldier, that the Arabs underestimated the Jews. They didn't appreciate their strength, their organisation and their cunning. Those who deserted to join the irregular Arab bands were under no illusion. They knew the Jews level of organisation and the ruthlessness of their cunning, and as such they were a valuable asset.

Leaving Palestine was, for the 'front-line troops,' the airborne and the infantry just a matter folding up their tents, packing the general equipment and transferring it all to an RAOC Returned Stores Depot.

Some of the divisions destined for redeployment in Egypt and other Middle East zones went south in convoys across the Sinai Desert The logistics of pulling out of Palestine was a long and difficult job for "rearwards services," RAOC and REME.. Several thousand tons of war and army surplus had to be taken away. Factory equipment and machinery had to be dismantled and that which could not be used in combat, sold locally along with tents, pots and pans and staff cars. Surplus weapons and ammunition were thrown into the sea. The announcement of the withdrawal had been anticipated and certain sections of the military were able to make preparations.

The military hospitals in Palestine were such an example. Bir Yacov was the largest and their evacuation plans were quickly underway, preparing sick and wounded for movement.

Attacks on the military were increasing and to add to the problem Arab civilians wounded in the crossfire were being admitted along with Arab Legion troops who were employed as guards.

Before Christmas I was transferred from the hospital to a convalescent camp at Nathanya.

After three months in the surgery ward at Bir Yacov it was a welcome change.

Just after New Year's Day there had been a CSE concert in the camp that night and the entertainers and patients had retired for the night. Just before midnight a sergeant came into the hut looking for the fittest men he could arouse. Fit meant being able to stand without crutches and no limbs in plaster.

Having only a limp I was chosen and called to the guardroom. It transpired that our Arab supernummary guards had been ambushed as they changed the watch, and their weapons stolen Thirteen in all, seven Sten Guns and six rifles. A highly suspicious situation to say the least, the guards were locked in the cells without any more ado.

Their story was that a large band of armed Arabs jumped out of the long grass and from behind rocks and took their weapons. Then they made off through a gap in the wire perimeter fence. It could have been true, although none of the staff or patients believed it.

The guards were only there to prevent theft; it was assumed that even the Stern Gang would not perform an act of terrorism against an establishment covered by the Red Cross.

Although the Jews were winning in the race to acquire arms by whatever method, all manner of arms were being bought and stolen by both Jews and Arabs.

Potential property buyers had also been looking over the camp a few days before the fateful night and as they were Jewish they were under suspicion. However the common but unprovable belief was that the weapons had simply been handed over to accomplices from outside.

The Orderly Officer's job was to find twelve men from the patients to take over perimeter patrol.

The only way each man could be armed was to take the weapons from the previous watch.

My partner and I were on the second watch at 0200hrs. I had the Sten gun and my fellow guard had the rifle. It was an eerie night and we did our duties with a fair amount of trepidation. After all, just supposing the ambush story was true?

The perimeter was a long one and we were supposed to meet periodically with the guards at either end of our stretch. Many of the camp buildings were painted white and within a couple of yards of the perimeter wire and on the other side of the wire was a plantation of some sort, probably an orange grove. There was no way in which we would have placed ourselves against a white background so we skirted around these to be on the safe side. We reached the meeting point and decided to sit on a rock to await the arrival of our fellow guards. We sat back to back and I let my Sten gun fall butt downwards between my knees. There was a loud bang and a single bullet flew upwards and passed within inches of my face. I hadn't checked the gun when I took it over and the safety catch was off and I was lucky it was not set for "burst."

Within minutes there was another burst of firing, this time from the direction of the two guards we were due to meet. We ran in that direction and found the two rolling about with laughter. Their patrol had included the huts where the entertainers were billeted and the female members of the troop had hung their smalls out on a line outside. The guard with the Sten gun said when he heard my accidental shot he got very nervous and mistook the fluttering of knickers to be suspicious movement and let off a burst of fire. That was his story. His partner said to us 'He simply did it for a laugh.'

The Supernumeries were released the next day, as there was no proof to any guilt.

Evidence of how stretched the British Army had become within the first month of the evacuation was shown when just a few days after being called upon for guard duty three patients from the convalescent depot were asked to act as escorts. Although it had a considerable element of danger it was an opportunity to see Palestine and escape the boredom of hospitalization.

As we drove the other two looked through the canvas opening to see where we were going and to spot mischief-makers. We were not long out of Nathanya when we were confronted by a ragged Arab standing in the middle of the road waving a very old Turkish rifle, and beckoning us to stop.

His 'road block' consisted of one or two smallish, easily passable boulders.

"Run the bastard down, sergeant," said the officer. It was fortunate that the sergeant ignored the order because, seemingly from nowhere, five or six others with the latest Lee Enfield MkV rifles joined the Arab. The Arab asked to see our work ticket. "Shoot the cheeky bastard, sergeant," said the irate officer.

It was eighteen months since I had fired a Bren gun and then only for a short burst. My fumbling hand was having difficulty fitting the magazine. Meanwhile the sergeant, who was wiser and older than any of us, showed the Arab the work ticket, even though it was doubtful whether he could read it. It could only have been seconds before the magazine was fitted, and no sooner was it in place than a face looked over the tailboard. The impudent Arab dropped down smartly when he saw his nose was only inches away from the end of my gun barrel.

We were allowed to move on to Tulkarm, an Arab stronghold.

Our destination was a military establishment the other side of town, but it was market day in Tulkarm.

We found ourselves caught up in a very typical crowded market scene that blocked the road.

We were beset with goats, asses, vendors and buyers. Cheeky Arab boys jumped on the running board and again would-be-thieves peered over the tailboard and, as before, vanished when confronted with the Bren gun. We ground our way through the melee and reached our destination. It was deserted except for an Arab supernumerary sergeant sitting in the guardroom with his bare feet upon the desk. It was a fine day for January, which was just as well because the guardroom had lost its corrugated iron roof.

The sergeant leapt to his feet, threw our officer a quick salute and fell into his boots.

It was at this point that we learned the purpose of our mission, which was to pay off the supernumeraries who had been left in charge of deserted military properties. The sergeant accepted his pay, signed a sheet in Arabic and gave another comical salute.

At the officer's bidding he ran over the plain to a walled clay-built village to find the rest of the guards. He returned with one man who drew his pay whilst the sergeant signed for the others and drew their pay. It was obvious they thought the British had gone and were not expected to return. When we got out of the lorry we found our tool kit had been stolen. It must have been taken in the confusion in Tulkarm.

We visited other installations on a route that took us to Nablus and on towards Jerusalem.

The lorry stopped and the corporal suggested that I stood to look out over the cab. They wanted me to see the view that lay before us. We were looking towards Jerusalem from the east. We were looking over a valley to a panoramic view of a mass of flat roofed buildings broken occasionally by towers, spires and domes. The sergeant was familiar with Jerusalem and named some of the prominent buildings. Although it must have been a mile away the most dominant structure was the Dome of the Rock. It was a view that I have seen so frequently since on photographs. Between us and the Dome of the Rock lay Kidron Valley and the steep walls of the Haram-Ash-Sharif, the plateau on which the majestically impressive Golden Dome on the right of the plateau. The smaller and less imposing silver domed Majid (Mosque) al Aqsa was on the left of the plateau. However it is the latter which holds a deeper religious significance for Muslims. Standing out prominently from the heart of this profusion of buildings was the tower and spire of the Church of the Holy Sepulchre.

Eventually we made our way back to Nathanya, stopping on the way at the Nuffield Club.

There we were treated to a splendid meal and we three tucked in whilst the officer and the sergeant checked the paperwork and counted the substantial unpaid cash at a distant table.

We said nothing but our meaningful exchange of glances conveyed our unspoken thoughts.

The last days of the Mandate were a time of opportunity for some.

On the return to camp we raced along the road so fast that our speeding lorry ripped the door off a stationary American car as the driver was opening it.

We were in bandit country and it would have been folly to stop.

Christmas 1947 was for the younger soldiers, their only Christmas in the Holy Land.

For some it was their second but for all it was the last. The end of the Mandate was in sight and our days in Palestine were numbered, we would be home in the coming months.

Those who had enjoyed previous army Christmases in Palestine were heralding the forthcoming event as the highlight of the year. Officers and senior NCOs would wait on the other ranks for Christmas lunch. This year promised to be especially relaxed, we were going home and like it or not, we had given into the terrorists demands.

At the Nathanya Convalescent Depot there was a shortage of officers and warrant officers so the patients had to queue for their Christmas lunch. However there were sufficient officers to dish the Christmas fare out. They judged the amount we should have by the amount served to officers in their mess, with the result that we ran short and many had to go without turkey and had to make do with roast pork. It wasn't a superb meal but it came a close second to a Sunday lunch at home.

In every camp throughout Palestine there were Christmas celebrations and some personnel managed to visit Bethlehem.

Staff Sergeant Alex Monaghan's Christmas was what he and the men at 614 AOD, Haifa, expected of their last Christmas in Palestine. He along with other senior NCOs did all the guard duties on Christmas Day to give the men a day free of all duties. For several weeks the other ranks had been preparing, planning and auditioning for the other ranks Christmas Day concerts. On Boxing Day at Camp 153 it was the senior NCOs day off and they too had a mess concert called 'The Tirah Follies.' It was a lively occasion with sergeants and warrant officers displaying their talents.

At the other end of the country 615 AOD, Rafah, Corporal Fred Page put on a highly professional show "Variety Christmas" for which he called upon an orchestra made up of musicians from his own depot and the nearby 612 Vehicle Group. In his cast were two of the Arab civilian workers.

For Daniel Gallagher, a private on detachment to 309 REME Workshops, with other personnel from 614 AOD it was to be an extra special Christmas because he was due to go back to the UK for demobilisation in January. REME workshops were an important part of the Sarafand Garrison and each unit was out to make Christmas the best ever. Their Christmas Day menu did not just cover the turkey lunch; each meal was a feast with its own menu. There was great joy and relaxation as the tension had eased. It was like an unsigned armistice. However in the midst of celebrations reality came back dramatically on Christmas Day. Twenty-one year old Danny and three comrades defied the out of bounds rule and visited the Café Galina, a Jewish café, located off the Herbert Samuel Esplanade in Tel Aviv. As they left the café they came under fire. Danny and twenty year old Craftsman D H Pickering were killed, their companions, Privates C and V R Birch were seriously wounded. They were operated upon at Hadassah Hospital then transferred to a British Military Hospital. The two dead men were buried at Ramleh Military Cemetery on Boxing Day, and the incident, not particularly significant in terms of the scale of atrocities in Palestine warranted just three column inches in the *Middle East Mail*. Its significance for British armed forces was that there really was no armistice and they were now involved in a conflict that had dropped to a new low, with a cowardly enemy who dared to call themselves soldiers.

The Jewish terrorist gangs were as active as ever, the entire civilian population was looking for weapons by whatever means possible, begging, stealing and if absolutely necessary, buying.

In addition there was a danger of being caught in the Jew v Arab crossfire.

It is generally believed that the conflict between Jews and Arabs, subsequently regarded as the "1948 War of Independence" by the Israelis had started even before the British Mandate ended. Any peace between the two sides had been fragile with some fatalities, for over twenty years.

Even this fragile peace ended in December 1947, five months before the end of the Mandate.

Jewish terrorists between 1945 and 1948 had taken hundreds of British lives and now the same terrorist tactics were to be used on the Arab population of Jerusalem.

They began their campaign by sticking warning notices on Arab homes, a tactic they had tried on British troops in their camps.

The conflict came closer to 614 AOD and Camp 153 when on December 11 the Irgun made a surprise attack on Tirah. They blew up the Muktah's house and killed thirteen villagers.

The situation worsened on December 13 1947 when Palmach Commandos lobbed two hand grenades into a crowd of Arab shoppers at Damascus Gate, Jerusalem killing six and wounding forty.

The Palmach claimed it was a meeting place for Arab gunmen.

That was the start of a frenzied campaign of violence against the resident Arab population that was also to spread to include other towns and villages of Palestine, eventually clearing 418 communities and creating 800,000 refugees. In retaliation the Arabs cut off Jerusalem's water supply with an explosion in the pipeline bringing water down from Ras-et-Ein an Arab village. The Royal Engineers immediately went into action to restore the supply.

Kataman was a middle class neighbourhood largely populated by Christian Arabs with the Christian Arab 'Hotel Semeris' at its heart. On New Years Eve the Haganah blew up eight abandoned Arab homes in an attempt to provoke a greater exodus from the neighbourhood. In the small hours of January 5 1948 the Haganah used a hand grenade to blast open the door of the Hotel Semeris.

The blast awakened the proprietors and their guests, but not soon enough for them to get out before two suitcases of TNT created an explosion that turned the hotel into rubble, killing twenty-six Christians. Two days later members of the Irgun, three of them in police uniforms drove to the Jaffa Gate in a stolen armoured police vehicle with two fifty gallon barrel bombs tightly packed with old nails, scrap iron and other iron fragments around a core of TNT. At the bus stop was a crowd of Arabs shoppers waiting for the Number 3 bus. The police vehicle with its deadly load was waved on through an Arab Legion checkpoint and an Arab roadblock to reach the terrorists' destination. When they drew level with the crowd they lit the fuse and rolled one of the barrel bombs out into the dumbfounded Arabs. The bombers sped away and clear of the explosion that killed seventeen innocent people.

On the way to their next target, no doubt tense with a mixture of fear and excitement when they ran into a traffic island and came under British fire as they tried to escape on foot through the Mamillah Cemetery. [*3]

Three were killed and the fourth was wounded and taken prisoner. He should have been executed because despite the deteriorating situation British Law still prevailed in Palestine but he was allowed to live. Eventually with injuries nothing worse than one leg being a few inches shorter that the other he was released.

Jews in the Jewish Quarter came close to dying of starvation when angry Arabs blockaded them in. British police decided to escort Jewish food supplies through to the stricken community after ensuring all involved were searched for weapons.

The British army still had a large presence in the city situated in Allenby Barracks: it was sufficient to curtail major daytime activity by either side. It was a different situation at night when there would be attacks by both sides. The Jewish policy of ethnic cleansing was intensifying. The Irgun so terrorised the Arabs in the Romema district that they sought the protection of the more moderate Haganah to help them abandon their homes. By December 17 the death toll in the conflict was one hundred and twenty six Arabs, ninety-five Jews and nine members of the British security forces.

Since the Jews introduced terror bombing into the conflict retaliation was in the mind of the Arabs.

It took a little while to set up an operation on a larger than usual scale. They took their cue from the Jaffa Gate incident and stole a police vehicle and loaded it with half a ton of TNT.

Two British deserters Eddie Brown a former police captain and Peter Madison a former army corporal dressed themselves in police uniforms and drove it to the target the offices of the Jewish owned *Palestine Post*.

The driver lit the fuse and walked away. The explosion was heard all over the city and the blast set fire to the building. Nearby houses had the windows shattered. In an attempt to minimise the significance of the bombing a single sheet edition of the *Palestine Post* was published next day, having been produced by another printing company. *[4]

There were casualties, not as many as the Arabs had lost due to bombs, but it awoke the Jews to the fact that bombing was not solely their prerogative.

Private Alan Moore arrived at his new posting with the 2nd Infantry Brigade OFP in the Syrian Orphanage, Jerusalem on Saturday afternoon 21 February 1948 and was immediately put on night telephone duty. Jerusalem by then was a hot spot of activity by both sides Alan had arrived in the early stages of what was to be a battle for control of Jerusalem. On his very first night of telephone duty he was to have his first taste of Arab fury. In the early hours of Sunday morning he heard the bang and felt the tremor of a huge explosion not far away.

It was the Ben Yehuda Street explosion that killed fifty-four people. Needless to say terrorist leader Begin immediately blamed the British and the Irgun was ordered to shoot any Englishman on sight. Gunfights broke out all over the city and the British lost almost a dozen men. The GOC took the unprecedented step to order all troops out of Jewish Jerusalem. The attack was not carried out by the British but was the result of a well-conceived plot by the Arabs. A convoy of three British army trucks headed by an armoured car had entered the city through a Haganah roadblock from the direction of Bab El Wad.

A tall fair haired man in a Palestine Police greatcoat and cap leaned out of the turret and jerking his thumb in the direction of the lorries said "They're OK, they're with me." One of the guards spoke to the British driver of the first lorry and then waved them on. Each truck containing over a ton of explosives was parked in a strategic position in Ben Yehuda Street. The fuses were lit with sufficient delay time to enable the perpetrators to retreat, and to be lost in the nearby streets and out of range.

The fair haired "policeman" was actually an Arab, Azmi Djaouni and two of the drivers were the deserters Brown and Madison. Every deserter had his reason or reasons for deserting before his official release. In the case of Eddy Brown it was revenge, the Irgun had killed his brother. *5

Without the conflict Palestine was a pleasant country in which to live. Many troops who served there during the war years married Jews and settled in Palestine. Many more married and came back with their wives to live in Britain. At one stage it was necessary to stop officers from marrying civilian girls in Palestine. Marriage to a Jewish woman was one of the reasons for some troops deserting in 1948. But many deserted and joined the Arabs in sympathy for their cause.

Alan Moore had moved to Jerusalem from Nathanya with the 1st Guards Brigade OFP as part of the consolidation strategy and the evacuation of many military sites. This arrangement remained until May 1948 when the camp at the Syrian Orphanage along with Alamein Camp and Allenby Barracks was evacuated and formed part of a large convoy to cross the Sinai Desert into Egypt.

Alan who would have been driving acted as escort on this occasion because he had been a patient in Sarafand Military Hospital for a short while. Alan said it was all a bit embarrassing, he was in a ward with conflict casualties and when asked 'What were you in for?' he replied 'A carbuncle.' It was on his leg and those who have suffered carbuncles in desert regions will know only too well how painful and debilitating they can be. Driving, for Alan was out of the question.

British armoured vehicles were a much sort after weapon by both sides and disposing of such vehicles was a major problem. Many had been taken to Egypt and many more had been destroyed. The Palestine Police for example had driven vehicles over the steep sides of a Wadi, into piles and set fire to them. It had been decided at Sarafand Garrison that the turrets should be immobilised and the vehicles then sold. Jewish civilian workers were given the job of putting an explosive into each turret to render them useless and beyond repair.

However the civilians were not doing what was required of them. On May 10 four days before the end of the Mandate a detail was dispatched from 3 Base Workshops, Khayat Beach to Sarafand to replace the civilians. REME Major G J Doel accompanied by Warrant Officer P C McCarthy and three lance corporals, WD McGregor. RT Rigby-Jones and RJ Sharpley were sent to do the job. On arrival they were offered money not to do the job. Ignoring the bribe they destroyed the turrets. *[5] On the way back to Sarafand they were ambushed, and though they fought bravely they were all killed.

The REME troops returning to the ambush scene to recover the bodies nearly came under fire from a Life Guards patrol. They were using a Life Guards armoured vehicle that had been in 3 Base Workshops for repair for a test run when they were spotted by a Life Guards patrol as they left Sarafand.

Thinking it was a vehicle in the wrong hands they alerted a unit further along the road. Fortunately they were correctly identified before the roadblock was reached and another tragedy was averted. Major Jim Emery remembers the incident well and he also remembers that Khayat Beach Military Cemetery was in the battle zone and the Arab gravediggers had fled. The men of 3 Base Workshops had the task of digging the graves and burying their comrades on May 11.

References
   1. *Palestine Triangle*
   2. *Palestine Post* May 3 1944
   3. *O Jerusalem*. L. Collins and D. Lapiere, Weidenfeld & Nicolson
   4. Ibid
   5. Ibid

13.

The Bitter End

December had determined the level and the ferocity of the hostilities between the Jews and Arabs that could be expected before we finally left Palestine. It was certainly going to make the withdrawal more hazardous especially when it was equally certain that terrorist activities by Irgun and Lehi against the British would continue. There were so many battles that only the serious ones were recorded. Each individual soldier may remember the events that concerned him but very few remember the date. What is clear in their minds are those last traumatic months of British rule, – the first five months of 1948.

Driving Army vehicles had now become one of the Army's most dangerous jobs; their precious cargoes were prime targets. Weapons and ammunition were top of the Jews and Arabs shopping lists but uniforms, blankets, work tickets and even AB64s the soldiers' identity card (Part 1) and Paybook (Part 2) were also worth killing for.

The Jews were clearly ahead in the arms race, the Palestine Arab would steal arms and ammunition but they did not have the same zeal, collective organization or callousness for it as the Jews. From well-informed military intelligence sources it was well known throughout the country that the Jews held considerable stocks of weapons in hideouts and had ample funds to buy more. Haganah representatives were buying arms in Europe and America with finance donated mostly by America.

Even though the Britain's wartime level of military stores in Palestine had been steadily reducing since the end of the war in Europe, there was still a lot to move and little time in which to do it. Up to 19 November 1947 the stock depletion had been governed by the demands from other theatres of military operation in the Mediterranean region. In 1946, No. 2 Base Ordnance Depot was scaled down to an Advance Ordnance Depot and re-christened 614 AOD.

The overall military strength had also been shrinking, reducing from its wartime peak. Units were being withdrawn, some were re-placed and some were not. Outgoing units handed in their stores and equipment at the Returned Stores Groups and the incoming units were drawing their requirements from 614 AOD.

Corporal Gus O'Brien worked in the Returned Stores Shed at 614 AOD and he remembers this period well, and some of the rare and unusual items handed in whose provenance had probably been lost forever. Receipts were given, but in many cases so frenzied was the receiving of stores, that tracing their origins was overlooked. Gus had many surprises, some very interesting and some very alarming. He remembers 'a ceremonial sword... for several days it had stood in the corner of the room and glistened at me. Then one day the major in charge of our group came in, saw the sword and took it into protective custody!!'

Staff Sergeant Freeman gave three or four unlabelled boxes to Corporal O'Brien for disposal. The boxes had lain in one of the store sheds for many years. When the Staff Sergeant was asked what was in the boxes, he replied 'Mustard gas.'

Not knowing whether it was a joke or not Gus decided to in-spect the contents of one of the boxes. Packed within the box were smaller boxes that looked like boxes of school chalk and in each of these were 24 glass phials in well-rammed sawdust. When one of the phials was held up to the light he saw that it contained a thick dark brown oily fluid. The phial was carefully replaced because the contents matched the description of mustard gas. The alarmed reac-tion of a captain who inspected the contents of the boxes confirmed Gus's suspicions.

The following Sunday, with a small party, Corporal O'Brien took the boxes in a lorry to Haifa docks where they boarded a de-stroyer. Using the depth charge rack the boxes were flung out to sea. Disposal of surplus weapons and ammunition at sea had been in progress for several months but at the start of 1948 the process was accelerated.

The hours of darkness were dangerous times to be out on the roads for Jews, Arabs and the British Army. Travel, other than in daylight, was to be avoided if at all possible. Before 1948 the Army and Palestine Police would impose a curfew on any trouble spot but a far graver situation was apparent after the battles of December 1947. There were occasions when a nighttime journey had to be taken. This brief description that Private John Leachman wrote for *Palestine Scrapbook* illustrates the hazards of travelling after dark.

"It was another starry night in the spring of 1948 when Jock Berwich and myself had to go on escort duty to the Rail Travel Office in Haifa to bring back some men who had arrived at the station. To get to Haifa we had to weave our way through several roadblocks. I'm not sure whose roadblocks they were: at least one was manned by the Arab Legion and one other could have been the Haganah. If any of them were manned by the Stern Gang they would have probably fought for our weapons and the vehicle.

The closer we were to Haifa the louder gun fire became from an ensuing battle between Arabs and Jews The stars, which had been so bright and clear back at 614 AOD were now hidden behind a veil of tracer bullet fire.

We picked up our passengers and began our return journey. The gunfire persisted, but this time the bullets were so close that we could only conclude that we were also under fire. With only the standard issue of five 303 rounds per man we were not in a position to retaliate effectively. In any case our brief in the closing weeks of the British Mandate was not to get caught up any battle between local factions."

From February 21 the 2nd Infantry Brigade was confined to camp until the evacuation duties on May 14. When they needed vital supplies the OFP formed convoys with other units in the Jerusalem area and, accompanied by armed escort vehicles, travelled through the raging battles. Once out of the danger zone they would divide to go to various destinations in the Haifa and Acre area during the precious hours of daylight.

To return they would meet up again at an assembly point to travel back through the conflict. If they missed the appointed reassembly time they were to stay overnight in the nearest British Army camp and return to base next morning to avoid darkness and travel when British armoured daylight patrols were on the road.

Drivers were mostly ambushed for their weapons and cargo but the Stern Gang and the Irgun would not hesitate to kill the driver and escorting troops. However there were occasions when Arabs would attack and kill if troops offered resistance as Rifleman Dennis Shelton testified.

Dennis was stationed with King's Royal Rifle Corps at El Bureij just south of Gaza. Their job was to take and hold some wells in the desert between Gaza and Beersheba. One day when returning to base they came across a gang of Arabs attacking an RAOC lorry.

Dennis said "We opened up on them, the ones who could still run, ran. We found two army bods, one RAOC, under the wagon, both badly wounded. We took them to our camp MO for treatment. I went in the ambulance with one of them to Rafah hospital. On the way their condition got worse, I was holding the side of one's head to keep his brains in."

Peter Allchorn was a driver in the Motor Transport Section at No. 1 Base Laundry Unit, Petah Tikva about 5 miles outside Tel Aviv. He was one of the last to leave the camp at Petah Tikva.

This is Peter's story:

'Early in 1948 we started to dismantle all the laundry machinery in readiness for shipment back to England, and this lasted right up to the evacuation time in May. Every few days we would make the trip to Haifa docks, a journey of about 50 miles. Some of the journeys were uneventful which was fortunate as it was only machinery and not arms we were transporting, so we had no escorts. However one incident did occur, I remember, just as we were about to cross a railway line the Arabs blew up the train right in front of us.

In those days not many service personnel could drive, so as the May deadline approached we tried to teach some to drive to enable us to get as much of the equipment into Egypt as possible. It was mostly desert so as long as they could drive in a straight line and get into gear they passed. My last memory of Palestine was the Jews and Arabs fighting to get into the rear of the camp as we were leaving through the main entrance.'

No. 1 Base Laundry left Petah Tikva as the Jews and Arabs were fighting to get into the rear of the camp. Top Left: Last trucks to leave loaded ready for the journey to Haifa docks. Top Right: The road was blocked by a train derailed by Arabs. Above: Laundry equipment arrives at docks ready for shipping to Cyprus.

Even though the massive job of evacuating men and materials was underway Jewish terrorists were still relentlessly mining troop trains, lobbing hand grenades into open trucks and attacking British military installations.

The civilian workers needed army transport and protection to get them to their workplace and help with the evacuation. Stealing weapons and other military equipment by both Jews and Arabs was at an all-time high whilst trust in Jewish civilian workers was at its lowest. Two hundred and fifty or so troops still marched every day to and from Camp 153 to the 614 Depot.

Originally they marched without weapons but now some of them were armed in case of an attack. The most vulnerable section of the march was a short stretch of the main highway between the lane from the camp and the Depot gates. It was there that a roadblock was established to halt all traffic until the troops had reached their destination at either end of the working day.

Private John Barr was a vehicle driver operating with his 4x4 full recovery vehicle out of Bat Galim. His story illustrates that even when operating in a tense situation the British army still expected a high standard of professionalism from young conscripts.

In January 1948, John in his Ford 4x4, towing two vehicles, accompanied by two other recovery trucks was taking the long hazardous journey to 612 Vehicle Group at Rafah when they were ambushed by Arabs. They were travelling along the dusty road through a wild terrain of rocks, cactus and scrub conditions that favoured bandits. The road, barely more than a track, twisted and turned over hillocks and through hollows requiring maximum concentration at the best of times but even more so when towing two other vehicles. John was preoccupied with his driving, putting his vehicle through frequent gear changes and wrestling with the steering column when an Arab seemingly from nowhere jumped on to the running board. John found himself looking into the barrel of a rifle. "I braked and flung open the door knocking him to the ground and jumped out after him. We were struggling on the ground when a volley of shots rang out and our party of six was hopelessly outnumbered and surrounded. Any resistance would have been futile," said John.

This ambush was familiar and occurred frequently in those final months of the British forces occupation. The Arabs only wanted guns, fortunately this was not an area for Stern Gang activity or they would have lost their lives and the lorry. One of the armoured cars that regularly patrolled the road came along and escorted the men and the vehicles to 612 VG where the six men were placed under close arrest.

In January 1948 more lorry convoys were making a one way journey south than going north, so it was several days before John and his pals could be taken back to Haifa and Bat Galim to face a court martial.

Troops leaving Haifa on a Z craft to embark on SS George II bound for Port Said, June 5 1948. *Photo: Brian Rivers*

With two blankets each and nothing underneath them but the hard cold steel floor of his vehicle they slept in their lorry. Although happy to have got out of the incident with his life and free from injury John knew there would be the inevitable court martial. With the demobilisation imminent and whatever the outcome of the trial, release into Civvy Street would be delayed.

At the court martial they were charged with stealing and selling their weapons. Eventually the six were found 'not guilty' and allowed to return to the UK on June 5 1948. John's demob was delayed by six months because of the court martial.

When a vehicle came under fire it was a standard procedure to stay with the vehicle no matter what the circumstances or temptations might be.

Peter Jackson of 612 Vehicle Group, Rafah, made regular journeys between Rafah and Haifa. As the journeys became more regular in 1948, the risk increased. Almost inevitably Peter and his escort were ambushed and under fire, they jumped out of the lorry and returned fire. The gunmen fled, the temptation was to chase them but they followed procedure and did not, but stayed with their beleaguered truck until the recovery vehicle arrived.

The overall evacuation strategy was to clear all that could be evacuated from the eastern side of the country and although the Mandate was due to end at midnight on May 14 1948 there would still be a corridor from the North, southwards to the Egyptian border via the Coast Road.

The worst single rail atrocity against British forces during the 1945-1948 conflict occurred on 29 February 1948 three months after Britain announced the evacuation.

Twenty-eight troops were killed and thirty-three injured when three electrically detonated mines exploded beneath the wooden coaches carrying 110 soldiers. The overnight Cairo Haifa train was approaching Rehovet along an embankment at 9.45a.m. when the tragedy occurred. The *Palestine Post* described the train as a troop train but half the train carried civilian passengers, mostly Jewish. They were in the front coaches and avoided injuries because on this occasion electrically detonated explosives were used to target the troops' coaches. Rehovet was notorious for it's terrorist activities because of its proximity to the Jewish neighbourhood and the cover provided by the surrounding orange groves.

This particular grove was so close that many of the bodies were thrown into the orange trees. A Royal Engineer eyewitness said arms and legs were scattered around. Two middle coaches were shattered and two damaged. Fortunately one further mine failed to go off, otherwise the damage and deaths could have been worse.

Because fewer troops were needed as the withdrawal proceeded the train was not one of the normally heavily laden troop trains that travelled into Palestine it carried personnel essential for the evacuation on the train either coming back from leave in England or fresh men to help with the removal of equipment and stores.

Settlers from Hatzofim were the first to reach the scene of the outrage. As they approached, the survivors, thinking they were terrorists, began shooting at them but two girls got through safely and assured the men that they had come to bring relief. The settlers helped bandage and care for the wounded and served coffee to the troops. A Red Shield ambulance later arrived but it was an hour before military ambulances could be summoned because the telephone lines had been cut.

Army sappers who were called to clear the wreckage examined an unexploded mine and found it contained 100lbs of ammonal and 40ft of wire leading to the orange grove.

Leslie Morgan and John Nisbet, part of a draft of 18-year-old ordnance clerks and storemen joined the train at Port Suez and were placed in the last two coaches when the explosion occurred.

Leslie wrote. "We were flung from our seats along with kitbags, rifles and sundry items from the seats and racks. A voice yelled 'Keep away from the windows.' Fortunately the coach in which I was travelling remained upright. We managed to compose ourselves and did not look out of the windows or leave the train. It was around a couple of hours later that we were able to dismount from the carriage and walk to the front of the train where a suitable conveyance was awaiting to take us to Haifa.

The sight that greeted us as we walked to the front of the train was one of utter devastation. Three coaches had been completely derailed and the wreckage lay on one side."

The OC of the train was Col. T. G. Gore who was also bound for 614 AOD to be the Chief Ordnance Officer. His duty was to supervise the evacuation of the depot and the stores that were being handed in by the units vacating the various camps and installations. Leslie's ultimate posting was to the Returned Stores Group at Kishon Camp by the river of Biblical fame, the Kishon Brook.

Brian Rivers, an 18-year-old subaltern was to have been on the same train, on his way with his fellow junior officers, to 614 AOD. However he was transferred at El Kantara to an earlier train to act as that train's OC.

His kit was not transferred with him. For a while he thought it was lost forever, until eventually it turned up. Officers and their kit normally travelled in the front coaches of troop trains.

John Nisbet, like Leslie Morgan, had been issued with a rifle and five rounds of ammunition.

Fearing an attack to follow the troops that could get to their feet put their bullets into the rifle and went to the windows. In the confusion John lost four rounds. He spent the rest of the journey under arrest and spent his first night at 614 AOD in the guardhouse.

Next morning an unrealistic Major Newman placed him under open arrest.

In a situation where every man is confined to camp working all day and on guard duty every other night, detention was a luxury the Army could not afford.

John Nisbet's next posting after Palestine was to 301 Mobile Laundry and Bath unit in Cyprus. From the brick built huts of Camp 153 they were now under canvas, both winter and summer.

Menachem Begin, the Irgun terrorist leader, gave retaliation for the Ben Yehuda Street explosion as his reason for mining the train.

In mid April Corporal Eric Long and Roy Pogson were sent on a dock's detachment to Haifa. There was an officer in charge and they were billeted in a large storage building with Royal Marine Commandos. The marines were responsible for security. The RAOC troops responsibility was to take into storage and arrange the movement of stores by ship to various destinations, including the U.K.

Eric Long writes… 'The stores and supplies which came from all over Palestine, included soap, stationery, motor transport spares, arms, medical supplies etc. We were kept very busy and the three of us worked eight-hour shifts round the clock, supervising the loading of ships.'

After the May 15 the little detachment left the storage building to sleep for six weeks on a troopship berthed out on a breakwater. A boat took them to the docks for work and leisure, but they had difficulty keeping to a curfew fixed at 22.30hrs when they went ashore in the evening.

Shipload after shipload of military supplies were being taken away day and night from the start of 1948. It wasn't just supply and troopships using the harbour, hospital ships taking away the sick and wounded were still weaving in and out of the dock.

The evacuation was creating problems for normal business traffic in the port.

So acute was the situation that on Friday March 5 an article appeared in the *Palestine Post* on the beneficial effect it was having on Tel Aviv port.

'Tel Aviv's little port is having the greatest boom of it's history. Stretched across the waters opposite, half the length of the city are ships of all descriptions, some with their holds loaded with supplies and others with ballast to load citrus. Hardly ever in the past two months have there been fewer than a score of ships anchored in the roadstead. In normal times there were seldom more than three or four. The busy times in the Tel Aviv roadstead were a reaction to the chaos and confusion in Haifa harbour. The Customs Sheds of the country's main port are choked with goods and importers think twice before taking their merchandise out into the highways.

Hence an unexpected burden was thrust upon Tel Aviv's poorly equipped port. Even the Government Authorities, whose attitude to the development of the Jewish port had been notoriously hostile, have been discharging cargoes of wheat, flour, barley and corn for the Food Control Department and the Government Agents, Messrs Steel Bros.'

Understandably Britain had been reluctant to develop a port in a predominantly Jewish city. There had of course been the shallow water port at nearby Jaffa, famous for receiving the shipment of the Cedars from Lebanon in Biblical times and in more modern times the exporting of oranges.

Until October 1947 the REME in Palestine were involved in the development of Palestine as a permanent British base with plans to set up more hospitals, barracks and administrative installations.

However the British withdrawal was on the cards and, like the RAOC who had depots to empty, REME had workshops with a large military and civilian workforce and thousands of tons of equipment to move.

The closure of 3 Base Workshops involved major workshops at Haifa, Khayat Beach, Kirat Motzkin and Tel Aviv. By early 1948 the civilian staff were disappearing as the tension between Arabs and

Jews increased.

923,000 square feet of covered accommodation had to be cleared and 10,000 tons of equipment and stores moved by the end of the Mandate. Normal staffing level was 90 officers, 3000 other ranks and nearly 5000 civilians.

As the civilian staff was shrinking, the burden on the military was getting heavier. As a gauge to the size of the job, was the demand for packing cases for the equipment and stores, which required 4000 tons of timber and 28 tons of nails.

At the point of departure the CO said, "Is that everything?"

The Major said, "Yes sir, everything but the chapel" and the CO said "We can't leave that behind!" Before you could say 'Holy Moses' the chapel was crated and on its way. *1

Infantry troops and their equipment had been leaving by road for several weeks but May 14 was the last day of the Mandate and the day that all installations outside an area specified by proclamation would be evacuated. Up to that point the British Army had protected certain vitally strategic civilian installations. One such installation was the water pumping station at Latrun between Jerusalem and Lydda. Michael Jefferson, a subaltern with the Lincolns' sent the account of his role at Latrun pumping Station to the Imperial War Museum, it reads as follows;

The pumping station was an isolated, essential facility about a mile from a well-fortified Palestine Police fort. It was most certainly not a position that could be held against any form of determined attack. It consisted of a series of small brick and plaster, domestic style buildings surrounding a pumping station house in a purpose built shed. It was situated on open rocky ground surrounded by low hills. Any interruption to the function of the pumping station would have a critical impact on the life of the already hard-pressed citizens of Jerusalem. We maintained round-the-clock patrols and irregular timed firing pattern of two-inch mortar parachute flares throughout the night to dissuade sneak attacks on the station. We received some wild, ineffective and inconsequential small arms fire from unknown sources.

We had running water; we had a field kitchen run by a corporal who had taken first prize in a divisional field catering competition. We were on reasonably generous rations that included highly 'tradable' bags of flour and sugar. Within half a mile of the pumping station was the Trappist Monastery of Latrun, which was renowned for the wine produced by the monks. The wine was certainly potable, despite the irreverent title bestowed on it by the cynical soldiery, 'Latrine Wine.'

A little judicious trading of flour and sugar with the Brother Hospitaler produced many gallons of excellent and highly potent Latrun 'Medoc.'

Our generous Quartermaster had insisted that due to our 'hard living' conditions we were entitled to a couple of gallons of Army Rum. It arrived in a small straw covered carboy, and I am sure it was first cousin of the potent brew issued to the troops in the First World War, before they went 'Over the top.' The local Palestinian village headman was happy to exchange a sheep for a bag of flour. Our Maestro of the field kitchen produced victuals fit for a General. The platoon certainly throve nutritionally.

Our relative tranquility was rudely disturbed on the morning of the May 13 when all hell broke loose. The Arab Legion, an elite Jordanian force, opened fire on a Jewish battalion of the Haganah dug in near Latrun, some 500 yards from our position. We were very close to the direct line of fire between the opposing forces. We sat uncomfortably beneath 40mm Bofors fire and 25 pounder shells, but took no hits. On the morning of May 14 we left Latrun in two Bren gun carriers and a three-ton truck. We had all our kit stowed on board the vehicles and preceded via the Lydda Road down towards the coast road and on to Gaza and Egypt.'

Whilst the British Army was busy with the evacuation, they had little time or inclination to participate in the ongoing battle between the Jews and Arabs. Their energies were spent on keeping the lines of communication to Egypt open and protecting properties that were still in British hands.

On the 15 May 1948 Lt. Gen.G.H.A.McMillan, General Officer Commanding British Forces in Palestine issued his proclamation together with a map showing the now occupied area marked in red, from Acre in the north to the Egyptian border in the south.

The sea was its western border, except for the bulge around the Jewish area Tel Aviv and it's environs. Mount Carmel was included at its widest point.

From Hadera, southwards the area narrowed but was wide enough for the road and rail communications but the rail link was out of action sometime before then.

Six key paragraphs contained the substance of the Proclamation.

1. The occupied area will be under military jurisdiction so far as may be necessary for the purpose of withdrawing His Britannic Majesty's Forces from Palestine, and will remain under such jurisdiction as long as the GOC determined.

2. It is not intended to interfere with the life of the inhabitants of the occupied area, only to the extent that it is necessary for the safe withdrawal of British Forces.

3. The withdrawal is expected to be completed on or before 1 August 1948 and the military jurisdiction in the occupied area will then be terminated by Proclamation.

4. All persons in the said territory must abstain from any actions of a nature calculated to prejudice the safety of British forces.

5. All laws, customs and rights and properties in the occupied area will be respected. All requisitions of services or property made by the British Forces will be compensated.

6. As long as the inhabitants of the occupied area remain peaceful and comply with the GOC's orders they will be subject to no more interference.

The 612 Vehicle Group at Rafah was the last post for vehicles that were to cross into the Sinai Desert and Egypt. It was a busy time at 612 and remained so until June 5, three weeks after the end of the Mandate.

Colonel Malcolm Stone, in 1948 a Captain, was charged with overseeing the destruction of armoured vehicles at the Vehicle Group. Many of these vehicles had gone to other military bases but there was a considerable number of American made Staghound armoured cars to be destroyed.

The Egyptian Army that was moving into the area as the British were leaving also had some Staghounds. This is Malcolm's memory of that critical period and how he referred to a very tempting offer:

'I was approached by a couple of Egyptian army officers who expressed an interest in purchasing some Staghound vehicles and offering all sorts of inducements. However we continued the destruction of these and other "A" vehicles by moving them in small groups outside the depot perimeter where sappers made short work of the process with demolition charges. The same officers then came along and asked if I could arrange for the wheels and tyres to be taken off and left outside the demolition area. When this did not happen they next suggested that I could easily arrange for the movement outside the perimeter to be delayed so that, because of the fading light, I would instruct that demolition would be left until the following morning and of course the vehicles would be left outside the perimeter until next day. Well I can only say that I was not tempted and that was the end of the affair."

There was an unfortunate incident when British convoys entering Egypt were mistaken by Egyptian pilots for Israelis invading Egypt. Consequently bombs were aimed at British lorries.

The next stage out of Palestine was to cross the Sinai Desert and Rafah, being almost on the border, was a suitable staging post for the British army leaving Palestine, as it had been for their entire thirty years earlier.

A key service was supplied by the RAOC when 52 Mobile Laundry and Bath Unit was moved to Rafah to provide laundry and bathing facilities for those who were leaving by road. Infantrymen, gunners, tank crews and drivers who had reached Rafah by the dusty roads welcomed the shower and change of kit before crossing the Sinai desert. Previously the unit with its dozen or so vehicles had been based at Kfar Bilu south of Lydda. The transport comprised of at least a dozen vehicles including, Matador tractors used for pulling the laundry units, 3 tonners for the bath units and the rest for other uses. There was a quad used as an all-round type of vehicle, previously used by the Royal Artillery for towing guns and transporting gun crews.

What couldn't be moved or was needed elsewhere had to be destroyed or in some cases sold. The sales included unarmed vehicles, workshop materials and military establishments. Top of the buyers' property list would have to be 614 AOD for its acreage, its purpose built storage sheds and it's link to the main railway line. Regimental policeman Ken Marshall remembers the day when Ben Gurion arrived at the Depot Gates with a party of Jews. Ken believes that Colonel Gore knew well in advance of the visit because of the preparations before hand. The Depot police were issued with Canadian battledress to replace the more ordinary Burton made standard British issue. It was a deeper, greener shade of khaki and Ken says

'The difference was not only in the colour but in the cloth and the cut.'

The policemen who were on main gate duty were issued with a service revolver in a holster instead of a Sten gun normally slung over the shoulder. To complete the impressive, sharp, vigilant appearance, the holster, belt and cross strap were blancoed white. The reason given for this change of ensemble was to look more efficient when other regiments came to collect stores and weapons.

One key installation that had to be vacated was 567 Command Ammunition Depot at Wadi Sarar. It was a potential prize for the victor and in the interests of remaining neutral could not be left with any of its stock. Sergeant Bill Edwards was an ammunition examiner sent there to ensure the safe disposal of unwanted ammunition by detonating several tons at a time in a demolition area outside the depot. The ammunition stores were guarded by members of the Arab Legion, armed with Bren and Thompson machine guns. When Bill and his team's work had been completed the Legionnaires escorted them safely to the Egyptian border. Bill recalls one perilous incident—

'One afternoon we had rounds of American ammunition to blow up. They were rounds of a largish caliber individually packed in waxed cardboard containers and in pristine condition. After emptying, the cartons were stacked separately. We did not suspect that all the cartons might not have been emptied by the Arab labourers, employees at the Depot.

We detonated the entire carpet of high explosives electrically from under the cover of a concrete bridge over the nearby wadi, and walked out to the site to judge the success, or otherwise of our efforts. Alongside us, some distance off, an ambulance was being driven containing invited sightseeing officers and as we walked we noticed that the pile of cartons was alight at one end.

Strangely, the pile was still standing, having been unaffected by the blast. It was then, before we reached it that the first shell exploded and we all threw ourselves on the ground. All the cartons had not been emptied. The ambulance instantly went into reverse gear.

Happily we all ended safely under the bridge, with shells still exploding. As shrapnel continued to fall a donkey stood beside our bridge, but I lacked the courage to rescue it and was relieved it came to no harm.

On another occasion little 'fox holes' were found scooped out very close to the demolition site. They had been made by Arabs, who lay there during the detonation of tons of high explosive, scavenging for unexploded munitions and copper from disrupted shells.

In 1947 and up until the end of the Mandate Staff Sergeant Alex Monaghan was the chief clerk at RAOC's Khayat Beach Sub Depot. Disturbances in the Haifa area hampered the attendance of many civilian workers, some couldn't make it every day, some would arrive tired, and some late.

One day, the reis (foreman) arrived both tired and late and he gave participating in the fighting during the night as his excuse. Alex discovered after further questioning that every night the reis rented a rifle to go out and fight with one of the bands of irregular militiamen.

A civilian pay office, staffed by an officer and a group of soldiers, was set up in Haifa for the purpose of paying money due to the civilians who refused to come into 614 AOD and Khayat Beach Sub Depots. The workers had come under fire on the way to work.

The situation at 614 AOD grew more critical as each week passed.

Civilian workers absconded especially the Jewish workers who were mostly clerical staff. However packing, crating and loading were the major concerns and a majority of the workers came from nearby Tirah. In any case it subsequently transpired that the stock records were lost overboard in the Bay of Haifa. Mistrust of Jewish employees was at a high level; spies and espionage agents were in most military establishments.

A prominent example that was to have an effect on security throughout Palestine was the case on 6 April 1948 when the Stern Gang made a cowardly attack on the 12th Anti Tank Regiment, Royal Artillery.

Menachem Begin's version of the April 6 attack is so different from the story of an eyewitness. In his book *"Revolt"* Begin gives a heroic account of a plundering raid on the 12th Anti Tank Regiment. The Royal Artillery was packing away their guns to leave Palestine when the sneaky attack occurred. Begin uses exaggerated terminology such as 'full frontal' attack – 'a few score against hundreds' – 'The whole camp was soon in our hands.'

Colonel G.S. Hatch CBE gave his more credible eyewitness account in *The Gunner* the RA Magazine.

'Three Army lorries pulled up at the barrier. After a moment the sentry walked out towards the cab of the first one, in which he could see a Major of the Royal Army Service Corps holding out some papers. As the sentry walked towards the cab to look at them he was not to know at the age of eighteen, he was about to die. A member of the IZL shot him at a range of one foot.

Simultaneously another marksman, dressed as a British soldier fired over the cab of the vehicle, picking off the sentry in the Bren gun post.-Hardly a full frontal attack.

Begin states 'the advance party overwhelmed the guard' a clear case of being economical with the truth. Colonel Hatch says of the four members of the guard who were rotating between spells of duty 'they were told to stand facing against the whitewashed wall and when they were in position they were all shot. None of them was more than twenty years of age.

The whole camp was not in their hands, in fact a thirty ton armoured track vehicle that was not in the terrorists hands was brought into action and bore down on their partially filled lorries, causing the occupants to leap out and flee. The Colonel was, in 1948, subaltern at 12th Anti Tank regiment. The Camp NAAFI Manager was never seen again after April 5.

He was Jewish. The planning of such an attack needed precise timing of the sort that could only be based on information supplied from the inside.

From November REME began its closing process and on January 31 1948 the workshops at Tel Aviv and Beit Nabala were vacated. All personnel and stores were transferred to HQ Workshops at Kiryat Motzkin. Khayat Beach workshop closed in mid-April and the buildings handed over to other units. By May the railway line to Egypt had been cut and REME Workshops last convoy to Tel-el-Kebir was on May 11.

Using their own transport and cranes 6000 tons of machinery and equipment was preserved, packed and moved to the docks to be documented and loaded. Surplus stores not required, and scrap were listed and sold locally. *[2]

The Jews occupied all of Haifa on April 25 and many Palestinians blamed Britain for allowing this to happen whilst the Mandate was still our responsibility. The scale of this evacuation was hard for both Palestinians and some at home to imagine.

Fighting between Jews and Arabs was foreseeable when Britain announced its intention in November. Jews especially wished to strengthen their tenuous position before May 15 and began pre-emptive terror tactics before real combat.

The Jews then turned their attention to Acre although Britain still had troops in the area. They showered the population with mortar bombs day and night but it was an outbreak of typhoid that overcame the city's inhabitants. An emergency conference at the Lebanese Red Cross Hospital in Acre was held on May 6. It was attended by Brigadier Beveridge, Chief of British Medical Services, representatives of the British Army, officials of the city and Mr. De

Meuron of the International Committee of the Red Cross. It was determined that the infection was water borne and there were at least 70 known civilian casualties. Acre was supplied with water by aqueduct from Kabri 10 kilometers north of the city. The aqueduct passed through Jewish settlements and there was a strong suspicion that the water had been deliberately infected at some point between its source and its destination.

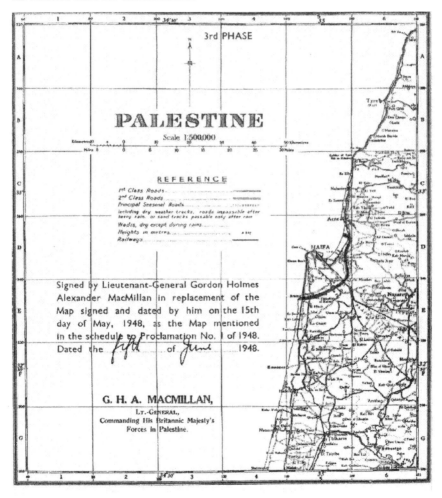

Official Map issued June 5, 1948, showing the remaining area to be totally evacuated by the target date of August 1.

Reprinted by 19 Fd Svv Regt RE Apr 1948

The Jews blamed lack of hygiene but in his reports de Meuron mentioned the little known fact that there were cases of disease among British soldiers. They were sent immediately to Port Said for hospitalisation. Nowhere else did the disease break out among either Palestinian refugees or British soldiers, including those serving in Egypt during the outbreak. Between September 1947 and January 1948 in Egypt when 10,262 people died in Egypt. However Arab claims that they had been poisoned were dismissed but became more feasible as the full extent of Israel's inhuman malevolence was revealed.

In a commanding position high on Mount Carmel was the 6th Airborne Radar station. Its purpose was to monitor shipping in the eastern Mediterranean. It was a strategic position from which the Royal Corps of Signals was able to pass on vital information to both the army and the Royal Navy. It was attacked in February 1946 by the Palmach, a commando style branch of the Haganah. It suffered some damage but remained operational until May 14 1948 when it was dismantled and most of the equipment was thrown into the Sea of Galilee. The 6th Airborne staff went to Haifa docks to leave by ship. One signaler with sufficient equipment was transferred to the 17th/21st Lancers camp to maintain contact with the remainder of the British Army. Corporal Alan Rose was amongst the last to leave. He remembers the station closing down and the sad duty of the Commanding Officer, Brigadier Cahoun was to shoot his horse.

References

1. Soldier Magazine July 1948
2. Ibid

EPILOGUE

Looking back and assessing our service time in Palestine the consensus of opinion was firm on several aspects.

Although we left behind 784 comrades in Palestine's military cemeteries we didn't come home in a blaze of glory. Our quiet retreat from Palestine was expressed in this poem by a young anonymous subaltern.

Exodus

Chased by no heavy chariots through the sea
Nor sent to safety through a lane of sand
I saw the British soldier in the Strand
Unburdened of his long captivity
Having no golden spoils of usury,
Not even one bright orange in his hand,
For the memory of the Partly Promised Land
But he was back where he was fain to be
And he shall not, I think – I think not half
Rebel against his leaders, nor repine
Like those who made of old the glittering calf
And longed for better food and the better wine,
He shall not murmur threats against the Staff
Nor shout once more to be in Palestine

The British Mandate was not cast aside in haste as some writers of history may suggest.

It took nine months from the announcement in November 1947 to the last troops leaving in August in 1948. We did not flee, chased out by a handful of terrorists, as one writer wrote. It was a very orderly, logistical exercise.

As the years have gone by the significance of that withdrawal has become painfully apparent. It was a seminal point in Middle East history that has resonated for sixty years. Most of us were not yet 21 years old and didn't fully realise the dreadful consequences that were to follow. Free from years of war, free from conscription we were on the threshold of a new life.

After most wars life returns to normality and displaced people have the opportunity to return to their own land. This was not to be in the case of the Palestinians. It took many years of witnessing their suppression, the taking of more and more of their land and the demolition of their homes, for Palestine veterans to realise normality would not return to the Holy Land.

There were several reasons for the slow dawning of the truth.

Our youth was the first obstacle. For ten years, through war and conscription discipline had been paramount. Independent thinking was restrained. The Army's evenhanded approach progressed into moral inertia in our civilian lives.

There was a worldwide sympathy for the Jewish race, and even we, who had experienced the Zionists' capability for violence, were no less sympathetic.

The conscript army performed its duty with remarkable resilience. No army before or since has coped with a terrorist situation so admirably. It needed more freedom by the British Government to bring a halt to the terrorist activities.

Following two days of violent terrorist activity at five military establishments and four attacks on military transport, a report in the *Sunday Express* of 1 March read 'Britain, unlike Germany, cannot repay terror with counter terror.'

Menachem Begin however claimed that we did counter terror with terror by declaring Martial Law following the attacks. *[1]

How did Martial Law affect the civilian population?

Government offices were closed, civil courts suspended and replaced with military courts, special permits were needed for transport between regions, and military commanders were authorised to set up courts for speedier trials, and curfews were introduced.

This writer had been in Palestine just four weeks when this occurred and now I am able to compare its effect with current Israeli counter terror tactics.

Menachem Begin firmly believes it was the actions of his Irgun that drove the British out.

Tom Segev, a modern Israeli historian summarised the situation when he wrote of the security forces 'Their hands were not stayed by weakness, however, but by a powerful sense of moral limitation on harsh behaviour towards Jews. *[2]

Tom Segev was born at the end of the Mandate and his father fought against the Arabs in 1948. The full story about Palestine has never been told and it is doubtful if it will ever be told.

What has been told is largely distorted by propaganda.

Palestine 1945-1948 was a massive and bloody conflict. It was so massive that the true total number of armed forces killed was never published.

A figure of 338 violent deaths between 1945 and 1948 was reported in *The Times* but it doesn't tally with the number of graves in at Khayat Beach and Ramleh. *[3]

Bombardier George Webb, author of '*Epitaph for an Army of Peacekeepers'* lists 784 who died in the three years. *[4]

Even after Britain agreed to withdraw the killings continued and a further 222 died before we left.

The Times included British civilians and policemen in their figures. George Webb's research related solely to military deaths. In addition to the 222 military deaths thirty-one members of the Palestine Police also died in the last six months.

Worldwide coverage of the events favoured the Jews. So effective was their propaganda that acts of terrorism against banks and police stations were glorified by some American newspapers. From its conception, the Zionist Movement saw the strategic advantage of an efficient propaganda campaign. It likened the British army to the Nazis, it sold the idea that Israel was a divine right and the Palestinians were a vicious race.

It took a female editor of a small Californian newspaper to expose the one sided reporting of the Israeli-Palestine situation.

So greatly distorted seemed the reports she was reading that she went to Gaza and the West Bank to see for herself. She found that a greater coverage was given to Israeli deaths.

She found for example that in 2004 twenty-two times as many Palestinian children were killed as were Jewish children, the largest single cause being a gunshot to the head.

Despite death threats, Alison Weir, author of the report and editor of '*If America Knew*' continues to expose the gross distortion.

Daily press releases are cranked out of the Israeli Press Office every day putting the Israeli point of view on every atrocity that Israeli's Defence Force commits.

Of course they don't' call them atrocities, and every violent act is justified.

Legitimate criticism of Israel whether it concerns Israel today or the annexation of Palestine in the first half of the last century will arouse agitated responses from local or international Jewry. Journalists and authors risk being labeled anti-Semitic if they publish a fair and forthright account of the Palestine-Israeli situation

Take the case of columnist and broadcaster, Brian Sewell, whose article appeared in the *Evening Standard* under the headline 'Bible Stories.'

Anyone who was in Palestine before 1948 and has subsequently seen the creeping advance of the partition line, the flagrant establishment of illegal settlements, the disregard of both international law and the Geneva Convention and the grotesquely savage treatment of the non Jewish population could only agree with Sewell's key assumption.

It was brought out in bold type at the top of the page 'At best the Israelis are prepared to tolerate a toothless Palestine... at worst, we should not doubt that there are Israelis who, setting aside the lessons of the Holocaust, see ethnic cleansing as the permanent answer.'

That was in October 2000, and today it is as true now as it was then. Since then more Palestinian homes have been bulldozed, more olive trees torn out of the ground.

Palestinian children shot on the way to school, peacekeepers murdered by Israeli snipers, and more land taken to turn the remaining bit of their country into a prison with an offensive 8m high wall.

Sewell's article created an angry response from Jewish readers including D.J. Schneeweis, the Israeli press attaché.

A short editorial comment stating the newspaper's view on the matter appeared on the 6 November 2000. It quite aptly put the question of anti-Semitism into perspective.

It made the following points: 'We welcome vigorous debate. We are not surprised that some people, perhaps most, do not agree with Mr. Sewell. But it would be a sad day for us all if it seemed that British Jewry, or even part of it, was demanding that the behaviour of the Israeli Government should be ring fenced and not subject to the same analysis and criticism as any other administration in the world, including our own.'

The article concluded. 'the Israeli government is conducting an intensely controversial policy towards the Palestinians, of which many Jews are as critical as many Gentiles. Mr. Sewell is perfectly entitled to his view. We will always uphold his right to express it.

Some may expect Israel's behaviour to be ring fenced and some Palestine veterans are endowed with a pre-notion from their service life to ring fence it. The anger felt at the time wanes and gives way to the happier memories of comradeship and the adventure.

In 2004 Britain's Palestine Veterans seized the opportunity to give every possible assistance to the BBC for the series 'Empire Warriors' which included the Palestine conflict. The film they produced was more than a disappointment after being ignored for so long it turned out to be a deprecation of the remarkable restraint of an army under provocation by a dishonourable enemy.

For three bitter years the terrorists committed nightly attacks on police stations and soft targets. Predictably the BBC only featured the three major incidents that shocked the world giving the terrorist leader Menachem Begin, and his gang countless opportunities over the years to fine tune his version of the events. The terrorist spokeswoman showed no remorse for the King David Hotel explosion that killed more civilians than military personnel.

On the other hand, Irene Lewis who, in 1946, was Corporal Irene Amos a clerk in the military wing of the King David Hotel featured favourably against the hard-bitten female terrorist leader. Recollecting the event plainly brought back the sadness and horror to her.

Following the programme people she met were impressed and better informed.

There is a danger of historically proven facts, clearly established, with the passage of time being deleted from the records for political reasons, a kind of moral weakness.

Current events have prompted H.M. Government to show more consideration for veterans of past conflicts. The expression 'laying the ghost' was oft said. Every 'ghost' that is, except the Palestine Veterans ghost. The spectre of the Palestine problem hovers over today's crises in the Middle East region.

Until our conflict is given the recognition it deserves with a satisfactory and just outcome to the Palestine problem, only then will our fallen comrades not have died in vain.

References

1. *The Revolt*
2. *One Palestine Complete*
3. *The Times* cited in *Palestine Triangle*
4. *Epitaph for an Army of Peacekeepers,* George Webb, Arcturus Press 2005

INDEX

Abbassia, 24
Abdul Illah, Prince, 15
Abu Sultan, 32
A Captain's Mandate, 176
Acre, 34, 85, 221
Acre Prison, 174
Acre Transit Camp, 49
A Day in the Life of a Fly, (film) 93
Aden, 18
Adler, John, RAOC, Editor *Palestine Post*, 130
Advance Ammuntion Coy. No. 28, 32
Age and Service Group, 56
Airborne Division, 6th , 55, 63-64, 97
    radar station, 223
Advance Ordnance Depot, 614, 133, 158, 178
Advance Ordnance Depot, 615, 96, 105, 136
Alakeefik Mary, 85, 86
Alakeefik Wheelers, 117
Alamein Camp, Jerusalem, 201
Alcock, Dave, 98
Alexandria, 13
Al Jiyah, 97
Allchorn, Peter, 206
Allenby Barracks, 62, 201
Allenby, General Sir Edmund H.H, 1.
Allen, Howard, WO II, 13, 24, 56
Almaza Transit Camp, 92
    commanding officer, 93
America, Special relationship with, 4
    a loan from, 182
American Press, 117
Amos, Irene, Cpl. ATS, 67-68
Anderson, Major G.W., 59

Anglo-Persian Oil Co., 2
Anthrax, 151-152
Anti-Semite riots, 182
Anti-Tank Regiment 12th, attack on, 220
Arab Legion, 76, 215
Arab National Movement, 6
Arab rebellion, 9
Arab refugees, 198
Arab Supernumery Guards, 76, 192
Arab workers, 178
    freelance, 106
Arabs, Christian, 198
"Archangel", Channel ferry, 14
Army Catering Corps, 134
Army Kinema Corporation (AKC), 103
Army Provost Marshall's Office, Tel Aviv, 65
Arnon River, 144
Athlit, 85
Astley, Malcolm, Cpl., 46, 133, 145
Atha, 374, Pte., 121
Attlee, Clement, 60
"Atlantic" paddle steamer, 20
ATS, 42, 67
    evacuation, 72
Australian troops, wartime, 103
Author, 43,146,155,185
Aziz, Bill, 105

Bab el Wad, 200
Baalbek, 145
Backhouse, Ron "Yorkie", 125
Baldwin, "Shorty", 105

Balfour, Arthur James, 3, 5
Balfour Declaration, 3, 10, 72
Ballad-es-Sheik, 159
BAOR Officers shop, Bad
  Oeyuhausen, 161
Barcilon, Hector, 175
Barclay's Bank, 188
Barclay's Bank, Tel Aviv, 61
Barker, Lt. General Evelyn, 71
Barr, John, Pte., 208
Barrass, R.H., Sgt., 48
Base Ammuntion Depot 531, 116
Base Ordnance Depot No. 2, 8, 17,
  28, 116
  manpower audit 1943, 17
Base Ordnance Depot, Shuaiba, 16
Base Workshops, No. 3, 179, 213
Basingstoke, 42
Basra, 15
Basutos, 81
Bat Galim, 208
Bay of Biscay, 18
BBC *Empire Warriors* TV documentary,
  228
BBC Radio, Christmas 1946 broadcast,
  145
Beach Gold, Normandy, 165
Bedouin Arabs, 157
Beer, George, bar owner, 122
Beersheba, 206
Beer Tavya, 64
Begin, Menachem, 20, 59, 182, 212,
  220, 226
Beirut (Beyrouth), 139
Beit Nabala, 221
Bell, Frank, 25, 56
Belsen, 55
Ben Gurion, 174
Ben Yehuda St. explosion, 200
Bethlehem, 8, 145
Bet Tsouri, Eliahu, 58
Bevin, Ernest, 61
Beveridge, Brig. British Medical
  Services, 221

Bible Lands, fitting custodians, 99
Bickell, Mr. Justice, 185
Billings, George, 43, 92
Birch, C and V.R., Ptes., 197
Birkett, Percy, 159
Bir Yakov Military Hospital, 114,
  147-148
Bitter Lakes, 56
Blackledge, Glyn, 186
Blackpool, 93
Box, Sgt. Major, 153
Bradley, RSM, 29
Briance John, Palestine Police, 84
British Army Fire Service, 107
British Army, two functions of, 74
British 'Betrayers', 179
British Criminal terrorist organisation
  (The British Army) 180
British Forces in Palestine (BFIP), 215
British Jews, 184
British Labour Party, 60
British Mandate, 112, 224
British Medical Services, 221
British Military Mission, 166
British Officers Club, explosion, 118
Brown, Eddie, police deserter, 199
Brown, Cpl. Wireless operator, 17
Brown, Ken, Sgt., 24, 30
Brutton, Phillip, Capt., 176-177
Bubonic plague, 130-131
Buck, Jeff, Sgt., 141
Buckshee Wheelers, 116
Burns, Denis, 41, 141
Burr, Sydney Palestine policemen, 8
Bush, George, W, 4

Café Galina, 197
Cahoun, Brig. C.O. 17/21 Lancers,
  223
Cairo, 5, 23, 93
Cairo-Haifa Express mined, 165
Cairo trams, 94

Camp 153, 28, 37, 49, 79, 86, 103, 115, 130, 145, 208
Dhobi, 160
Cape Finisterre, 45
Carmichael, Hoagy, 137
Carob tree, 101
Cartwright, Eddie, 104
Cassels, Major General, James, 64
Casualty Receiving Station (CRS), 112
Caunt, James, newspaper editor, 184
Cedars of Lebanon, 139
Chambers, Leo, 37, 90, 156
Chapman, David, 138
Chester Military Hospital, 148
Cholera epidemic, 52
Christian Arabs, 198
Christie, Ian, Sgt., 141
Christmas 1947, 192, 196-197
concerts, 196
Churchill, Winston, 14, 21, 59, 70, 93, 178
Church of Scotland Club, 41
Church of the Holy Sepulchre, 145
Cigarettes, Players, 50 free, 127
CIGS (Chief of Imperial General Staff), 22
Civilians, decontaminating of, 131
Clark, Brian, Sgt, 8.
Claude Butler cycles, 117
Clegg. John, 19
Clerk and Storemen's School, 75
Cockram, CSM., 84
Colchester, 13
Coldstream Guards, 53, 75
Collective fines, 8
Collins, Herbert, Major, taken hostage, 71
Collins, Irene, Mrs. 72
Colonial Forces, 81
Combined Services Entertainment Company (CSE) 103, 105,115
Connah's Quay, 148
Cooper "Duff", CSM, 89
Cosgrove, John, 179

Cox, Stan, 141
Creech-Jones, Arthur, Colonial Secretary, 71
Crewe 'Pinky', shooting accident, 118
Cross, Brian Cpl., 40, 91, 118, 156, 161
Cunningham, Lt.General, Sir Alan, 64
Cycle Trades Federation, 117
Cyprus, 20, 138-140

Daily Express, 180, 185
Daily Mirror, omnibus edition, 102
Daily Routine Orders, 80, 126
example of, 119
Damascus, 53
Damascus Gate, Jerusalem, 198
Danish paratroops, 103
Daroutis Hotel, 71
Davidson, Major, 51
Dayan, Moshe, 9
D.D.T., 130
Dead Sea, 7, 62
Dean, Albert, 184
Deebs Mr., 144
Deir,Yassin, 170
Denniston, J.G, Major-General, 167
De Meuron, Mr. International Red Cross, 221-222
Derna Camp, 165, 166
Deolali Transit Camp, 47
Depot Defence Force, 76
Derbyshire, 156
Derby Synagogue, arson attack, 182
Detention Barracks (glasshouse) Jerusalem, 153-154
Deversoir Convalescent Depot, 142
Devlin, Pat, Constable, PP, 159
Dewsbury, 171
Dill, Lt. General, J G, 143
Displaced persons, 41, 225
Disraeli, Benjamin, 3
Djaouni, Azmi, 201
Dodge lorries,ten stolen, 156
Doel, G.J., Major, death of, 202

Domenico Major, 153
Dome of the Rock, 195
Dover Castle, 41
Doyle, Bunny, 104
Draft Conducting Officer (DCO), 48
Draper, Harold, 'Brummie', 37, 43, 97
Driberg, Tom, MP (Lab.Maldon), 185
Duchense, Martin, Police Sergeant, 159
Dysentery, 151

Edelman,Mr. MP (Coventry W), 181
Eden, Anthony, 59
Education, British Army, 143
Edwards, Charles, O.C Sub Depot, 78
Egerton, Alan, 83
Egypt, 13, 30, 50, 75, 92, 138, 183, 215
    Italy invades, 15
    Army life in, 104
Egyptian Army, 166
Egyptian Border, 210
Egyptian vultures, 95
Eighth Army,28
El Aden, 25
El Alamein, 23, 26
    memorial, 16
El Arish, 31, 96
El Bureij, 206
El Kantara, 30, 96
Elijah, 136
Ell, Les, Gunner, 68
Emery, Jim, Major, 202
Empire Warriors, BBC TV, 228
Epitaph for an Army of Peacekeepers 226
Esdraelon, Plain of, 53
Evacuation strategy, 210
Even-handed approach, army's, 225
Evening Standard, 227
European Jews, 189
Eyles, Charlie, Sgt., 32, 145
Exodus, 83

Famagusta, 140
Fareidis, 127
Farnborough, 175
Farrow, John, 56
Fayid, 53, 75
Fayid Militray Hospital, 142
Fede and Fenice, immigration ships, 64
Feeney, Commander, ATS, 163
Feltham Holding Depot, 42
Feltham Officers' Mess, 167
Fertile Crescent, 2
Fisch, Mrs. Civilian Welfare Officer, 164
Flanagan, Michael, S/Sgt., 176
Forgotten Allies, 11
Foulkes, CA, Sgt., 48
France, 37
Free from infection (FFI), 95, 139
Freeman, S/Sgt., 175
French Consulate, 67
French Mandate, 22
'Full Monty', 129
Fursland,Rex, 151

Gallagher, Daniel, death of, 197
Gallagher, Mr. W, MP (West Fife. Con.), 185
Garden of Gethsemane, 145
Garrison Club, 140
Gath, 33
Gaza, 52, 97, 215
Gaza Detention Barracks, 148
Geneifa, 183
General Gordon's Expeditionary Force, 36
Genesis 1948, 176
George Crosses, 70
Georgic II, 209
Georges-Picot, Monsieur, 1
Gerrard, Dennis K.C., 186
Gibraltar, 45, 56
Godfrey, Danny, 153-154

Golden Dome, 195
Golden Sands Holiday Camp, 140
Goldsmith's Officers Club, explosion, 118
Gold Star beer, 134, 148
Gore, Margaret, 175
Gore, T.C. Lt. Col., 50, 90, 161-177, 211, 218
Gourock, 17
Government Printer, Jerusalem, 143
Gray, 763, Pte., 7 days CB, 121
Great Bitter Lake, 141
Green, Peter, 135
Greenwood, Arthur, 60
Grieves, S/Sgt, 170, 173
Grigg, Edward, 58
Gruner, Dov, 71
Guard duties, 120
Guards Brigade OFP, 201
Guinness, 148
Guy, Col. C.O. 612 CVG, 156

Habbiniya, 15
Habforce, 15
Hadar-HaCarmel, 90
Hadera, 216
Hagannah, 9, 169
Hagannah Palmach, 63
Haifa, 20, 24, 25, 49, 62, 86, 90, 102, 141, 158, 209
Haifa, capture of, 221
Haifa-Kirkuk pipeline, 2
Haifa Military Hospital, 146
Haifa Oil terminal explosion, 118
Haifa Police HQ, attack on, 188
Haj Amin el Husseini, 57, 189
Hakin, Eliahu, 58
Halse, R.C. Col. Army Legal Department, 168
Hammerman, Pte., 24
Hammond, Arthur, Pte., 41, 146
Haram-Ash-Sharif, 195
Harding, Dennis, 156

Hardwick, John, Sgt., 48, 76 86
Harold, Sid, 115
Harris, 378, Pte., 48
Harris, Jack. Lt., 55, 138
Harris, Len. Cpl., 110, 134, 160
Hatch, Col. G.S., CBE, 220
Hatzofim, 210
Hayman, Jack, Sgt, 37.
Haywood, Stan, 39, 66
Heath, Stan, 47
Hebron, 33
Hecht, Ben, Hollywood scriptwriter, 179
Hejas-Damascus Railway, 52
Heliopolis, 92
Herbert Samuel Esplanade, 63
Herbert Samuel Way, Haifa, 137
Herzle, Theodore, 4
Hewitt, Harold, S/Sgt., 24
Hewitt, SQMS, 5
Hibbs, Jack, 43
High Commissioner, 123
Hilsea Barracks, 19
Hiscock, Joe, Sgt., 8
Histadrut (Jewish Trade Union), 189
Hitchcock, Brig., 28
Hitler, 5, 187
H.M.S. Aux, 17
Homer's Illiad, 110
Horrocks, Walter, Cpl., 40, 96
Hotel Semeris, 198
Hotel Yarkon, 66
Hot Springs (Kallihoe), 144
House of Commons, 58, 181
Houses of easement, 114
Houses of Parliament, 115
Howard, Major Bill, 7, 143, 162
Howe, Andrew. S/Sgt., 51, 90
Howells, Freddie, 103
Hughes, Keith, 125
Humber Scout Cars, 79
Hyreres Transit Camp, 41

If America Knew, 227
Immigrants, Jewish, 5
Indian Division, 4th, 27
Infantry Brigade, 2nd, OFP, 200
Infantry Brigade 61st, 157
Indian Ocean, 18
Infantry Division,3rd, 55, 87
Ingle, Ken, 19
Intelligence Corps, 180
Iraq, 15
Irgun attacks Tirah, 198
Irgun Zvai Leumi (IZL), 179, 220
    posters in camp, 132
'Isle of Thanet' Channel ferry, 38
Israeli Defence Force, 227
Italy, 37
Ivers, Dennis Michael, S/Sgt, 161,
    170

Jackal hunting, 112
Jackson, Peter, 209
Jaffa, 37
Jaffa Police, 156
Janner,Barnett MP (Leics. W. Lab),
    181
Jefferson, Michael, 2nd. Lieut., 214
Jeffery, John, Cpl., 68
Jenkins, Capt. Green Howards, 53, 86,
    121
Jerusalem, 37, 153, 198
Jerusalem HQ, 7
Jerusalem Military Hospital, 118
Jewish Agency, 57, 180
Jewish Brigade, 21
Jewish civilian employees, 117
Jewish journalists, 117
Jewish National Fund, 6
Jewish National Council, 182
Jewish Irish black and tan, 149
Jewish Rottenburg Project, 108
Jews, Muslims and Christians waded
    together, 144
'Jews of America' article, 179

Jisr-el-Majami, 33, 53
Johnson, Craftsman, 100
Jones, Penny, 163
Joppa (Jaffa), 143

Kabri, 222
Kantara, 14
Karlsruhe, 41
Kataman neighbourhood, 198
Kendal, Kim, 104
    sister, Kay, 104
Kent, Derek, Sgt., 183
Kfar Bilu, 112, 217
Khamsin, 95
Khan Yunis, 157
Khartoum, 47
Khayat Beach Mary, 85-86
Khayat Beach Sub-Depot, 78-80, 85,
    155, 219
Khayat Bus Co., 137
Kidd, Charles, Cpl., 34, 116
King David Hotel, 7, 70, 178
    explosion, 66-71
King Feisal II, 15
King Ibn Saud, 9, 57
    letter to Roosevelt, 9
    letter to Truman, 72
King's Regiment, 130
King's Royal Rifle Corps., 206
King's Rules and Regulations (KRR's),
    115
Kingsway, Haifa, 131
Kirby, Trevor, Constable PP, 69, 116
Kishon Brook, 211
Kishon Camp, 88
Kishon Railway workshops, 65
Kishon Returned Stores Depot, 211
Knapp, Jim, 141
Kollek, Teddy, Mayor of Jerusalem, 84
Kurzman, Dann, 176
Kyrenia, 141

Lady Chatterley's Lover, 133
Lake Huleh , 11
Laker, Judge Windham, taken
    hostage, 72
Lambert, R.C. Major, S.I.B., 172
Lancers, 17/21st, 223
Latrines, types of, 113-115
Latrun Detention Centre, 117
Latrun 'Medoc', 215
Latrun pumping station, 214
Lawrence, D.H., 133
Lawrence, T.E., 52, 157
Leachman, John, Pte, 205.
Lebanon, 117, 138
Lebanese Red Cross Hospital, 221
Levant Fair, 26, 82
Lewis, Irene, Cpl. ATS, 67
Lehi (Lehamei Herut Israel), 21, 88
    alliance with Irgun, 60
LIAP (Leave in addition to Python),
    101, 138
Liberty ships, 30
Life Guards, 202
'Little Death Ships', 12, 20
Liverpool Assizes, 185
Lloyd-George, David, 2, 5
Lloyd, Ken., Sgt., 165
London Hebrew Society, 4
London University Matriculation
    Exams, 144
Lucas, Capt., 161
Lord Gort, High Commissioner, 58
Lowther, C.H.E. (Kit) Brig., 166
Lyneham, 54
Lydda, 52, 217
    railway goods yard attacked, 62
Lydda airport, 51

MacDonald, Harry, S/Sgt, 176.
Machin, Ray, 43, 92
Machin, May, 127
McCardle, 'Scouse', 84
McCarthy, P.C. WOII, death of, 202

McDonnell, Cpl, 52
McDowall, John, Pte., 16
McGregor, W.D. L/Cpl, death of, 202
McMillan, Lt.Gen. GHA (GOC BFIP),
    215
McNeill, Major, 12
Madison, Peter, army deserter, 199
Majid (Mosque) al Aqsa, 195
Malta, 14, 54
Mamillah Cemetery, 199
Mandate, last days of, 195
Mann, Capt. G.M. (M.O), 152
Mannion, Joseph, Pte., 129
Marshall, Ken, 218
Marsh, Peter, Cpl., 176
Martial Law, 118
    effects of, 225
Martin, Clifford, Sgt., 179-180
Mason, Pte., 135
Mayes, George, Lt. Col. Acting C.O.
    614 A.O.D, 168
Mediterranean, 139
Medloc, 13
    C. Route, 41
Meiri, David, (alias Begin), 59
Mellor, Capt., 86
Meyer, Golda (Mrs. Meyerson),180
MI 5, 170
Middle East Mail, 197
Middle East School of Artillery
    (MESA), 124
Military Dispersal Unit (MDU), 129
Military Police, 34, 43
Military properties deserted, 194
Mine filling factory, 98
Mitchell, Frank, 164
    C.O. Palestine Store Co., 130
Mobile Laundry and Bath Unit
    (ML & BU)
    No.3 Qastina, 87, 146
    No. 52 , 41
    move to Rafah, 141
    No. 301 Cyprus, 212
Monaghan, Alex, S/Sgt., 43, 85, 219

Montague Burton, 129
Montefiore, Sir Moss, 4
Montgomery, Major-Gen. Bernard, 23, 188
Moore, Alan Pte., 200
Morecambe and Heysham Visitor, 184
Morgan, Leslie, Cpl., 165
Moss, Jack, 83
Mount Carmel, 49, 81, 99, 116, 128, 134, 159, 216
  Radar station, 223
Mount Herzle, 59-60
Mount Olympus, 140
Moyne, Lord Walter, 58
Mufti of Jerusalem, 57, 189
Muncey, Bill, WO I, 47, 89, 161
Musa-El-Alami, 57-58
Mustard gas, 204
M.V. Batory, 38

NAAFI, 69, 79, 95, 134, 140
Nablus, 108, 165
Nathanya, 64, 180
  Convalescent camp, 150, 192
National Geographic Magazine, 36, 92
Nazareth, 145, 165
Nazi propaganda, 21
Nazism, 20
Neale, Joe, L/Cpl., 127
Nelson Bar, 118
Neujean Jules, 124
Newman R.S.T., Major, 49, 86, 122, 161-177
Newman, T. Sgt. RASC, 70
New York Herald Tribune, 178
Nicolas, George, Craftsman, 16, 95
Nicosia, 140
Nisbet, John Pte. 211
North Africa, 27
Nuffield Club, 195
Nutt, Dennis, 89, 128

O'Brien, Gus, Cpl., 53, 76, 83, 91, 100, 131, 157
Old Dalby, 67
Olive harvest at Camp 153, 157
One Palestine Complete, 123
Orange Growers' Association, 157
Ordnance Directorate, Cairo, 166
Ordnance Mobile Workshop, 7
Osborne, 322, Pte. (3 days C.B.), 121
Out of bounds, 26 Haifa
  establishments, 122

P & O steamship Co. 52
Page, Fred, Cpl., 98, 105
Page, Walter H. U.S. Ambassador, 4
Paice, Mervyn, Sgt., 179-180
PAIFORCE, 15
Palestine, 1
  1917 population of, 1
  Jewish population, 2
Palestine Police Force, 5
Palestine Past and Present, 143
Palestine Police Old Comrades Newsletter, 159
Palestine Post, 60, 199, 213
  office explosion, 200
Palestine Railways, 14
Palestine Scrapbook, 91, 100, 162
Palestine Veterans assist BBC, 228
Palestinians, non Jewish, 62
Palmach commandos kill shoppers, 198
Paperback books, 132
Parachute Battalion, 5th, 64
'Paris by the Sea', 139
Parker, Ken, Pte., 78-80, 99, 129
Parker, Sydney, Pte., 16, 17
Parliamentary Labour Party. 60, 178, 190
Passen, Pierre Van, 2
Pay parade, 82
Pauncefoot, Lt, 76.
Pepper, Claude, Senator, 58

Perkins, Sydney, Sgt., 23
Petah, Tikva, 21, 206
Phillips, Arthur, Sgt., 50
Phillips, Ivan Lloyd, 62
PIAT (Projector Infantry Anit-Tank), 169
Pickering, D.H. Pte. Death of, 197
Picturegoer, 128
Pictureshow, 128
Piehards, feral dogs, 87
Pine Tree Holiday Camp, 139
Pioneer Corporal accidentally shot, 118
Pogson, Roy, 212
Poland, 55
Pope, Stan, 136
Port of Tel Aviv, 213
Port Said, 13, 41, 45, 56, 92
Portsmouth, 75
Port Suez, 47
Postal charges, 123
Postmaster General, Jerusalem, 68
POW Camp, Bologna, 25
Price, Ken, Sgt., 70
Private soldiers pay, 141
Proclamation from G.O.C., 215-216
Purple Heart, the, 147
Python Number, 56

Qastina, 146
Qastina airfield, 63
Queen Alexandra's Nurses, 126
Qyrat (Kyrat) Motzkin, 23, 179

Radio Palestine, 113
Rae, D.T. Capt., 66
Rafah, 22, 130, 208, 217
Rafateers, 615 AOD entertainers, 105
Rail atrocity, worst ever, 210
Rail Marshalling yard, Rafah, 23
Ramat David, 99
Ramat Gan Police Station, 63

Ramat Hakovesh, 157
Ramleh, 11
Ramleh Military Cemetery, 188
RAOC Returned Stores Depot, 191
RASC soldiers accidental death, 118
Ras-et-Ein, 198
Rashid, Ali, 15
Rayon, Jamel Mohammed, 109
'Rearward Services', 22
Red Cross, 192, 222
Red Sea, 18
Red Shield ambulance, 211
Red Triangle YMCA newsletter, 144
Read Hall Barracks, Colchester, 13
Refugee ships, Milos and Pacific, 21
Regimental Orders, examples of, 121
Regimental Police, 82
Rehovet, 129, 130, 210
REME Workshops. evacuation of, 213-214, 221
Reynold's News, 185
Riding stables, Elia Gordon's, 117
Rifles stolen, 82
Rigby-Jones, R.F. L/Cpl. death of, 202
River Jordan, 53, 62
Rivers, Brian, Lt. Col., 86, 110, 163, 211
RMS 'Queen Elizabeth', 19
Road block, near Camp 153, 208
Robertson, Pat, Major, 177
Roosevelt, President, 9, 57
Romena District, Jerusalem, 199
Rommell, General, 23, 30
Roper, Jeff, 87
Rose, Alan, Cpl., 223
Rothschild, Lionel Walter, 3
Royal Army Ordnance Corps (RAOC), 6, 24,50,74-75,92,117,191
    Holding depot, 42
Royal Army Service Corps (RASC), 27, 75, 123, 134, 158, 178
Royal Artillery, 218, 220
Royal Corps of Signals, 52, 223
'Royal Daffodil', channel ferry, 39

Royal Dragoon Guards, 176
Royal Electrical and Mechanical
  Engineers (REME), 16, 74-75, 90,
  95, 105, 202
Royal Engineers, 27, 198, 210
Royal Marines, 173, 212
Russell, Thomas, Flt/Lt, 66
Russell, James, 157

Sail makers, 127
Sailors, depot guards, 91
Salamanca Barracks, 32
Salt, Wally, 75
Salvation Army, 95
Samuel, Herbert, 5
Sand Fly fever, 151
Sarafand, 7, 22-23, 32, 82, 133,
  201-202
Sarafand Military Hospital, 146
Sarafand Workshops, 24
Saudi Arabia, 9, 57
Schneeweis. D.J., Israeli press attaché,
  228
Schiff, Soloman, Deputy
Superintendent P.P, 21
Sea of Galilee, 223
Segev, Tom , Historian and writer, 226
Seven Pillars of Wisdom, 157
Seven Sisters Hill, Jerusalem, 116
Sewell, Brian, 227
Shafto's Cinema, Tel-el-Kabir, 38
Shamir, Ishtak, (real name:
  Yzertitsky), 20
Sharpley, R.J. L/Cpl. death of, 202
Shawcross, Sir Hartley, Attorney
General, 185
Shaw, John, Secretariat Chief, 67
Shelton, Dennis, Rifleman, 206
Shepherd and Turpin, inventors of
the Sten Gun, 84
Shepherds' fields, 8, 145
Sherwood Foresters Camp, 132
Shirley, Judy, 104

Shite hawks, 95
Shuaiba, 15
Sicily, 30
Sidi Haneesh, 32
Silver, Bernard Isadore, 171, 173
Silver, Mr., 171
Silverman. S, MP Nelson and Colne
  (Lab.), 181
Simon the Tanner, 143
Sinai Desert, 31, 217
Sinton,Jock, S/Sgt., 156
Slade, G.O. Mr., 186
Smith, E.A. Sgt. PP, 70
Smith, Henry, Brigade Ordnance
  W.O., 158
Soloman's Temple,143
Southampton,42
South Staffs. Regiment, 130
Speck, Walter, 31
Special Investigations Branch, (SIB),
  82, 161
Special Night Squads, 8
Spinney's Restaurant, 122
SS Lancastrian, 19
SS Laurentic, 7
SS Mooltan,19, 95, 128
SS Patria, 21
Staghound armoured vehicles, 217
Stamp, Col. Former CO 614 AOD, 168
State of Israel, 176
Stern, Abraham, 21
Stern gang, 21, 208
Stone, Malcolm, Lt. Col., 166, 216-217
Stevenson, Alan, 136
Strathnaver troopship, 158
Streicher, Julius, 185
Suez Canal, 3, 14, 142
Sulieman, Ali, 105
Sulieman, Christian Arab, 150
Sunday Express 70, 225
Surtees, Sister, Q.A Nurse, 149
Sykes-Picot Agreement, 1
Sykes, Sir Mark, 1
Syria, 11,22, 24

Syrian border, 112
Syrian orphanage, 200
Styler, Capt. , entomologist, 100

Tabitha, 143
Taft, Robert, Senator, 71
Tantura, 170
Tarran, John, Sgt., 17, 28, 143
Taylor, Bill, PP, 21
Tel Aviv, 61, 155, 213
Tel-el-Kabir, 27, 30, 50, 141
The Gunner, 220
The Revolt, 66
The Shia, Jewish undercover unit, 164
The Times, 10, 174-175, 180, 226
Thomas Cook, 36
Thompson, D.C. Assistant Secretary, 70
Thorburn, Major, 107
Tiberius, 122, 165
Tilbury Docks, 46
Tirah, 108-111, 198
  likeness to Derbyshire, 110
Tobruk, 15, 165
  fall of, 25
  taking of, 26
Toc H, 65
Toulon, 39
Transit Camp 156, 142
Transit Camp 312, 38
TransJordan, 62
TransJordan Frontier Force, 83
Trappist Monastery, Latrun, 215
Tremaine, Edgar, 166
Tripolitania, leave ship, 139
Troodos, 140
Troopship , convoy of 16 ships
  Andes, Cameronia, Diomede,
    Highland Monarch,
  Idrapoera, Indian Prince,
    Manchester Port,
  Nea Hellas, Niger Stroom, Orcades,
    Phemlus,

Reina del Pacifico, Stirling Castle,
  Strathallan,
  Warwick Castle, Windsor Castle,
    Volendam , 16
Truman, Harry S. U.S. President, 61, 72
  secret writings of, 187
Tulkarm, 194
Tuqan, Ibrahim, 6
Turks, 99
567 Times, newssheet, 100

Umm Qasr, 15
UNSCOP (United Nations Special
  Committee on Palestine), 190
Uris, Leon, 83

Vendors, Egyptian, 50
Venereal disease, 93
Venus Bar, Haifa, 125
Vernon's Pools, Liverpool, agents for,
  133
Vichy France, 11, 22
Victoria Barracks, Portsmouth,13

Wade, Jim, 31
Wadi Sarar, 23, 89, 98, 153
Wagstaff, Alec 'Waggy', 100
Waller, Pat. Capt., 82
'War of Independence 1948', 197
Watson, Lt. Col.'Pip', Border
  Regiment, 163
Walker, Cpl., 31
Webb, Col. Assistant Chaplain
  General, 144
Webb, George, Sgt., 226
Weir, Alison, writer, 227
Weir, R.A. Col., 162
Weizmann, Chaim, 4, 22, 59
Welfare's 181 Camp, 140
Welfare food parcels, 122

Wells, Bob, 86
West African soldiers, 113
White, John, 43, 99, 126, 178
Whitehead, Jack, Pte., 165
Withdrawal dates decided, 190
Whiting, Capt., 31
Whitmell, RSM., 50, 88, 97
Williams, Emlyn, 148
Williamson, H.G. Rev, 143.
Wilson, Dave, Major, 65
Wilson, Woodrow, 4
Wingate, Orde, 8
Womens' Voluntary Service, 140
Wood, Frank, 'Chopper' Cpl., 164
Woolf, Mr. Jewish trader, 131
Workshops, 3 Base,, 179, 213
Workshops 309, 83
World War II, outbreak of, 13

Yafo (Jaffa), 143
Yellop, Ray, S/Sgt., 141
Yalin Mor, Nathan (real name
    Friedman-Yellin), 20
YMCA, 7, 69, 141, 143-144
York Demob Centre, 129

Zagazig, 31
Zgornicki, Pte., 24
Zionism, 2, 61, 181
Zionist(s), 3, 9, 181
    and the Turkish Government, 4
    Churchill disenchanted, 178
    propaganda, 71
Zionist Congress, 4
Zionist Movement, 5
Zulficar, Suzy, 164

Other books written by soldiers who served in Palestine
1945 – 1948

Brutton, Phillip	*A Captain's Mandate*	Pen and Sword Books	1996
Glubb, John Bagot	*A Soldier With the Arabs*	Hodder and Stoughton	1957
Farran, Roy	*Winged Dagger*	Collins	1948
Hall, Trevor	*Enduring the Hour*	Arcturns Press	2005
Webb, George	*Epitaph for an Army of Peacekeepers*	Arcturus Press	2005
Wilson, R.D.	*Cordon and Search*	Gale and Polden	1949

ISBN 142510765-6